AN ESSAY

ON

MARITIME LOANS,

FROM THE FRENCH OF

M. BALTHAZARD MARIE EMERIGON;

WITH NOTES:

TO WHICH IS ADDED

AN APPENDIX,

CONTAINING THE TITLES

DE EXERCITORIA ACTIONE, DE LEGE RHODIA DE JACTU, *AND* DE NAUTICO FŒNORE,

Translated from the Digests and Code of Justinian.

AND THE TITLE

DES CONTRATS A LA GROSSE AVENTURE *OU* A RETOUR DE VOYAGE,

FROM THE

MARINE ORDINANCE OF LOUIS XIV.

BY JOHN E. HALL, ESQ.

Gallia causidicos docuit facundia Britannos. *Juvenal.*

THE LAWBOOK EXCHANGE, LTD.
Clark, New Jersey

ISBN 9781584773979 (hardcover)
ISBN 9781616191764 (paperback)

Lawbook Exchange edition 2004, 2011

The quality of this reprint is equivalent to the quality of the original work.

THE LAWBOOK EXCHANGE, LTD.

33 Terminal Avenue
Clark, New Jersey 07066-1321

*Please see our website for a selection of our other publications
and fine facsimile reprints of classic works of legal history:*
www.lawbookexchange.com

Library of Congress Cataloging-in-Publication Data

Emerigon, Balthazard-Marie, 1716-1785.
    [Traité des assurances et des contrats à la grosse. English]
    An essay on maritime loans / from the French of M. Balthazard Marie Emerigon; with
notes, to which is added an appendix containing the titles De exercitoria actione, De lege
rhodia de jactu, and De nautico foenere, translated from the digests and code of Justinian,
and [an English translation of] the title Des contrats à la grosse aventure ou à retour de
voyage, from the marine ordinance of Louis XIV, by John E. Hall.
    p. cm.
    Originally published: Baltimore: Published by Philip H. Nicklin & Co. ; Philadelphia:
Farrand & Nicholas; Boston: D. Mallory & Co. ; Portland: Lyman, Hall & Co. ; Albany
: D. Farrand & Green; Middlebury: Swift & Chipman, 1811.
    Includes bibliographical references and index.
    ISBN 1-58477-397-9 (cloth: alk. paper)
    1. Insurance, Marine—France. 2. Bottomry and respondentia—France. I. Title: Maritime
loans. II. Hall, John E. (John Elihu), 1783-1829. III. Title.

KJV2862.E4413 2003
346.44'08622—dc22   2003058945

Printed in the United States of America on acid-free paper

AN ESSAY

ON

MARITIME LOANS,

FROM THE FRENCH OF

M. BALTHAZARD MARIE EMERIGON;

WITH NOTES:

TO WHICH IS ADDED

AN APPENDIX,

CONTAINING THE TITLES

DE EXERCITORIA ACTIONE, DE LEGE RHODIA DE JACTU, *AND* DE NAUTICO FŒNORE,

Translated from the Digests and Code of Justinian.

AND THE TITLE

DES CONTRATS A LA GROSSE AVENTURE *OU* A RETOUR DE VOYAGE,

FROM THE

MARINE ORDINANCE OF LOUIS XIV.

BY JOHN E. HALL, ESQ.

Gallia causidicos docuit facundia Britannos. *Juvenal.*

BALTIMORE:

PUBLISHED BY PHILIP H. NICKLIN & CO:

Also by

Farrand & Nicholas, Philadelphia; D. Mallory & Co. Boston; Lyman, Hall & Co. Portland; D. Farrand & Green, Albany; and Swift & Chipman, Middlebury.

A. Miltenberger, Printer,

1811.

TO

JOSEPH HOPKINSON, ESQ.

COUNSELLOR AT LAW

IN THE

SUPREME COURT OF THE UNITED STATES.

THIS VOLUME

Is dedicated as a slight memorial

OF THE

RESPECT AND GRATITUDE

OF

HIS PUPIL.

ADVERTISEMENT.

BY THE TRANSLATOR.

THE title, under which this translation appears, has been adopted as a generic term to designate the two species of contract known in our law under the terms of Respondentia and Bottomry. Such a title is a desideratum in our legal language which is attempted to be supplied by translating the term *nauticum fœnus* from the civil law. The words *gross adventure*, from the French, are likewise used, occasionally, in the work, to convey the same general idea. When the principle, inculcated by the authour, applied, exclusively, to either of the contracts, there was no difficulty, as the words *bottomry* and *respondentia* are familiar to the lawyer, however uncouth they may appear to a scholar.

The translator would have good authority for dwelling upon " the infinite labour, unwearied study and reflection" which his authour has displayed in collecting " the decisions and authorities, applicable to the purpose of his work. He held a distinguished rank among the advocates of his own country,"* and when he undertook to pay that debt which, it is said, every man owes to his profession, he brought to the task, a mind in which " great learning was united with great practical knowledge." " His book is, of all the foreign publications on this subject, the most useful to an English lawyer."†

---

* Park on insurances, *Introd.* 11.
† Marshal on insurance, *Introd.* 22.

His treatise on Maritime Loans is now, for the
first time, presented to the English reader, with all
that attention to fidelity, which is the humble praise
of a translator; and it is hoped that where he has
ventured to exceed the province of an interpreter,
he may not be considered as aiming at idle orna-
ments or useless appendages. The notes are confined chiefly to the explanation of technical terms
in the Civil and French law, and such local usages
as appeared to be necessary to the elucidation of the
language of a foreign jurist. The references to
English authorities, include the most important
cases: but they are given very briefly, because they
may be found with great facility, by turning to the
chapters which have been devoted to this subject
by Park and Marshal. In the United States very
few cases have occurred: such as have been seen
by the translator are noticed.

As this treatise is professedly a commentary on a
part of the celebrated ordinance of *Louis XIV.* and
those texts of the civil law which treat of Maritime
Loans, it was deemed not improper to translate and
add them to the volume.

Throughout the whole work, the translator has
endeavoured to explain his originals with perspe-
cuity and accuracy. If he be found to have done this,
he has fulfilled his duty to the reader. If his labours be rewarded with this approbation, it will be
an encouragement to him to offer to the publick a
translation of the treatise on Insurance by *Emerigon*
and the *Consolato del Mare:* which works are nearly
ready for the press.

Baltimore, October 1809.

TABLE OF CONTENTS.

CHAPTER I.

	Page.
Introduction,	17.
General observations.	18.

SECT. I. *Texts of the Roman law relating to maritime loans.*

L. 1. ff. de naut fœn.	ib.
L. 3. ff. eod.	19.
L. 4. ff. eod.	ib.
On the §. 1. of the L. 4. ff. eod.	20.
L. 5. ff. eod.	21.
L. 6. ff. eod.	ib.
L. 1. c. de naut fœn.	22.
L. 2. c. eod.	ib.
L. 3. c. eod.	ib
L. 4. c. eod.	ib
Opinion of Paulus.	ib
L. 26. c. de usuris.	ib.
L. 122. §. 1. ff. de verb. oblig.	23.

SECT. II. *Definition, denomination, legality and nature of the contract of maritime loans.*

§. 1. Definition.	24
§. 2. Denomination.	25
§. 3. Legality of the contract	26.
The different constructions which have been given to the chap. *naviganti extra de usuris.*	27.
It is a contract of a particular kind.	30.
The legality of it is undoubted.	31.
§. 4. It is more of a real than a personal nature.	32.
Is it mutual ?	ib.
Each party is interested.	ib.

	Page.
It is gambling.	33.
It is conditional.	ib.

SECT. III. *It is the essential quality of this contract that there is a risk and that it should be borne by the lender.*

§. 1. Bottomry by way of wager.	33.
Clause [voto per pieno] of interest or no interest.	33.
§. 2. The risk should be borne by the lender.	34.
It cannot properly be called bottomry until the risk has commenced.	ib.
What will be the consequence if the money be expended on shore before any risk has commenced ?	ib.
If the risk ceases ?	ib
Whether the contract be void ?	ib.

SECT. IV. *Difference between bottomry, loan, partnership and insurance.*

§. 1. Difference between bottomry and loan.	36.
§. 2 In what respects it differs from partnership.	ib.
§. 3. Its affinity with insurance.	38.
§. 4. The difference between them.	39.

SECT. V. *Notice of certain maritime associations.*

Page.

§. 1. Joint concern in the fitting out of a ship. 41.

§. 2. Joint concern in the profits of an adventure. 42.

§. 3. Consignment of an adventure on commission. *ib.*

CHAPTER II.

Of the form of the contract.
SECT. I. *Of the external form.*

§. 1. It may be made before a notary or under a private signature. 44.

Can it be made verbally? 45.

§. 2. Does it create a lien on the property of the party. *ib.*

Must it be comptrolled, acknowledged and registered? *ib.*

§. 3. If it has been executed by private signature, does it enjoy the same privileges as if it had been executed by a publick act. 46.

SECT. II. *Internal form.*

§. 1. What ought to be mentioned in it. 47.

Is it necessary to stipulate that the lender run the risk? *ib.*

§. 2. Blank bill of lading. 48.

§. 3. Bottomry united with other contracts. *ib.*

CHAPTER III,

Of maritime interest.
SECT. I. *General rules on the subject of maritime interest.*

§. 1. Maritime interest is an essential part of the contract. 49.

§. 2. Is it necessary that the interest should be paid in money? 50

Implied interest. *ib*

§. 3. What is the law where the parties have neglected to insert a stipulation for interest. *ib.*

§. 4. What is the law where the lender incurs no hazard? 51.

Page.

§. 5. What is the law in case the ship perish? *ib.*

SECT. II. *Rate of maritime interest.*

§. 1. The rate of maritime interest is unlimited. 52.

§. 2. Interest or premium at so much *per* month. 53.

§. 3. The unexpected arrival of peace or war. *ib.*

§. 4. The whole of the maritime premium is due the moment the risk commences. *ib.*

SECT. III. *What if the vessel never return?* 58.

SECT. IV. *Common legal interest*

§. 1. When the maritime risk ceases, the common legal interest commences. 60.

§. 2. May there be a charge of legal interest on the maritime interest? 61.

CHAPTER IV.

SECT. I. *General observations upon the action against ship owners (actio exercitoriâ) for the acts of the master.*

§. 1. Of the owner (*exercitor.*) 64.

§. 2. Of the master. 65.

SECT. II. *It is a general rule that the owner is bound by the acts of the master.*

Of a substituted captain. 68.

SECT. III. *Are the owners responsible for the contracts of the captain which are made at the place where they reside?*

§. 1. Of a captain who borrows money upon bottomry at the place where the owners reside. 69.

Text of the laws. *ib.*

The part owners who do not consent are not bound by such loans. 70.

Of the action *de in rem verso.* 71.

§. 2. Packages shipped on board without the knowledge of the owners. *ib.*

Page.

SECT. IV. *Of a part owner who refuses to contribute his proportion.*

§. 1. Do the part owners who refuse to contribute lose their shares or interest in the vessel? 73.

§. 2. Money may be taken up on bottomry on their account. 73.

§. 3. Whether a recusant owner may require the vessel to be sold. 75.

The will of the majority is to govern. ib.

SECT. V. *Of a captain who borrows money at gross adventure in the course of the voyage.*

§. 1. Text of the laws 77.

§. 2. Is it necessary that the captain should be authorized by the magistrate of the place to take up money at gross adventure? 79.

§. 3. Ought it to be a publick contract? 80.

§. 4. The loan must be made expressly for the necessities of the ship. 81.

§. 5. Is the captain authorized to take up money at gross adventure in order to complete his cargo? 82.

SECT. VI. *Various questions on the points which are treated of in the three preceeding sections.* 82.

§. 1. What is understood by the terms, *the residence of the owners.* ib.

Residence in the same bailiwick or county. 83.

Residence not in the same bailiwick. ib.

§. 2. Is the captain at liberty

Page.

to borrow money at the port where the vessel is fitted out without the consent of the owners who are domiciliated elsewhere? 84.

§. 3. If the owners or their correspondents be on the spot? 85.

SECT. VII. *Of an unfaithful captain.*

§. 1. the owners are no further bound by the acts of the captain than as those acts relate to the voyage. 86.

§. 2. Penalties against a faithless captain. ib.

§. 3. The infidelity of the captain who has squandered the money shall not prejudice a third person who contracted with him *bonâ fidê.* 87.

§. 4. The lender is not obliged to prove that the loan was properly applied. ib.

Of a fraudulent bottomry or Respondentia bill.*

SECT. VIII. *Of an imprudent lender.*

§. 1. Is it necessary that the ship should actually be in need at the time of the loan? 81.

§. 2. If too much has been borrowed? 89.

If the ship arrive in a port where the money cannot be expended? ib.

§. 3. Of a captain who is prohibited from taking up money at gross adventure. ib.

§. 4. It is lawful for a party, according to circumstances, to avail himself of the exceptions established by the law of *Lucius Titius.* 91.

* This paragraph was inadvertently omitted in the body of the work, (p. 88.) and is therefore introduced in this place.

§. 5. If a bottomry bond which appears to have been subscribed by the captain in the course of the voyage and executed for the necessities of the ship, be fraudulent, it lies upon the owners to prove the fraud. Thus it was decided in Sweden, in a case reported by *Loccenius,* lib. 2. cap. 6. n. 12. (But it is not sufficient that the captain has been unfaithful: it must be shown that the lender was an accomplice. *Supra.* §. 3. and 4, and see the following section.

Page.

Sect. IX. *Of a captain who sells a part of his cargo in the course of the voyage.* 92.

Sect. X. Of the several actions given by the civil law in such cases, viz. the *actio principalis, accessoria* and *contraria.* 96.

§. 1. The Roman law. *ib.*

The action against the owner was given in addition to that against the master. *ib.*

It was optional to sue the master or the owner. *ib.*

This choice did not destroy the right of action against the master. 97.

If the master were a slave? *ib.*

When the person elected to sue the owner the action became a principal suit. *ib.*

It was *in solidum* and for the whole. *ib.*

There was no limitation against the *actio exercitoria. ib.*

§. 2. The new law. 98.

When the voyage is ended does the captain cease to be master? *ib.*

Can actions be instituted against him? *ib.*

When judgment is obtained against the master it may be executed upon the owners. *ib.*

Do the powers of the captain cease on the loss of the ship? 100.

Sect. XI. *Of abandonment by the owners in order to avoid being bound by the acts of the master.*

§. 1. Are the owners bound to answer jointly and severally for the acts of the master? 101.

The obligation of the owners for the acts of the master is more of a real than a personal nature? 102.

§. 3. Of a captain who is also supercargo. 103.

§. 4. If the owners abandon ship and freight? 104.

§. 5. May the captain borrow

Page.

money to be paid at an appointed time or draw bills of exchange? 105.

§. 6. The form of an abandonment made by the owners in order to avoid being responsible for the acts of the captain. 113.

§. 7. Exception on account of the ransom of the vessel.

Sect. XII. *Is the captain personally bound by the contracts which he makes in that capacity?*

§. 1. Is the person who contracts as agent for another personally bound? 114

Where an agent expressly states himself to be such or it is otherwise known? 115.

Whether he may be personally bound notwithstanding the designation of his quality. 115.

§. 2. Custom of merchants. 116.

Sect. XIII. *Stipulated penalty against a captain who violates his engagements.*

§. 1. The penalty stipulated by the captain may be rigorously exacted. 118.

Of a clause, that the freighter may exact the penalty stipulated with damages and interest. 122.

§. 2. Is the lien or privilege of mariners and of lenders at gross adventure in any way affected by the stipulated penalty above mentioned? 123.

CHAPTER V.

What things may be pledged in a maritime loan.

Sect. I. *Maritime loan on the ship or the cargo.*

§. 1. On the ship. 124.

§. 2. On the goods. 125.

§. 3. On the ship and the goods. 126.

§. 4. If it be expressed *on a certain vessel* without going farther? 127.

Page.

SECT. II. *Maritime loan on the freight, profits and wages.*
§. 1. On the freight.   130.
On the profits.   131.
§. 2. On the wages.   ib.
§. 3. Penalties inflicted by
the ordinance for the violation of the provisions
here treated of.   134.
SECT. III. *Maritime loan on a thing which is already at risk.*   135.
SECT. IV. *Is it lawful to lend any thing but money in a maritime loan?*
§. 1. What may be lent.   138.
§. 2. Union of the contract
of maritime loan with
others of a different na-
ture.   139.

CHAPTER VI.

Of cases in which maritime interest is not due.
SECT. I. *Of a return in conse-quence of their being no risque.*
§. 1. If there be no risk, it is
not a contract of mari-
time loan.   146.
§. 2. It is of no conse-
quence that the borrower
was unable or unwilling
to put the goods on board 147.
The borrower may retract
and rescind the contract
by his own act.   ib.
§. 3. The contract is not a
maritime loan but in pro-
portion to the value on
board.   149.
Of legal interest.   150.
The one half *per cent.* on the
premium to the underwri-
ter   ib.
SECT. II. *Of a fraudulent borrower.*
§. 1. Whether fraud is presumed against the person
who borrows beyond his
interest.   151.
§. 2. Punishment of a fraudulent borrower.   152.
He must restore the money
notwithstanding the loss

Page.

of the vessel.   152.
Whether he ought to pay
maritime interest.   153.
Whether he ought to pay
legal interest.   ib.
If the vessel return safely
ought he to pay maritime
interest?   ib.
SECT. III. *Proof of the lading*
§. 1. If the vessel be lost the
borrower must prove the
lading.   156
Whether the borrower
ought to pay a tenth part
of the loss.   156.
If the borrower carry the
money with him?   156.
Whether he must prove the
special employment of
the money.   157.
Whether he must prove
that the money was fur-
nished before the risk
commenced.   ib.
§. 2. The proof of the proper employment of the
money is never imposed
upon the lender.   158.

CHAPTER VII,

Of the risks.
ECT. I. Losses and averages
occasioned by the perils
of the sea.   158.
§. 1. Simple average.   ib.
§. 2. Gross average.   161.
§. 3. Clause, free from average.   163.
§. 4. Clause, that the risk of
the lender shall be con-
fined to certain specified
perils.   165.
SECT. II. *In general, the len-ders only bear the perils of the sea.*
§. 1. The perils of the sea
are the only risk he bears. 166.
§. 2. Internal defect of the
thing.   ib.
§. 3. Loss occasioned by the
act of man.   167.
Loss by contraband   197.
Observations on the text of
Art. 12. h. t.   168.
§. 4. Dangers by land.   169.

xiv

CONTENTS.

CHAPTER VIII.

Page.

Time and place of the risk.
Sect. I. *Of a contract of maritime loan for an entire voyage.*
§. 1. What is meant by an entire voyage. 179.
Contract for a voyage out and home. 170.
In case of doubt, it is to be presumed that it was for the voyage out and home. *ib*
§. 2. If the vessel do not return? *ib.*
Sect. II. *Contract for a limited time.*
§. 1. Losses which occur during the term are borne by the lender. 173.
The peril ceases with the time limited. *ib.*
§. 2. Clause, at so much a month not exceeding one year. 174.
Terms of the clearance. *ib.*
§. 3. Of a ship which is not heard of. *ib.*
§. 4. If the ship return before the expiration of the term. *ib.*
§. 5. Unlimited time. *ib.*
§. 6. Time of demurrage. *ib.*
Sect. III. *Of contracts for an entire voyage, with a designation of it or limitation of time.*
. 1. If there be a limited time and a designation of the voyage. 175.
For the voyage not exceeding six months, and *pro rata*, if it be longer. 176.
For the voyage at two per cent. a month 176.
Agreement that the first six months shall be due notwithstanding any accident subsequent to that time. *ib.*
§. 2. Agreement, that after a certain time the borrower shall pay one half

Page.

per cent. a month on the principal and interest. 178.
§. 3. Agreement, that in case of war the principal and interest shall be transmitted in bills of exchange. 179.
§. 4. Agreement, that in case of peace, the interest stipulated at so much *per month*, shall be reduced to the usual course of the place. *ib.*
Sect. IV. *Place of the risks and change of the ship.*
§. 1. Of a change of the voyage 180.
§. 2. Change of the ship. *ib.*

CHAPTER IX.

Of the payment of maritime monies.
Sect. I. *Is a bottomry bill negotiable?*
§. 1. Is it negotiable, if drawn payable to order? 182.
§. 2. Nature and effect of this negotiation. 183.
Guarantee in case of insolvency of the debtor. *ib.*
Sect. II. *In what manner, and at what time and place ought the money to be paid.*
§. 1. It ought to be paid in money. 18
§. 2. Ought it to be paid immediately on the safe arrival of the thing which was the subject of the loan? 185.
§. 3. If the money has been lent on the outward voyage or for a limited time. 186.
Risk of the money which is not demanded at the place where the term expires. *ib.*
§. 4. Competent judge. 187.
Provisional judgment. *ib.*
Arbitrations. *ib.*
Sect. III. *Of prescription or limitation of actions* 187.

CHAPTER X.

Page.

Of security.

SECT. 1. *In general, the security contracts the same obligations as the borrower.* The security is discharged by the renewal of the contract. 190.

SECT. II. *Whether the security is responsible for the fraud of the borrower.* 192.

SECT. III. *Of the obligation in solidum of the securities.* 195.

CHAPTER XI

Of the extinction and nullity of the contract of maritime loan.

SECT. I. *Comparison of the 11th 16th and 17th articles, h. t.*

§. 1. If there be an entire loss? 203.

§. 2. If there be a general average? *ib.*

If there be a particular average? *b.*

§. 3. Of a total loss. 204.

Opinions of Valin and Pothier. *ib.*

§. 4. If the goods of the borrower are landed before the accident. 205.

§. 5. Of unseaworthiness or stranding. 206.

SECT. II. *Of the right of the lender to the things saved.*

§. 1. Of the nature of the action which lies for the lender to recover the thing saved. 207.

Is the interest due in proportion to the amount saved. *ib.*

The things saved are pledged to the lender. 208.

Lien on the freight. *ib.*

Abandonment is not necessary. *ib.*

Apportionment between the assurer and the lender. 209.

SECT. III. *Does the contract become void by the ill success of the voyage?*

Page.

§. 1. General observations. 210.

§. 2. Relinquishment of the voyage before its commencement. 211.

Relinquishment of the voyage after it is commenced. *ib.*

§. 3. If the vessel, in consequence of an accident, never return. 212.

§. 4. If, owing to particular occurrences, the speculation of the borrower is not successful. 213.

CHAPTER XII.

Lien of the lender upon the effects at risk.

SECT. I. *View of the Roman laws relating to liens on the ship and cargo.* 215.

SECT. II. *Laws of France on the same subject.*

§. 1. The law *interdum* has been adopted among us. 217.

Can the ship be charged with hypothecation? *ib.*

§. 2. The lender on the hull has a lien upon the ship. 220.

If the vessel do not put to sea? *ib.*

The lender on the ship has a lien on the freight. 221.

If the borrower on the hull have relinquished the freight? *ib.*

Does the lien extend to the whole ship and freight? *ib.*

§. 3. Lien of the lender on the cargo. 222.

Effects landed before the accident. *ib.*

§. 4. Lien of the lender on the vessel and cargo. 223.

§. 5. The lien embraces both the principal and interest. *ib.*

§. The lien attaches though the bill be private. *ib.*

And although the holder do not prove the useful employment. *ib.*

SECT. III. *Priority of liens on a ship which has not commenced her voyage.*

Text of the ordinances.

1st *Rank.*

Vendor of the ship.   224.
The workmen.   ib.
Material men.   ib.
Concurrence of the above,
  persons.   ib.
If the vessel was built for a
  stipulated price.   225.
2nd. *Rank.*
The lender at bottomry.   229.
Money lent by a third person, [*not at bottomry.*]   230.
Joint owner who furnishes
  the proportion of his partner.   231.
SECT. IV. *Priority of liens on
  a vessel which returns
  from her voyage.*
1st *Rank.*
Mariners.   232
2nd *Rank.*
Creditors for loans made
  during the voyage.   233.
Owners of merchandize sold
  during the voyage to supply the necessities of the
  ship.   234.
3rd *Rank.*
Creditors for loans made before the departure of the
  ship.   235.
Material men.   ib.
Workmen.   236.
4th *Rank.*
Shippers of small adven-
  tures.   ib.
5th *Rank.*
Creditors for the premium
  of insurance.   237.
6th *Rank.*
Money left by renewal.   ib.
7th *Rank.*
The vendor.   239.
SECT. V. *Priority of liens on
  the cargo.*
1st *Rank.*
Charges of unlading.   241.
2nd *Rank.*
Freight and general ave-
  rage.   ib.
3rd *Rank.*
Furnishers of particular articles, during the voyage
  for the safety of the thing. ib.

4th *Rank.*

Lenders before the depar-
  ture.   ib.
Lenders at an intermediate
  part.   ib.
Does the vendor of the merchandize come in con-
  currence with the lender
  on the cargo?   212
SECT. VI. *Claim of property
  —Severance of
  property.*
Vendor's right of lien.   246.
Severance of property.   ib.
SECT. VII. *Of those who have
  priviledged or concurrent
  claims, on the property
  saved and the policies of
  insurance.*
§. 1. Salvage.   253.
Seamen's wages.   ib.
Other creditors.   ib.
Lien on the freight.   ib.
§. 3. Lien on the policies.   ib.
§. 3. Concurrence between
  several different creditors.   259.
SECT. VIII. *Of priority in
  cases where there are secret part owners by assignment from the original
  owner.*
§. 1. General observations.   259.
§. 2, Are those who lend at
  risk to the assignor preferred to the assignee?   260.
§. 3. Are those who lend at
  risk to the assignee preferred to the assignor   260.
§. 4. What if the interest assigned had been modified
  by a contract of maritime
  loan.   ib.
What if the assignee had
  given bills of gross adventure to the assignor
  as the consideration of
  the interest assigned?   261.
De Exercitoria Actione.   267.
De lege Rhodia de Jactu.   279.
De Nautico Fœnore, Digests.   288.
Same title from the Code.   292.
Des Contrats à la grosse.
  Aventure.   294.

AN ESSAY

ON

MARITIME LOANS.

THERE is a great resemblance between contracts of Maritime Loan and Insurance. They
frequently appear to be governed by the same
rules. They are twin brothers, to whom maritime commerce has given birth: yet each has a
character peculiar to itself.

But we cannot dispute the promogeniture of
Maritime Law. It enjoys certain privileges of
which Insurance is deprived. But Insurance has
acquired an extensive empire ; and its nobility,
though less ancient, surpasses the other in dignity.
I mean *among ourselves ;* for in Marseilles, the borrowers, are, in general, a kind of people not much
favoured with the gifts of fortune, to whom money
is trusted, in this way, very sparingly.

C

CHAPTER I.

General Observations.

Although Insurance was but little known to the Romans, yet the contract of which we treat was in general use among them.

That which we term money lent at bottomry or respondentia, or, to use a more general expression, money lent at maritime interest and risk, was called by the Romans, *pecunia trajectitia*. Not that it was given by one person to another merely for the purpose of having it transported from one place to another, but because it was lent to a person, to be employed by him in maritime commerce, upon condition of returning it, in case of a successful trade, with maritime interest. And there was a stipulation that it should not be returned, nor should interest be paid for the loan of it, if the vessel should happen to be lost by the perils of the sea, in the prosecution of a specified voyage. *Pecunia nautica quæ et trajectitia et maritima dicitur, est, quæ periculo creditoris in navem recepta, trajicienda committitur. (a)*

a Calvinus.

SECTION I.

Texts of the Roman law relating to Maritime Loans.

L. 1. ff. de naut. fœn.

The law 1 *ff. de naut. fœnor.* says, that *trajectitia pecunia** is that which is transported beyond sea, *trajectitia pecunia est, quæ trans mare vehitur:* that is

---

* So called, because it was given to the borrower to be employed by him in commercial speculations upon and beyond seas.

to say, that which is transported beyond sea at the risk of the lender, and to be employed in merchan, dise for the advantage of the borrower.

If this money be expended in the same place in which it has been furnished, it is not said to be *tra-jectitia*: *cæterùm, si eodem loci consumatur, nor erit trajectitia;* but if it be expended in the purchase of merchandise in the place where it was lent, which merchandise is afterwards embarked at the risk of the lender, it preserves its quality of being *trajec-titia. Sed videndum, an merces ex eâ pecuniâ com-paratæ, in eâ causâ habeantur : et interest utrum etiam ipso periculo creditoris navigent; tunc enim trajectitia pecunia fit.* We perceive by this last sen tence, that the essence of maritime loan consists in the hazard of the lender.

The money is not at the risk of the creditor un- L. 3. fl. til the vessel has set sail. *In nauticâ pecuniâ, ex* eod. *ea die periculum spectat creditorem, ex quo navem, navigare conveniat:* that is, the lender incurs the hazard from the moment that it commences.

This is a text which demands attention. It is of L. 4. fl. no consequence, says Papinian, if the money has eod. been furnished, in the first instance, upon condition that the maritime peril shall not be incurred by the creditor : nor if the peril has ceased to be at his risk by the completion of the term or condition stipulat-ed : in either case, nothing is due but common le-gal interest: *utrubi, majus legitimâ usura fœnus non debebitur.* But in the first case, that is, when the money of the creditor never has incurred the mari-time hazard, *(trajectitiâ pecuniâ sine periculo cre-ditoris acceptâ)* it is, beyond dispute, only a loan at ordinary interest: *in priore quidem specie, semper.* In the second case, on the expiration of a certain term or the fulfilment of a certain condition, *(post diem præstitutum et conditionem impletam, periculum esse creditori, desierit)* the legal rate of interest shall be chargeable in consequence of the want of maritime interest: *in alterâ verò discusso periculo.* In either case the creditor cannot retain the pledge or lien that has been given to him and which would enable him to demand a maritime interest, not due to him: *nec pignora vel hypothicæ, titulo majoris usuræ, tenebuntur.*

Upon this text, I shall remark, 1st, That, according to *Papinian*, we cannot apply the term *trajectitia* to money furnished for a transmarine voyage, upon a condition that it shall not be at the risk of the lender; but that in such a case, it is an imperfect contract, which does not authorise the demand of maritime interest.

2d. It was lawful to lend upon bottomry, or for an entire voyage, or for a limited time; but as soon as the lender ceased to run the risk *(discusso periculo)* the common and not the maritime interest was to be paid.

3d. The lender was not prohibited from demanding pledges and hypothecations as an additional security; provided that it was not a pretext for exacting maritime interest after the sea risk should be at an end.

On the §
1. of law
4. ff. eod.
(a) L. 4.
§. 1. ff. de
naut fœn.
L. 23. de
oblig. et
act. L.
122. ff de
verb.
oblig.

When the money was only furnished for a part of a voyage, it was usual, in consequence of the difficulty attending epistolary correspondence, to despatch a slave, for the purpose of demanding the principal and interest at the place where the risk ceased to be at the hazard of the lender, and to stipulate for the payment of a pecuniary penalty in case the borrower should not perform his obligation.*(a)*

The penalty was due at the expiration of the term, unless no person had appeared to demand payment.*(a)* This penalty could not afterwards exceed the common legal interest beyond which it was not lawful to exact any thing.*(b)*

et act. Cujas. (*b*) d. L. 4. §. 1. ff. de naut. fœn. ib. Cujas.

(a) L. 2. 8. 9 ff. de naut. fœn.
L. 23. ff. de oblig.

The law, *periculi pretium,* 5 *ff. de naut fœn.* is very obscure. The text is certainly corrupted. We may however infer that in contracts of hazard, that which is received beyond the principal is a premium paid for the risk: *periculi pretium est.* And in such cases the simple agreement, not clothed with an express stipulation is sufficient to augment the obligation. *In his omnibus, et pactum sine stipulatione ad augendum obligationem prodest.*

That which is received, then, beyond the principal is less an interest than an increase of the debt, in consideration of the peril to which the money is exposed.*(c)* And as *Dumoulin* says, in the explanation which he has given of this law (upon usurious contracts after No. 102,) *valet sine stipulatione, nec subest taxationi usurarum, quia augmentum sortis non est usura, sed periculi pretium.(d)*

(c) ib. Cujas.

(*d*) vid. L. 7. ff. eod.
Kuricke, quœst. 26.

I have lent you, at maritime interest a sum of money on merchandise laden on board your vessel; in consequence of which you have hypothecated, not only these goods, but others, which are on board of other vessels. If the vessel, which was the object of the contract, be lost, my principal and interest are also lost and I cannot resort to the other goods, upon which I had run no risk. This is the decision of the law 6 *ff. de naut. fœn.* because, as is observed by *Cujas* upon this law, (lib. 25. *quœst.* Pauli) the principal obligation being extinguished, the hypothecation, which was only accessary, is also at an end. *Cùm principalis obligatio non consistit, nec pignoratitia, quæ sequitur, locum habet.*

L. 6. ff. eod.

L. 1. C.
de naut.
fœn. Money lent on Bottomry or at Respondentia, the risk of which is incurred by the creditor, cannot bear extraordinary interest longer than while the risk continues. *Trajectitiam pecuniam, quæ periculo creditoris datur, tandiu liberam esse ab observatione communium usurarum, quamdiù navis ad portum adpulerit, manifestum est.*

L. 2. C.
eod. If you do not encounter maritime hazards, you cannot claim a greater interest than is allowed by law.

L. 3. C.
eod. The lender is not prejudiced by a loss, which happens at sea through the fault of the borrower.

L. 4. C.
eod. Until the vessel is arrived at her port of destination, the perils of navigation are at the risk of the lender, who has agreed to incur them. But if there be no stipulation to that effect, the borrower runs the risk. *Sine hujusmodi verò conventione, infortunio naufragii non liberabitur.**

Opinion
of Paulus. Paulus, *lib.* 2. *sentent. tit.* 14. decides that money to be transported is susceptible of an indefinite interest, because of the peril which the creditor takes upon himself. *Trajectitia pecunia propter periculum creditoris, quamdiù navigat navis, infinitas usuras recipere potest.*

L. 26. C.
de usuris. *Justinian* seems to have wished to reduce the maritime interest to one *per cent.* per month.*(a)* *Doumoulin, (b)* says that the law of *Justinian,* relates

a See the
novels
106. 110. b contrats usur. n. 91, &c.

---

* But then he cannot stipulate for or receive any more than his principal with legal interest. The contract, in that case, is a mere hypothecation or pledge of the vessel or goods, for the security of the money which has been lent; but it is not properly speaking, a maritime loan.

And bottomry bonds may be given for security of mercantile or other debts, either in places where the owners dwell, or in foreign places by their order. *Bee's Adm. dec.* 348.

only to navigation at ordinary seasons, when there was little danger: but that when the danger was considerable, he enforced the law *periculi pretium*, 5 ff. *de naut. fœn.* of which he endeavours to give a new explanation.

It seems to me that it was easier to say, that the law of Justinian was applicable to money which was to be transported, the risk of which was not run by the creditor, who is comprehended in the law 4. ff. *de naut. fœn.* This explanation is not at variance with the law 26. C. de usuris, nor with the text of the novels, 106, 110.

Calimachus residing at Beritus, a village in Syria, received a sum of money at bottomry from *Stichus*, a slave of *Seius*, for a voyage from Beritus to Brandusium and back; with a warranty that the vessel should sail from Brandusium before the ides of September. A slave was embarked to attend the execution of the contract. And it was agreed that if the vessel should not leave the port of Brandusium on her return voyage to Beritus before the ides of September, the principal, together with maritime interest and the expences of the slave, who was despatched, should be paid at Brandusium, in order to be sent to Rome. Both the outward and inward cargo were hypothecated to the lender. The Ides arrived, and the vessel had not sailed. *Erotus*, the slave appointed to go in her, instead of demanding the money, consented that the vessel should put to sea for Beritus, although the stipulated term had elapsed. The vessel was lost. The law decides that it was not the loss of the creditor, because the slave had no power to prolong the term. *(a)* [L. 122, § 1. ff. de verb. oblig.]

Upon all the texts which I have explained, you may read the learned commentaries *Stypmannus (b)* and *Locenius. (c)*

a Ibid. Cujas, lib. 2. obs. 11.

b part 4. cap. 2.
c lib. 2. cap. 6.

An Essay on

The *Guidon de la Mer, (a)* says, that the contract
of bottomry, such as is now customary, has very little
resemblance to that which was formerly in use. But
this assertion is not true, except as it regards the
form which modern rules have given to this contract
whose origin is lost in antiquity. *L'origine di questo
contratto è molto antica, percio di essa ne fanno es-*
b Targa, *pressa mentione le leggi tanto civili, quanto canoniche;*
cap. 32. n. *mà di forma, o piu tosto diri forma, è moderno. (b)*
5. p. 131.

SECTION II.

Definition, denomination, legality and nature of
Maritime Loan.

§ Defini- I adopt the definition which M. Pothier gives of
tion.   this contract.

a n. 1. h. " The contract of maritime loan," he says *(a)*
t.   " is an agreement by which one, who is the lender,
lends to an other, who is the borrower, a certain
sum of money, upon condition that if the thing
upon which the loan has been made, should be lost,
by any peril of the sea, or *vis major*, the lender
shall not be repaid, unless what remains shall be
equal to the sum borrowed; and that if the thing
arrive in safety, or in case that it shall not have been
injured, but its own defect or the fault of the master and mariners, the borrower shall be bound to
return the sum borrowed, together with a certain
sum agreed upon as the price of the hazard incurred."

This definition is taken from the Roman laws,
formerly cited. It is to be found nearly the same
in all our books. *(b)*

b Stypm.
part. 4   cap. 2. n. 13. p. 378. Kur. jus Hans. lit. 6, p. 761. Locc. lib. 2. cap. 6. n.
2. p. 988. Targa, cap. 32. n. 6. Lubeck, de avariis p. 126. Wolfius and his glossarist
§.680.681. 2. Black cap. 30. p. 461. dict. de Savary verb. contrat *d* la grosse Prevôt de
le Jannès, principes de jurisprud. tit. 20. n. 556.

We have just seen that in the Roman law the contract of maritime loan is commonly called *pecunia trajectitia*, and sometimes *pecunia nautica, fœnus nauticum, (a) &c.*

§. 2. Denominati- on.

a Kuricke jus. hans.tit. 6. p. 761. Lubeck p. 126.

In the Guidon de la Mer, *(b)* it is called *bome- rie,* from a Flemish word which signifies a *keel* or bottom. Wolf *(c)* makes a distinction between *pecunia trajectitia,* money lent to be transported, and *bomerie.* By the former he means money advanced upon merchandise, and by the latter, that which is given upon the body of the vessel.* But the nature of the contract is the same in both cases.

b ch. 18.

c § 680

Among us the contract is called *gross adventure,* because the lender exposes his money to the perils of the sea and contributes to the gross or general average. It is also called a loan on the return voyage (*à retour de voyage,*) because the lender generally runs all sea risks until the safe return of the ship.(*d*)

d Valin. 2. Poth. n. 1. h. t.

In many countries of Italy the contract of bottomry is called hypothecation. I ship certain goods on board a vessel and receive a sum of money from the captain, for which I hypothecate the vessel to him and stipulate to pay him a maritime interest. If the vessel return, I pay the freight of the goods, the sum which I have received and the stipulated interest. If the vessel perish, the captain loses his money and I lose my goods.

He who furnishes the money is termed the lender and he who receives it, the borrower.(*e*) In the Roman law the lender is termed the creditor.

e Savary verb. con- trat *à la* grosse.

---

* In like manner we distinguish between money lent at Respondentia, which answers to the *pecunia trajectitia* of the Romans, and *Bottomry,* a term which is derived from the same source; and corresponds with the French word *bomerie.*

D

The condition is said to be fulfilled, when the vessel arrives in safety at her destined port; and it is not performed when the voyage is not completed.(*a*)

c Cujas, in loc. cit.

§ 3. Lawfulness of contract.

* It is beyond doubt that this contract, without which commerce would languish extremely, is lawful. The interest which the lender claims, in case of a successful voyage, is the price of hazard, *periculi pretium* and has nothing in it which resembles usury.

Nevertheless it seems to me that it is declared to be usurious by the 19th chap. *extra de usuris Naviganti, vel eunti ad nundinas certam mutuans pecuniæ quantitatem, pro eo, quod suscipit in se periculum, recepturus aliquid ultra sortem, usurarius est censendus.*†

---

* The stat. 6. Geo. 1. c. 18. enacts that during the continuance of the Royal Exchange and the London Assurance Companies, which were subsequently erected in pursuance of this statute by 8. Geo. 1. c. 15. § 25. all other corporations or bodies politick, sole or aggregate, and all societies and partnerships for assuring ships or merchandise at sea, or for lending money upon bottomry, should be restrained from so assuring or lending. All bottomry securities contrary to this act are made void, the contract is deemed usurious and the offenders are to be punished as in cases of usury. But private persons are not prohibited from lending at bottomry in the same manner as they might have done before the statute was enacted. Nor does it prevent the South Sea or East India Company from advancing money on bottomry on ships or goods on board ships or to persons employed in their service. §. 26.

† This is a text of the Canon law, which our author has introduced, as we presume, merely to show the different opinions which have been entertained upon the subject. The various interpretations that have been given to this text can be of no practical use even in France, for there the extravagants, i. e. Papal constitutions, which are a part of the Canon law, have never been considered as in force.

Upon the strength of this text certain writers en- Different interpretations of the cap. naviganti. *a* Introd. de assecur. n. 26, &c.
veigh against this contract and term it usurious.
Straccha (*a*) has entered into an elaborate disserta-
tion upon this subject, which has been censured by
the generality of civilians. But they do not agree
in their interpretations of the chapter, *Naviganti.*

Some say that the chapter ought to be understood First Interpretation.
of cases where the money has been furnished upon
bottomry for a voyage, which may be performed
without just fear of peril : *quod ibi simultanteè, dici-*
tur de mutuante naviganti, intelligitur de navigante *b* 2. Dumoulin contr. usur. n. 95. p. 38.
in flumine, vel ita tutò, ut cesset justus timor peri-
culi.(*b*) But there is no voyage without some damage, be it more or less.

The lender upon bottomry is not declared to be Second interpretation.
an usurer, he is only presumed to be so : *usurarius*
est censendus. This legal presumption, they say, is
admitted in courts though not in conscience.

If I stipulate for a maritime interest in consideration of a loan, I am guilty of usury : but if the interest be to be paid in consideration of the risk to
which my money is exposed, my conscience is safe.
Fagnan upon this chapter n. 21. and 24. says,

Ego ad concilianaas opiniones, puto sic distin-
guendam : aut quæritur, an ejusmodi, contractus
censeatur usurarius in foro externo, et quantum
ad judicium ecclesiæ : aut quæritur, an sit usura-
rius in foro animæ, et quoad Deum. In primo
casu, existimo contractum judicari, usurarium, et
ita procedere opinionem Canonistarum; quia, cum
creditor recipit in se periculum rei mutuatæ, et
aliquid accipit ultra sortem, ecclesia judicat princi-
pale objectum illius ess ex lucrum ex mutuo; ita ut
non sit audsendns si dicat, se non recipere ratione
mutui, sed solùm ratione periculi; quia cum hoc
consistat in intentione, non pertinet ad Judicium
Ecclesiæ, quæ nón judicat de occultis.

In secundo autem casu, id est in foro animæ, vera videtur Theologorum distinctio: Nam si mutuans recipiat aliquid ultrà sortem ratione mutui, seu eâ intentione ut lucretur ex mutuo, quamvis periculum in se suscipiat, absque dubio est usura, quæ solâ voluntate committitur; sed si verè non intendat lucrari ex mutuo, sed tantummodò accipere per mercedem, seu pretium periculi, in foro interiori, et quantum ad Deum non est usurarius.   Itaque tota hæc res ab intentione distinguitur, et specificatur.

In dubio autem cum non distinguit an lucrum recipiat ratione mutui, vel ratione periculi, ceusetur recipere ratione mutui: et ideò usura est: et sic arbitror posse conciliari dissidentes opiniones: quod nota.

Third interpretation.

Maritime loan or gross adventure is composed of three different contracts: 1. The contract of partnership, as to the profits of the voyage. 2. The contract for the sale of an uncertain portion of these same profits, if a portion have been agreed upon. 3. The contract of assurance, by which the lender takes upon himself the risk as much as to the principal; as to the portion stipulated, which is indicated to him on the profits.   [In this circuitous manner we arrive at the lawfulness of bottomry and evade the Pontifical decision. (*a*)

u de Luca de credito. disc. 3. n. 9. de usuris. disc. 3. Casaregis disc. 14.   62, Targa ch. 32.

Fourth interpretation.

Some doctors get over the difficulty, by adding a negative to the text of the Decretal.*   They pretend that we should read *usurarius non est censendus*. Indeed, what follows the text seems to require this particular negative.   Ille quoque *qui dat decem solidos, ut alio tempore totidem sibi grani, vini, vel olei mensuræ reddantur: quæ licet tunc plùs valeant, utrùm plusvel minùs solutionis tempore fuerint valituræ, verismiliter dubitatur: non debet ex hoc*

---

* A technical term by which the laws of the Papal powers are denominated.

usurarius reputari. Ratione hujus dubii etiam ex-cusatur qui pannos, granum, vinum, oleum, vel alias merces vendit, ut ampliùs, quàm tunc valeaut in certo termino recipiat pro eisdem: si tameu ea tempore contractûs non fuerat venditurus.

Now, if it be not equally usurious, when I give you to-day ten crowns, upon condition that you shall deliver me wine, oil or fruit to the value of the money, according to the market price, a year hence: if it be not equally usurious when I sell you, to-day, a certain quantity of cloth, grain, oil or other merchandise for the price at which those arti-cles may be sold six months hence—if, in these cases, the uncertainty of the event makes the con-tract lawful, the same must be said in favour of bottomry. The words of the text, *ille quoque qui dat decem solidos—non debet ex hoc usurarius repu-tari,* imply that the lender on bottomry, who is be-fore spoken of ought not equally to be esteemed an usurer. Puto igitur negationem omissam, esse in-serandam. Stypmannus, part. 4. cap. 2. n. 181. p. 399. Fachin, lib. 2. cap. 47. Cabassut, lib. 6. cap. 8. Gibalinus, de usuris, lib. 2. cap 4. art. 3. n. 25.

This opinion is warmly disputed by the Cardinal de Lucca. *(a)* He treats it as the result of error and ignorant temerity : *de errore et indoctâ temeritate.* *a* de usu-ris, disc. 3. n. 7. 8. and 9.

Molina, *(b)* after having reduced to three princi-pal conclusions the different opinions of the jurists upon the chapter *naviganti,* finishes by telling us that we may take which we please : *ex his tribus expositionibus, elige quem malueris.** *b* de just. et. jur. disput. 318. vol. 2. p. 283.

---

* Much learning and ingenuity have been wasted by many very sensible writers in attempting to prove the immorality and wicked-ness of usury. Some cite a proposition of Aristotle, which is probably misunderstood, that money is naturally barren and therefore cannot produce. But these same writers, by admit-ting that there is no immorality in receiving legal interest de-

The De-
cretal na-
viganti
should be
set aside.

To use this liberty in its fullest extent, I think that we should set aside the whole chapter, with its commentary. The Decretals, inserted in the body of the Canon Law, not having been published in France nor adopted by our Sovereigns, they have not, in themselves, the force of law. *We may cite them as an authority which is highly respectable but they must not prevail over the civil law.* (Edit du mois de Mars 1769, concernant l'administration de la Justice dans l'etat d'Avignon and le Comtè Venaissin, tit. 3. art. 1. Hericourt, Loix Ecclesiastiques, tom 1. p. 13. 107.)

Bottomry
is a con-
tract of a
particular
nature.

Bottomry is adopted in all commercial countries.* It is not a sale nor a partnership, nor a loan, properly speaking, nor an assurance, nor a contract composed of different kinds : *undique collatis mem-*

---

stroy this absurd argument. Those who quote the Holy Scriptures, *Lev.* xxv. 35. 36. 37. and many other texts, seem not to be aware that the mosaical laws were chiefly political and not moral precepts. Besides, the Jews were expressly permitted to take usurious interest of a stranger, though not of a brother. *Deut.* 19. 20.

There is no more reason in this declamation against usury, as a moral offence; than there would be in censuring those who demand a high rent for a house or an extravagant hire for a horse. But it is proper that the law should interpose between the cupidity of some and the wants of others, and therefore a legal rate of interest has been established : and it is proper that avarice and oppression should be despised, and therefore the practice is considered as disreputable. Nevertheless it may be doubted whether laws against usury do not operate to the prejudice of those whom they are intended to protect, by making them pay, not only for the use of the money, but for the danger of detection, which the lender incurs. "Laws excessively good," says Montesquieu, " are the source of excessive evils."

* To constitute a right to hypothecate the ship, there must be urgent necessity, in a foreign port, and a total want of sufficient personal credit and the bond may be sued in the admiralty though it was made on land—3 Mod. 244. for the service at sea is the principal consideration. 4. Burr. 1950. 2. Ld. Raym. 1044. 2. Wils. 265. 1. Ld. Raym. 576. Hypothecation cannot be made to a consignee. Hopkinson's Rep. (in Bee. 339.)

bris; but it is a specific contract known to the law. It has a character and qualities peculiar to itself. It has been introduced into commerce for the advantage of society. It is such as has been defined above. It is different from all other contracts and forms one of a particular kind. *(a.)* *a* Pothier n. 6. h. t.

The legality of this contract is recognized by all our lawyers. *(b.)*   Its legality is not disputed.

b. Kuricke, quœst. 24. Locc. lib. 2. cap. 6. n. 3. p. 988. Rocc, n. 50. Casaregis, disc. 14. n. 1. Targa cap. 32. Daix, sur le statut. de marseille, p. 377. Covaruvias, variar. resolut. lib. 3. cap. 2. n. 5. Stypmannus, part. 4. cap. 2. n. 108. p. 385· 2. Valin, 2. •

Fagnan, (d.) who argues that bottomry is presumed to be usurious *in forc exteriori,* is compelled to acknowledge that his opinion is at variance with that of most of the Theologians: *contrariam opinionem, videlicit nauticum fœnus nullo jure improbari, amplectuntur communiter Theologi; quia quod in hac specie ultrá sortem accipitur, non datur ratione mutui, nec propter nudum interesse inter usurii temporis, Sed propter justissimam causam, id est, propter periculum quod in se suscipit creditor, contra naturam mutui.* He cites St. Thomas, St. Antoninus and a crowd of other writers.   *d* inloc. cit.

In the opinion of all these grave Divines the contract of Bottomry is authorized by our marine ordinance, and it contains nothing in itself which is contrary to justice, provided there be no fraud : for, as *Pothier* observes, *(b)* the usury which is prohibited by the Civil and Ecclesiastical laws is that which consists in exacting something beyond the sum lent, by way of reward for the loan, *vi mutui;* but, in this contract, the maritime profit which is stipulated beyond the sum lent, is not a reward for the loan, but the price of the risk, which the lender undertakes to the exoneration of the borrower.   *b* n. 2. h t.

---

* The authors whose names are here quoted are of various nations. He does not therefore allude to the French lawyers exclusively.

§ 4.
The con-
tract of
bottomry
is more of
a real
than a
personal
nature.

In considering the nature of this contract, we shall find that it is rather real than personal.* Commerce is its sole object. The maritime interest, which is the price of the risk, is considered, to some purposes, as a part of the profits of the voyage. If the ship perish, the lender can claim nothing; and if nothing has been exposed to the waves of the sea, there has been no contract of bottomry.

Is it
mutual?

a Pothier
n. 3.

† Pothier *(a)* says that " this contract is unilateral, or, on one side only; because the lender is under no obligation to the borrower by the contract. " No one" he continues "is bound but the borrower, who engages to return the money borrowed, with maritime profit, if no accident of *vis major* shall occasion the loss of the effects upon which the loan has been made."

Each par-
ty is in-
terested

" In this contract continues the same author, *ib.* n. 4. there is an interest on each side; and it differs, in this respect, from an ordinary loan, which is a contract of benevolence, that concerns the interest of the borrower only and imports, on the part of the lender, nothing but the pure service which he renders the borrower by granting the use of his money without reward. But the contract of maritime loan is made for the interest of the lender as well as for that of the borrower. The lender does not contemplate the rendering of any service to the borrower, but he expects to receive the maritime interest, which is stipulated, if he is not prevented by some accident."

---

* The civilians denominate *real contracts*, those from which an action *in rem* results, and those which require an action *in personam* are called personal contracts. It is of no consequence in the former case, whether the subject of the contract be land or moveable property. The word, *real*, in the Civil Law, does not apply, as with us, exclusively to land.

† *Synallagmatique.* A term derived from the Greek, which is applied, by the French, to contracts that are mutually obligatory.

"Maritime loan is to be ranked he adds, *ib.* n. 5. among the number of aleatory or gaming contracts," [inasmuch as it depends, in a great measure upon chance.] "The risk of the loss of the effects upon which the loan is made and which the lender runs, is valued at a price which is the maritime profit; and this the borrower binds himself to pay in case of a safe arrival."

(margin: Conditional. It is an aleatory or gaming contract.)

The borrower contracts to return the sum lent and to pay him a certain stipulated interest for the use of it. But this contract is not made, even for the return of the principal, but with a condition, that no accident of *vis major* shall happen, which shall occasion the loss of the effects upon which the loan is made. *(a)*

(margin: a ib. 33. Targa cap. 33. not. 4. p. 141.)

SECTION III.

It is essential to this contract that there be a risk, and that that risk be incurred by the lender.

At Leghorn and in other parts of Italy it is lawful to lend money at bottomry by way of wager. If the vessel arrive in safety, the principal and maritime interest become due to the lender; and if the ship perish, all is lost to him although the borrower has not employed the money which he received in commerce nor has had any property at stake. *(b)*

(margin: §. 1. bottomry by way of wager.)

(margin: b Cassaregis disc. 14. 15.)

The stipulation, *interest or no interest* is a real wager. I have spoken of it in my treatise on insurance. *(c)* terest. c Cassa. disc. 62. n. 27. et seq. ch. 1. Sect. 11. §. 4.

(margin: Clause, interest or no interest.)

This is not permitted among us. To constitute this contract the money must be invested in something which is exposed to the dangers of the sea; and in case of loss, it is incumbent on the borrower to prove property to the amount of the loan. *(d)*

(margin: d Art. 3. 14. h. 1.)

E.

§ 2. The peril must be borne by the lender.

It is not less essential to this contract that the peril be borne by the lender: *periculo creditoris.*(a) by the lender. *a* L. 1, 3. 4. 5. ff. de naut. fœn. L. 1. 2. 4. C. eod. Pothier n. 16. h. t. Stypm. part. 4. cap. 2. n. 14. p. 378.

It is not properly bottomry until the risk commences.

It cannot properly be said to be a contract of bottomry until the day that the risk commences; *ea die periculum spectat creditorem.*(b) commences. *b* L. 3. ff. de naut. fœn.

If the money be expended on land before the commencement of the risk?

From which it follows that if the borrower expend the money on shore without exposing it to the dangers of the sea, it is not a contract of bottomry, although it may be so called in the instrument of writing, *si eodem loci consumatur, non erit trajectitia.(c)*

c L. 1. ff. de naut. fœn. [Vezey 154. 1. Ld Raym 578. 2. ib. 982. Bee 346.]

If the risk cease ?

As soon as the risk ceases, either by the safe arrival of the vessel or by the expiration of the stipulated term, the contract ceases to bear maritime interest.(d)

d L. 4. ff. de naut fœn. L. 1. C. eod.

If the contract was, ab initio, void.

If the contract was void in its commencement, the maritime interest is not chargeable, because no maritime dangers were borne by the lender.*

---

* A bargain on a mere contingency, where the reward is given for the risk, not for forbearance, will not be within the statute. *Cro. Eliz.* 643. *Button v. Downham.* If therefore a man give or lend money not to be paid if the event should be one way, but double if the other, and it is uncertain which way it will happen, it is not within the statute: for the reward is given for the risk and not for forbearance. But if under colour of such an hazardous bargain the real treaty is for a loan, with an usurious reward for that loan, and to evade the statute, the contingency inserted is of little moment, being no ingredient between the parties: the court or a jury on the whole may pronounce such a contract usurious, notwithstanding the colour of contingency, if they are satisfied the reward is given for forbearance, not for the risk.

The intent of the bargain is the material thing: if that was borrowing the money, it is within the statute, whatever colourable contingency is inserted: and this is the sense of all the resolutions in the several cases. 5, *Co.* 69. 70. 2. *And.* 15. *Mo.* 397. *and Mason v. Abdy.* But where the principal was fairly and truly put in hazard, and such as none would run for the interest the law allows, there is no case where it has been held within the statute. The slightness or reality of the risk seems to be the only rule directing the judgment of the court. Cro. Eliz. 741. Bedingfield v. Ashley; and in 3. Keb. 304. Long. v. Wharton, which, though inaccurately reported, seems to me to be good law.

I cannot see two contracts bearing a greater similitude than this [bond by A. aged thirty in consideration of a loan of £ 5000. to pay £ 10,000 if he survive B. aged 78.] and bottomry. A life may be insured ; so may a ship, which may sink the day after : so may the party die : one is as much an adventure as the other. It was endeavoured to distinguish *bottomry* from every contract upon this, that though above what the law allows upon a loan, yet bottomry contracts were established in favour of trade, there being a risk of the principal and they being necessary for trade and commerce. But whatever favour the court may show to such contracts, they will never establish them upon the destruction of a statute ; and the princ ple of the court thereon was, that the bottomry bond was not within the statute ; nor could it be ; for it is plain that a real risk was run, that the principal may never be payable ; therefore it cannot be given for forbearance, but grounded merely on the contingency, the risk. But as a colourable contingency in case of a life annexed to the payment may make that bond usurious, so will a colourable contingency annexed to a bottomry contract : as in a bond, if one out of twenty ships bound from Newcastle to London, arrived safe ; that would be a contingency thrown in to evade the statute, which would be too hard for such a bond : so if such a contract is made, if the packet should return to *Dover* from *Calais* at a season of the year when their is no danger : and this I may say with the more security, as *Joy v. Kent, Hard.* 418. is an express proof of it ; where a bottomry bond was sent to be tried whether it was an evasion of the statue ; which would not have been so if it could not have been an evasion. Indeed Lord *Hale* throws out expressions very favourable to trade, but so inaccurate in that book, that I do not think they could be such as came out of the mouth of so great a man. One of the first cases of bottomry, which came in question, was *Sharpely v. Harrel,* Cr. I. 208. what the court goes on there, is the real risk of receiving less ; which is cited again in *Roberts v. Trenayn* 2. Roll. 47. and Cr. I. 508. which differed from the other. In *Soome v. Glen,* as in 1. Sid 27. the resolution is founded on the real hazard of the principal, which cannot be within the statue. *Per* Burnet, I Earl of Chesterfield v. Jansen. 2. Vez. 143.

SECTION IV.

Difference between contracts of bottomry and those of loan, partnership and insurance.

§. 1. Bottomry and loan. Bottomry is different from the contract of loan, because: 1. The peril of money, simply lent, concerns the borrower: whereas money lent at bottomry is at the risk of the lender.*(a)*

a L. 11. C. sicertum petatur. Locc. lib. 3. cap. 2. n. 4. p. 1012.

2. In a simple loan, interest is not due but by positive stipulation,*(b)* whereas maritime interest is implied in the contract itself.*(c)*

b Sententiæ Pauli lib. 2. tit 14. ib. Cujas, L. 3. ff. 3. de usur. L. 24.ff. de præsc. verb.

c L. 5. §. 1. ff. de naut. fœn. ib. Cujas.

3. In a simple loan, the interest, among merchants, could not exceed the rate fixed by the Prince, or, at most the custom of the country; whereas bottomry may carry any interest.*(d)*

d Supra §. 1. Poth. n. 2. h. t.

4. Legal interest is calculated annually, in a successive manner and separate from the principal: *seorsim ab ipsâ sorte ;* whereas the whole maritime interest is due jointly with the principal and at the same time; *simul et semel;(e)* and as *Dumoulin* observes,*(f)* the maritime interest is an augmentation of the principal : *augmentum sortis.*

e Styp. part. 4. cap. 2. n. 3. p. 379. Targa cap. 33. not. 18. p. 148. *f* Contrats usur. n. 102.

§. 2. Difference between bottomry and partnership. We say in common that the contract of bottomry is a kind of partnership which is formed between the lender and the borrower.*(g)* But in order to constitute a partnership, the capital, the loss or the gain should be equally borne by both parties. Here nothing is common between them. There is therefore no partnership. *Non est contractus societatis, quia periculum non est commune ; nec etiam lucrum commune.(h)*

g Savary, verb. contrat à la grosse. Encyclop. verb gros-se aventure 1. Denizart 581. *b* Dumoulin contr. usur. n. 98.

In fact, partnership is an agreement between two or more persons, by which they hold all or a part of their goods in common : or it may be for a parti- cular voyage, a particular work or other affair, in which they are to bear the loss or reap the profits equally. *(a)*

a L. L. 1. 5. 52. 67. ff. pro socio.

But money lent at gross adventure belongs properly to him who has received it. The profits of the voyage belong to him exclusively, with the exception of the maritime interest which he is obliged to pay. The sea risks are borne by the lender. It is certain, then, that a contract of maritime loan, is not a partnership and we need not regard the opinions of those authours whom I have just cited ; nor that of *Casaregis*, *(b)* who thinks that he perceives a species of partnership in this contract. *Modernus contractus cambii maritimi*, he says, *redolet speciem societatis nanigationis cum navarcho.* But this system has been invented by the ingenuity of the Transalpine * writers in order to elude the pretended decision of the chapter *Naviganti.*

b disc. 7. n. 2.

There is nothing, however, to prevent us from uniting the contract of maritime loan with that of partnership, as we shall show more fully in a future chapter. *(c)*

c ch. 3. Sec. 4.

You may load a vessel for the fish trade, a cruize or a mercantile voyage and I furnish a certain sum, upon condition that if the ship perish I shall lose my money, but that if she return in safety, my

---

* The transalpine writers (*ultra-montains*,) are those who live *ultra montes.* In France, the word is used, to designate the inhabitants of those countries which are subject to the Papal power. In order to determine the degree of respect that is due to an author, particularly those who treat of maritime law or the laws of nations, it is frequently a matter of some consequence, to know where he lived and when he wrote. The modern decissions of most of the French and English Admiralty courts afford an illustration of the truth of this remark.

advances shall be returned and I shall also be entitled to a proportion of the profits of the voyage : *est species cambii maritimi, quod contrahatur per quamdam species societatis, quod scilicet super navi pis-* *a* de Luca, *catoriá, vel piraticá, seu etiam mercantili ineatur* de credito *societas, in quá unus ponat pecuniam, et alter na-* cap. 3. n. 8. *vim el industriam, sub mutuo periculo. (a)* But this is rather a partnership than a maritime loan. *(b)*

b (Fagnan, ad cap. naviganti, n. 28.) vid. infrà ch. 2. Sect. 2. §. 3. and ch. 12. Sect. 9.

§. Affinity   The contract of maritime loan approaches more between nearly to that of Insurance.   There is a strong ana- Insurance and mari- logy between them.   In their effects, they are con- time strued on the same principles. *(c)* loans.

c Cleirac, on the Guidon de la mer, ch. 12. art. 2. p. 331. valin, on art. 11. h. t- and art. 6. des assur. p. 12. 46. Pothier n. 6.

In the one contract, the *lender* bears the sea risks, in the other, the *underwriter.*

In the one, the maritime *interest* is the price of the peril; and this term corresponds with the *premium* which is paid in the other.

The rate of the premium or interest is greater or less according to the duration and nature of the risk.

In either case it is incumbent upon the plaintiff to prove that the condition has been fulfilled.   " In case of a suit, it lies upon the lender, in order to *d* Cleirac, render the contract of maritime loan executory, to on the show that the ship has arrived at her port of desti- Guidon de la mer, nation in safety; and in an action on a policy of In- ch. 18. surance, it lies upon the assured to prove the loss, art. 2. pag. 331· capture or shipwreck of the vessel. *(d)*

Neither of these contracts acquire a legal existence until the risk is commenced.   If the money borrowed be not employed in maritime commerce, *non erit trajectitia,* and it ought to be returned with common interest: if the assured do not put any thing on board, the policy ceases, *defectu materiæ* and he is released by paying one half *per cent.*

In each contract, it may be laid down as a genelar rule that the subject of the risk should be on board at the time when the accident happens.

In general, the assurer and the lender are exposed to the same sea risks, during the time and in the places fixed by the parties.

In general, the assurer and the lender are not responsible for the barratry of the captain, or for losses occasioned by the fault of the assured or the borrower.

We cannot assure nor take up money at gross adventure, on freight to be carried or on eventual profits, &c. * Assurance and maritime loan are different in many respects.

1. In case of shipwreck, the lender has a lien §. 4. Difupon all the effects saved, without admitting the ference borrower to any participation with him: on the con- between trary if the whole of the property is not covered by contracts. the policy, the assured takes a part of the goods saved, in common with the assurers.

---

* But by a declaration of the french government in 1779, freight, actually earned, was permitted to be insured; and it was provided that in case of loss, it should not be included in the abandonment of the ship, unless it were expressly so stipulated in the policy. But freight though actually earned, can in France be insured only by the *freighter*, when he agrees to pay the freight at all events. Le Guidon ch. 15. art. 1. Valin, on art. 15. p. 58. Pothier, h. t. n. 36. 1. Emerig. 225.

In Italy, *Rocc. not.* 96. England and the U. S. freight may be insured, provided the risk on freight has been commenced. Mar. 76. In the U. S. it is common to insure commissions and eventual profits.

 2. The lender does not contribute to particular averages, but the assurer does: (unless there be an agreement to the contrary.) *(a)*

b vid. in-
fra ch. 7.
Sect. I.
 3. By the clause, free from average, the assurers are covered, even from general average: it is not so with respect to lenders. *(b)*

c ib.
 4. By the policy, the assurer may restrict himself to particular sea risks; but against lenders such a limitation would be void. *(c)*

d vid. in-
fra ch. 5.
Sect. 4.
ch. 6.
Sect. 4.
 5. We may assure merchandize which is actually at hazard; but it is not permitted to take money at bottomry on a vessel which has sailed, unless she is in the course of her voyage and for intermediate necessities. *(d)*

e vid. in-
fra ch. 5.
Sect. 3.
 6. Mariners are never permitted to assure their future wages; but they are allowed, under certain modification, to take money at gross adventure upon the wages which they expect to receive. *(e)*

f vid. n-
fra ch. 11.
 7. The formality of abandonment which is necessary in insurance is unknown in the other contract. *(f)*

g vid. in-
fra ch. 9.
Sect. 3.
 8. The limitations of actions established respecting actions on policies have not been applied to contract of maritime loan. *(g)*

h vid. in-
fra ch. 3.
Sect. 3.
 9. The assurer who insures for a gross premium on a voyage out and home, is bound to refund one third of that premium if the vessel do not return; but the whole sum is due to the lender, although the vessel do not return. *(h)*

 10. In assurance, we must attend to the dates of the policies in order to regulate the return premium, but they are not regarded in contracts of maritime

loan, effected for the same purpose and in the same place.

11. The assured may stipulate that in case of a- *a* vid. in-
bandonment, he shall not be obliged to pay fra ch. 12.
Sect. 2. §.
freight: the same indulgence is not granted to the 2.
lender on the vessel. *(a)*

12. The policies of Insurance made on loose sheets
of paper create a lien on the property of the parties,
provided they are executed before sworn brokers
or notaries; but the other contracts do not create *b* vid. in-
such a lien unless they are recorded by a notary in fra ch. 2.
Sect. 1.
his publick register, in the same form as ordinary
contracts. *(b)*

13. The assured ought to run the risk of one *c* vid. in-
tenth.* But the same law is not imposed upon the fra ch. 6.
Sect. 6.
borrower, who may borrow upon the whole inter- §. 1. &c.
est which he has at stake. *(c)*

SECTION V.

Notice of certain Maritime Associations.

We must not confound contracts of bottomry
with certain maritime associations, of which it may
be well to say a few words.

We made a distinction, formerly, between the §. 1. Joint
concern
owner of a ship and the victualler. The first fur- in the fit-
nished the vessel, and the second, the provisions. ting out
of a ship.
They were partners in the profit and loss in proportion to the value of what they respectively fur- *d* Guidon
nished. *(d)* We find traces of this species of mari- de la mer
ch. 18.
time contract in the *ordonnance de la marine.* *(e)* art. 1. 3.
19. Ord. 1589. art. 59. *e* art. 2. h. t. and art. 7. tit. des assur. and ch.

---

* With us no such rule prevails : a person may assure his
whole interest.

a ch. 36. 37. *Targa* (*a*) treats of a contract *di colonna*, This contract takes place between the owner of a ship, the captain and the mariners, who agree that the voyage shall be for the common benefit of all.* See b ch. 13. Sect 3. my treatise on assurance, where I speak of mariners hired for a share of the profits. (*b*)

§. 2. Joint concern in the pro- fits of an adven- ture. When I intrust a package to the Master of a vessel to be sold for our joint account, two contracts take place: the contract called *mandatum*,† by which I give him power to dispose of my property, and the contract of partnership, in virtue of which the profits are to be divided between us. This is what is denominated, in Italy, *accomenda*. c Conso- lato del Mare ch. 207. 218. Targa, ch. 34. 35. Casaregis disc. 29. n. 4. 20. et seq. Valin, One party runs the risk of losing his capital, and the other, his labour. If the sale produce no more than the first cost, the former takes the whole of it, without giving any thing to the latter. It is the profits only which are to be divided between the partners, according to their agreement. (*c*) art. 1. h. t. p. 3.

Consign- ment of an adven- ture upon commis- sion. In order to avoid the risk of making fruitless voyages, merchants have been in the habit of receiving small adventures on freight *at so much per cent*, to which they are entitled at all events, even if the adventure be lost. This is what the Italians d Targa ch. 34. call *implicita*. (*d*) 35. Casa disc. 29.

---

* The Greek vessels at this day, and our New England *Whalers*, as they are called, are owned and navigated in this manner and under this species of contract. The captain and his mariners are all interested in the profits of the voyage in certain proportions, in the same manner as the captain and crew of a privateer, according to the agreement between them. Such agreements were very common in former times; all the mariners, as well as the master, being interested in the voyage.

It is necessary for the reader to be informed of this fact, in order to understand many of the provisions of the laws of Oleron, Wisbuy, the Consolato del Mare, and other ancient codes of maritime or commercial law.

† In the English law, called *authority*.

But all this has no relation to the contract of maritime loan. Yet we are apt to confound them sometimes.

There is no doubt but that the admiralty has jurisdiction: 1. of contracts of bottomry: 2. of those which relate to the equipment of a ship and the recovery and distribution of freight; 3. of contracts with mariners who are to be paid out of the profits or freight: 4. of the transportation, properly so called, of the cargo and adventures. But the Consular Court ought to have cognizance of, 1. the manner in which adventures and other merchandizes are disposed of on land: 2. the distribution of the profits made out of them: 3. the right to commissions: 4. every thing that relates to commercial transactions in foreign countries.* Vid. my treatise on Insurance. *(a)* _a_ ch. 20. sect. 2. §. 3.

In the last Section of the twelfth chapter, I shall speak of the cession of interest in the vessel and cargo or in particular goods. This contract forms a kind of partnership, which unites itself sometimes with that of bottomry. *(b)* Cession of Interest.

_b_ Suprà Sect. 4. §. 2. and infrà. ch. 5. Sect. 4.

---

* Previous to the French Revolution, the *Court of Admiralty* had cognizance of all maritime contracts and *the Court of the Judge and Consuls,* of all matters relating to commerce by land. But since that eventful epoch the two jurisdictions have been combined in one, which is exercised by the *Tribunal de Commerce.* Matters of Prize are determined by the *Council of Prizes* sitting at Paris

CHAPTER II.

Of the form of the Contract.

We have no printed form of the contract of maritime loan.* It is drawn up in such a manner as the parties may find suitable. It is sufficient if the language be clear and unequivocal. It must contain proper clauses and nothing must be stipulated which is contrary to the nature of the contract.

If it be obscurely written, we must interpret it as well as we can. It is enough if we can ascertain the intention of the parties, without expecting that illiterate men should express themselves with the precision of a lawyer; *voluntas eoram amplectenda est, et verborum captationes dicidiosæ condemnendæ, si imperitus notarius sic non loquitur, aut sic formulam non concipit, quomodo Scævola Africanus. (a)*

a D'Artré, de laudimiis cap 1. §. 4.

SECTION I.

Of the external form.

§. 1. Whether the contract may be

"The contract of maritime loan may be made before a Notary or under private signature." (a) made before a Notary or under private Signature. a art. 1. h. t.

This should be said with an exception as to money taken by captains who trade to the ports in the Levant.† The instrument when made there should

---

* Vid. Appendix.

† Constantinople, Smyrna, Thessalonica, Tripoli, Tunis, Cairo, Candy, Algiers, &c.

be executed before the chancellor * of the consu-late of France, or it will be void. (*a*)

a Declaration du 21, Oct. 1727. art. 30. infra ch. 4. Sect. 5.

Notwithstanding the opinion of *M. Vali.* (*b*) I believe with *M. Pothier* (*c*) that parol evidence of the contract would not, at this day, be admitted. (*d*)

May it be made verbally?

b art. 1. p. 3. *c* n. 27. *d* vid. Emerig. on Ins ch. 2. Sect. 1.

The contract of maritime loan when made before a notary creates a lien in the same manner as every other publick contract. † But if it be made on a loose sheet of paper, although drawn up and signed by a notary it will not give any lien. ‡

§. 2. Does it create a lien on the property of the party?

This contract is subject to the *demi-controle;* § and if it be by private signature, the petition, when a suit is brought upon it, must pray, that a day of ged and registered ?

Must it be comptrolled, acknowledged and

---

* Chancelier, is an officer under the consul in a foreign port, who exercises the functions of Notary Publick and Register or clerk of the consular court, in those places, as in the ports of Levant, where the consul enjoys a judicial authority. His acts have, in France, the same effect, as if they were the acts of a similar officer within the limits of the Empire.

† In France every contract which is made in due form before a Notary Publick has the effect of a judgment with us, by creating a lien upon the property of the parties. An obligation, for instance, executed before a Notary is equal to a judgment of record, and is therefore said to have a lien, *porter hypotheque.* Nay more, it is executory without a judicial writ. It is only necessary for the party to obtain an exemplified copy and place it in the hands of an officer of the court, who, without further authority, may levy on the property of the debtor, to the amount which is specified in the instrument. For this reason, those instruments are said to have *execution parée,* (executio parata.) As these expressions frequently occur in the pages of writers on French jurisprudence, it was presumed that this explanation would not be deemed superfluous.

‡ It will, nevertheless, if the loose sheet remain as a record in the office of the Notary Publick; but not if it be delivered to the party in the original, or, as it is termed by the French writers, *en brevet.*

§ The formality of comptrolling is a merely fiscal regulation, for the purpose of raising a duty to the state. It is also

hearing be assigned to the borrower, three days after the date of the summon, in order that he may
come in and acknowledge the contract, in default
of which it will be taken as proved. The petition
must also pray that the contract be registered in the
registry of Admiralty, to serve as occasion may require. It is not until after this proof and enrolment
that the lender may obtain a judgment against the
borrower, who delays the performance of his contract.

It is surprising that these contracts, which are in-
finitely more beneficial than those of insurance,
should be perplexed with restrictions, that are prejudicial to commerce and of no advantage to the
parties.

§. 3. When it is made under a private signature, whether it is entit- led to the same pre vileges as if publick- ly execu- ted.
M. Pothier, n. 29. says "the instrument under
private signature, when it is acknowledged or proved, is equally authentick with that which is executed before a notary-publick, as against the borrower and his heirs. But it is not so," he adds,
"as to third persons, against whom the lender may
wish to enforce the privileges attached to his contract. The date of instruments under private signature is not regarded as against third persons, if it
be not proved by some other means than the instrument itself."

The rule cited by this authour relates only to liens
against purchasers. It is otherwise when the ques-

a Emerig. des ass. ch. 16. Sect. 5. §. 3.
tion is of mere priority. (*a*) I know that frauds may
be committed, but human laws can not prevent every evil. The contract of maritime loan under private signature is legal for this reason alone, that

however, a check upon the Notaries, because, as this formality must be observed in a very short time after the execution of
the deed, it prevents the antedating of it; a practice, which is
substantially a forgery and deserves to be punished with equal
severity.

the form has been adopted by the Ordinance ; and *a* vid. 1.
as contracts of assurance correspond with those Valin.
made before a notary-publick, the same law pre- tit.de la
vails as to contracts of maritime loan. (*a*)
tit. des Contracts à la grosse vol. 2. p. 3. infrà ch. 4. Sect. 5;

a vid. 1.
Valin.
art. 16.
tit.de la
saisie, p.
344. and
art. 1.

———◆:◆———

SECTION II.

Of the internal form.

The contract should contain the names of the §.1. What
borrower and the lender, and those of the captain the con-
and the vessel: it ought to mention the amount should
lent, the rate of interest, the times and places of contain.
the risk, to state whether the money is lent on the *b* Pothier
bottom or the cargo, jointly or separately, and all n. 30. in-
other lawful stipulations which the parties may think frà ch. 5.
proper to make. (*b*)

§.1. What
the con-
tract
should
contain.
b Pothier
n. 30. in-
frà ch. 5.
Sect. 1. §.
4.

Thus a promissory note for *value received* in mo- c Savary
ney lent at gross adventure, without further expla- Parere *
nation, would not be called a bottomry bond. (*c*)

c Savary
Parere *
57. Valin.
art. 2. p.
4.

According to the laws, 2. *and* 4. *C. de naut.*
fœn. it is necessary that, by a special clause, the Is it ne-
lender should undertake to bear the maritime risks.(*d*) cessary to
With us, this agreement is presumed. It is suffici- the lender
ent that you lend at maritime interest upon the ves- risks ?
sel or cargo, or both, to put the risks of the sea
upon the lender. (*e*)

Is it ne-
cessary to
state that
the lender
incurs the
risks ?

d Kuricke, jus hans. tit. 8. art. 1. p. 761. *e* Infrà ch. 4. Sect. 5. 6. 7.

---

* The French, or rather the Italian, word, *parere* signifies
opinion. Savary has published a collection of *pareres* or opinions on subjects of commercial law, which is much esteemed.

§. 2. Blank bottomry bills. Promissary notes in blank are prohibited by the Edict of 1716; and with much greater reason should the law be so as to bottomry bills, on account of

a infrà ch. 6. Sect. 3. the privileges attached to this species of contract and to prevent abuses. (*a*)

b infrà ch. 5. Sect. 4.

Suprà ch. 1. Sect. 4. §. 2. Sometimes this contract is confounded and united with others, such as those of partnership and freight, examples of which may be seen hereafter. (*b*)

c ch. 3, Sect. 7. I could add several other points respecting the internal form of these contracts; but it will be sufficient to refer to what I have said in my Treatise on Assurance, (*c*) where I have spoken of the internal and external form of a policy. In the same place the reader will find a collection of rules on the interpretation of contracts.

CHAPTER III.

Of Maritime Interest.

"The greatness of martime interest is founded upon two considerations: the dangers of the sea,
which render it proper that we should not incur
such hazards without a prospect of uncommon advantages; and, the facility, by which the borrower
effects extensive speculations in consequence of the
loan. On the other hand, common legal interest,
not being supported by such reasons, is either entirely prohibited by the Legislator, or, which is *a* Mon-
more reasonable, it is restricted by proper limits."(*a*) tesq. liv.
22. ch. 20.

SECTION I.

General Rules on the subject of maritime interest.

" We cannot call that a contract of gross adven- §1. Mari-
ture which does not contain a stipulation for the pay- time interest is an
ment of a maritime interest. That is, the borrow- essential
er must be bound to return, not only the principal part of
this con-
but an additional sum or some other compensation tract.
for the risk incurred. If a person lend a sum of
money to a master of a vessel for a certain voyage,
with an agreement that it is not to be returned in
case of loss or the capture of the vessel by a *vis
major*, and does not stipulate for a maritime profit,
it cannot be called a contract of gross adventure.
But it is merely a contract of loan, mingled with *b* Pothier
a donation of the money lent in case of the loss or n. 19. h. t.
Emerig.
capture of the vessel, which donation would be- des assur.
come valid upon the delivery of the money, provi- ch. 3.
Sect. 11.
ded the parties were able to contract. (*b*) §. 2
G

In general, maritime interest is payable in money; *solet pretium hujus periculi, ut plurimùm, in
numeratâ pecuniâ consistere.* (*a*) But, as Pothier
observes, we may stipulate for any other thing. (*b*)

a Locc.
lib. 2. cap.
6. n· 4.
b Emerig. des ass. ch. 3. Sect. 10.

§. 3. Inte-
rest by
implica-
tion.

If it be true then, that the lender may stipulate
for any thing by way of interest, that is for any advantage to himself, in case of the safe return of
the vessel, this advantage, whatever it may be,
should be such an implied interest as will give the
legal character of gross adventure to the contract.
For example, a captain, in time of war, being at
Smyrna and in want of money to victual his ship,
borrows of a French merchant 1000 piastres, Tur-
kish money. Upon the safe arrival of his ship at
Marseilles, he engages to return this money at the
rate of a French crown for each piastre, the perils
of the sea being at the risk of the lender. This is
a real contract of gross adventure. The difference
between the two coins constitutes the maritime
premium and the price of the risk. This case is
not within the 11th art. of the Declaration of 1779.*
The captain, therefore, upon his safe arrival, should
be obliged to pay the full sum of 3000 livres, which
would, in fact, be paying a premium of about 20
per cent. on the sum borrowed.

§. 3. The
law,
where the
parties
have ne-
glected to
insert a
stipula-

Straccha (*c*) maintains that no more than common legal interest can be recovered in cases where
the parties have neglected to make a stipulation
for the payment of maritime interest. In this opinion I do not coincide. When a contract is fulfil-
tion for interest. *b* Introd. de assecur. n. 24.

---

* The article to which our author refers is as follows. Every article, the price of which shall be expressed in a policy of
Insurance, in foreign or in other than the current money of this
kingdom, and the value of which is fixed by our edicts, shall
be estimated at the real value of such foreign or other money
in *livres tournois*. We expressly prohibit any stipulation to the
contrary under pain of its being declared void. 2 Emerig. 629,

led *bonâ fidê*, it is the province of equity to supply the omissions of ignorance or inadvertence. The lender incurs the perils of the sea and the borrower derives an advantage by employing his money in commerce. It becomes necessary, then that a maritime interest should be paid, in order to place the parties upon an equal footing and to preserve the spirit of the contract. Thus, in the case stated, the maritime interest should be ascertained by the customary rate, at the time and in the place where the contract was made.

Maritime interest is not due to a lender who has run no risk, even if it should so happen in consequence of the act of the borrower. §. 4. If the lender run no risk.

We have before seen (*a*) that the Italian lawyers, in order to elude the chapter *naviganti*, have supposed that this contract is composed of those of partnership, sale and insurance. But, if he who has lent his money at gross adventure, become the insurer, it is necessary that he should have a premium, for there can be no insurance where there is no premium, stipulated or implied. Casaregis (*b*) says that the parties are presumed to have agreed that the premium due in such a case, should not be paid but by the merchandize at risk, and that if every thing be lost, the premium perishes also: *quamobrem sequitur, quòd amissa navi, illud quoque præmium amittatur.* §. 5. If the ship perish? *a* ch. 1. Sec. 3. §. 1. *b* disc. 65.

Such subtleties are unknown in France. The contract is a contract of maritime loan and nothing more. The lender cannot demand the principal, nor premium, nor maritime interest, if the thing upon which be lent his money, he entirely lost by the accidents of the sea.

SECTION II.

Rate of maritime interest.

§. 1. The rate of interest is unlimited.   In the first chapter, I quoted those texts of the law and principles which prove that maritime interest is not subject to the limits of ordinary legal interest, but that it may be regulated by the degree of danger to which the lender exposes or believes he exposes his money.

a ch. 33. n. 19. p. 149.   Targa *(a)* says that if the rate stipulated be excessive, it is in the power of the court to lessen it.

b n. 2. h. t.   Pothier *(b)* observes that "although maritime profit, at however exorbitant a rate it may have been fixed, in the contract of gross adventure, is always considered *in foro exteriori* as nothing more than the price of the maritime perils and is therefore lawful: yet, if the intention of the parties was to comprehend in that profit, besides the price of the risk, a compensation for the loan and the credit given by the lender, this profit would be, as to that compensation, unlawful and usurious *in foro conscientiæ.*"

But every thing which belongs to the *forum conscientiæ* may be taken notice of *in foro exteriori,*＊ when a contract contains clauses which are repugnant to the nature of it or when a fraud is proved. Law is not a human institution; it is a science as immutable as its authour. The duty of judges consists in making it respected. *Hanc igitur video sapientissimorum fuisse sententiam, legem neque hominum ingeniis excogitatam, nec scitum aliquod esse populorum, sed æternum quiddam, quod universum mundum regeret, imperandi, prohibendique sapientia*

＊ Or, in our own legal language, equity is a part of the law.

———*Lex vera atque Princeps, apta ad jubendum et ad vetandum,* ratio est recta summi jovis. *(a)* [a Cic. de. leg. lib. 2. cap. 4.]

Maritime interest or premium is generally stipulated at so much *per cent.* for the entire voyage or by the month, &c. *(b)* [§. 2. Interest at so much per cent a month or for the voyage. b Poth. n. 20. h. t. (infrà. ch. 8.)]

The stipulated rate of interest is not affected by the unexpected arrival of peace or war, unless the event was provided for in the contract. Such has been held to be our law notwithstanding the opinion of Pothier, n. 22. h. t.(*c*) [§. 3. Whether affected by war or peace. c Emerig. des. assur. ch. 3. Sect. 3. 4. 5.]

It is a general rule that the moment the risk commences, the whole maritime premium becomes due, although the contemplated voyage is interrupted or the risk cease before the expiration of the stipulated term. Pothier (*d*) says that "when the lender has begun to incur the risks although he has not borne them all the time that he contracted to bear them, the voyage having been shortened, the entire maritime profit is not the less due to him, provided no accident of *vis major* has occurred to occasion the loss of the goods upon which the loan was made. The ordinance having made this provision with regard to the premium on a policy of insurance, a parity of reasoning requires a similar rule as to the contract of gross adventure.(*e*) [§ 4. The whole interest is due from the moment the risk commences. d n. 40. h. t. e Emerig. des assur. ch. 16. Sect. 2. and the following section.]

SECTION III.

If the Vessel do not return?

If the money have been borrowed for the voyage out and home and the vessel do not return, it should seem that one third of the premium should be de-

a Valin, art. 15. h. t. page 17. Poth. n. 41. (*) ducted, according to the principle which has been adopted in matters of insurance.*(a)*

I should cheerfully submit to the authority of these writers, if their opinion did not appear to be at variance with the principles of our jurisprudence. 1. The general rule, they say, is, that as soon as the risk is commenced, the whole premium and the maritime interest becomes due. 2. According to *b* tit. du fret. the 9th Art.*(b)* " if the vessel, having been freighted out and home, be obliged to return in ballast, the whole freight is due to the master." In such cases it has pleased the Legislature to allow a return premium of one third; but this is *stricti juris.* Until there shall be a new law reducing the maritime interest and freight to two thirds where the vessel does not return, the borrowers, as well as freighters, must be governed by the general rule.

c Case 1. Francois Boulle, v. Ganteaume and Oliver, 7th August 1736, Case 2. Among my notes I find two decisions*(c)* by our admiralty† in which it was decided, that the entire maritime interest is due though the vessel do not return. Valin, to whom I transmitted my notes, has, through mistake denominated these decisions arrêts of the Parliament of Aix, and Pothier has fallen into the same error.‡

Anow. v. Heirs of Galmi. 18 Aug. 1741.

---

* *Sed quære*, where the premium is stipulated in the shape of interest by the month; how can it be apportioned, or on what *data* can it be ascertained how long the voyage would have been, and how long the risk continued?

† The authour alludes to the admiralty court at Marseilles.

‡ Before the revolution an appeal lay from the *Court of Admiralty at Marseilles, to the Parliament of Aix in Provence,* which probably occasioned the error of Valin and Pothier. But it seems that the two decisions quoted in the text were acquiesced in without any appeal.

In the year 1740, Pierre Evesque, master of the vessel called *La Marie Fortunee*, borrowed, 3000 livres upon gross adventure, from Francois Boulle. This sum was to be employed in merchandise, *to and from* the French West India Islands, at a maritime interest of twenty-two *per cent.* and the whole was to be paid one month after the safe arrival of the vessel at Marseilles. Jean Baptiste and Eustache Evesque, brothers of Pierre, the borrower, became jointly bound with him for the performance of the contract. The vessel arrived in safety at Guadaloupe, and the whole outward cargo was landed. On the 11th of September 1740, the vessel ran aground and was wrecked in a hurricane. The captain and his cargo were lost. On the 6th of July 1741, Francois Boulle filed a claim against the heirs of Pierre and his securities, praying that they might be condemned *in solido* [*jointly and severally*] to pay him the 3000 livres, together with the twenty-two *per cent.* and common legal interest upon the whole from the time it became due. A sentence was rendered for the whole sum on the 19th June 1742. On appeal, this sentence was confirmed, 17th June 1743.*

Case 3.
Francois
Boulle
v
Pierre
Evesque
et al
1740.

In the year 1746 Jean Baptiste Pons, a shipping merchant, lent to Matthew David, captain of the Pink, *la Vierge de Caderot*, and to Francis Isnard, the mate, 297 livres, upon the merchandize of the said Pink for an outward voyage to the French Islands and to return to some port in the kingdom, at a maritime premium of 100 *per cent.* In her voyage to the islands, the vessel was captured by the English. Captain David ransomed her by means of a bill of exchange of 1050 sequins of Venice, which he drew upon Veyrier of Marseilles, his owners, and left Francis Isnard, his mate, as a

Case 4.
Jean-
Baptiste
Pons
v
Mathew
David
and Fran-
cis Is-
nard
1746.

---

* Of course, by the Parliament of Aix.

hostage. Veyrier asked Pons and the other persons interested, whether they would take the ransom upon their own account. They answered that they were bound to contribute to the ransom as soon as a liquidation should be made. The vessel arrived at Guadaloupe, where she was sold by the captain, who supposed he had become the owner, in consequence of the ransom. He embarked in another vessel and arrived at Bourdeaux.

Pons filed a petition against David and Isnard jointly, for the 297 livres upon the return voyage, together with maritime exchange* of 100 *per cent.* and the common legal interest from the time of captain David's return to France; offering at the same time to contribute to the ransom at the rate of 28 liv. 18 s. *per cent.* The captain demanded two deductions. 1. He wished the contribution to the ransom to be deducted with relation to the time of the ransom itself, so that it should be subtracted from the principal, and thus the interest would be diminished likewise. It was decided that the ransom was an extra charge, which did not, *ipso jure*, diminish the capital, although, by the ordinance,(*a*) a lien is given on the goods for the amount of contribution,

a Of jettison art. 21.

---

* The French writers, when they speak of the consideration given for maritime loans, employ a variety of words in order to distinguish it according to the nature of the case. Thus, they call it interest when it is stipulated to be paid by the month or at other stated periods. It is a *premium* when a gross sum is to be paid at the end of a voyage, and here the risk is the principal object which they have in view. When that sum is a *per centage* on the money lent, they denominate it *exchange*, considering it in the light of money lent in one place to be returned in another, with a difference in amount between the sum borrowed and that which is paid, arising from the difference of time and place. When they intend to combine these various shades into one general denomination, they make use of the term *maritime profit*, to convey their meaning. As we shall occasionally use these expressions in the course of this translation, this explanation may not be entirely useless.

which takes place here by analogy on the money borrowed, yet it does not authorize a set-off until default
of payment.* 2. The captain also prayed a deduction of one third of the maritime interest, because
the vessel had not returned. It was decided that this
deduction takes place only in cases of insurance.

On the 21st of January 1750, a sentence was rendered by which David and Isnard were condemned
jointly to pay 297 livres, with maritime interest, at
the rate of 100 *per cent.* and common legal interest
from the time of the arrival of the captain at Bordeaux, deducting 28 livres 18 s. *per cent.*† with 5
per cent. interest from the date of the advance made
by Veyrier, to effect the ransom.

In the year 1746, Antoine Collury, of Port Ma- Case 5
hon, Minorca, lent to Balthazard Brusquo and Je- Joseph
rome Ferro, officers of a Felucca, 120 pieces of Mi- Coulet
norca coin, for a voyage to and from Genoa, at the Baltha-
rate of 16 *per cent.* payable on the return of the Brusquo
vessel at Mahon. The vessel arrived at Genoa, and Je-
where she landed her cargo and she did not return to Ferro,
Minorca. The contract was assigned to Joseph 1750.
Coulet of Marseilles. A sentence was rendered, on
the 13th March 1750, condemning Brusquo and
Ferro to the payment of the 120 pieces, with 16
per cent. and also common legal interest from the
termination of the risk.

---

* And as payment cannot be demanded until the interest has
accrued, the set-off or deduction must be made from that in the
first instance.

† The sentence does not express whether this proportional
deduction was to be made from the principal of the money lent or
from the gross amount of the principal and maritime-interest. It
seems that it was calculated on the principal only and deducted
from the amount of the principal and interest, otherwise it would
be at variance with the principle which appears to have been laid
down by the court.

Case 6
Armelin
v.
Jean-Bap-
tiste
Margerel
1758. In the year 1758 Jean-Baptiste Margerel, mate of the Pink called *la Vierge de la Garde* commanded by captain Clastrier, borrowed of Armelin, six dozen skins of Morocco leather, for which he executed a respondentia bond, binding himself to pay 270 livres and 100 *per cent.* free from average, on the safe return of the vessel to Marseilles. The vessel arrived in safety at Cayenne. Margerel's adventure produced 960 livres, which he received in paper money. The vessel was then declared not to be sea worthy. Margerel, not being able to find a vessel by which he could make a return shipment, was obliged to convert his money into a bill of exchange upon the Royal Treasury, which was never paid.

Armelin filed a petition against him, claiming the 270 livres, together with maritime and legal interest. Margerel replied that his contract was conditional and that he was only to be bound in case of the safe arrival of the vessel: that the vessel never did return, having been declared unseaworthy: that he had not been able to find a vessel by which he could ship goods in return for Marseilles, and that, consequently, according to the 17th art. of the ordinance, *hoc titulo,* the contract was reduced to the value of the things saved, to wit, a draft on the Royal Treasury which he offered to deliver up.

On the 27th of June 1760, a sentence was rendered in favour of Margerel, by which the plaintiff was non-suited. From this decision Armelin appealed. He contended that the goods had been safely landed, before the vessel was condemned as not seaworthy and that as Margerel had disposed of them according to his own discretion at Cayenne, the contract was still in force.

An arrêt passed, 30th June 1761, on the report of M. de Corriolis, in these terms:

" Our aforesaid court has annulled the appeal and judgment appealed from; and proceeding to give a new judgment without regard to the offer which was made by Margerel upon the service of the summons of the 20th of May 1760, and doing right on the petition of the said Armelin——it has condemned the said Margerel to render and restore to Armelin the produce of the sale of six dozen pieces of Black Morocco, which he received from Armelin and sold at Cayenne: and this he is to pay in the same paper money which he received in payment. For this reason Margerel shall exhibit to Armelin his journal and ledger, in order to show the nett profit of the sale: or he shall pay, if he shall prefer so to do, the 270 livres with maritime interest of 100 *per cent.* and common legal interest, in money: and he shall make his election within three days after notice of this arrêt, otherwise he shall be debarred from that privilege.

This arrêt decides, 1. That notwithstanding the loss of the ship in the course of the voyage, the contract of gross adventure is in full existence as to effects landed. 2. That the borrower, who has not been able to send the returns by another vessel, is obliged to give an account of the proceeds of the outward shipment. 3. That if he do not render this account, he ought to pay the principle, together with maritime and common legal interest.

In the year 1775, *Pierre Rathier*, mate of the vessel called "*la Marie Elizabeth*," received, by way of maritime loan on goods, the sum of 600 livres from *Jean-Pierre Plasse*, on a voyage to the French west Indies and thence back to Marseilles, at the rate of 15 *per centum.* *Ginezy* joined in the bond, agreeing to be bound by the contract of Rathier. The vessel arrived at Guadaloupe and discharged her cargo. On the 6, September 1776, she was lost in a hurricane.

Case 7.
Jean Pierre Plasse
v.
Pierre Rathier and Etienne Ginezy
1779.

M. Plasse commenced an action against the debtor and his security to enforce the payment of the
600 livres, together with maritime |and common le-
gal interest. In the month of January 1779 a sentence was rendered in his favour. From this sentence, the defendant, *Ginezy*, prayed an appeal.
But after some altercation, he submitted to it and
paid the judgment and costs, because the goods
of the borrower had been shipped in another vessel
and were amply sufficient to cover all expences.

It results from this series of decisions among us,
that if the goods, upon which the loan was made,
be safely landed, no deduction from the maritime
rate, is to be made, although the vessel do not return or be lost on her voyage. If the borrower
squander the goods or their proceeds, or dispose
of them according to his own pleasure, instead of
shipping them in another vessel, he is bound to repay the sum borrowed, with the maritime interest
entire. *Vide infrà (a)* where the question concerning maritime interest is treated *de novo* according
to the text of the 13, article *hoc titulo.*

a ch. 8.
Sect. 1.
§. 1.

———✳:✤———

SECTION IV.

Common legal interest.

§.1.When   Upon the termination of the maritime risks, if
the mari- the borrower delay the fulfilment of his contract,
time risk
ceases,   the charge of common legal interest attaches *ipso*
the com- *jure*, although it may not be judiciously deman-
mon legal
interest   ded.* *Discusso periculo, majus legitimâ usurâ non*
commen- ces.

---

* If the risk be not commenced the contract will become a
simple loan ; even though the borrower covenant to perform the
voyage. Marsh. 647. 1. Vern. 263. If the lender has insured his principal, *Marshall* thinks he should receive one half

debebitur. (a) *Exinde, communis prœstatur usura,* a L. 4. ff. de naut. says the glossary upon L. 1. C. eod. (b) fœn.
b Styp. part. 4. cap. 2. n. 197. p. 392. Locc. lib. 2. c. 6, n. 11. p. 994. Targa, cap. 33. n 2. Wolf, §. 680.

Such is our law, as it may be collected from the c infrà ch. 9. decissions cited in the preceeding section, saving §. 2. the modifications of which I shall treat hereafter.(c)

Will the maritime interest carry common legal §. 2. May there be a interest from the moment it becomes due? will it charge of carry interest from the date of the judgment? legal inte- rest on the maritime interest ?

M. Pothier, in his remarks on n. 51. h. t. after having said that the principal of money lent at gross adventure carries common legal interest only from the date of the judgment, in which he directly con-tradicts the provisions of the laws, adds that "the same rule does not extend to maritime interest; this profit being an accessory which is given by way of interest on the sum lent; *nautica usura, nauticum fœnus.* You cannot demand interest upon it. It would be interest upon interest, a compound inte-rest which the laws prohibit: *accessio accessionis non est.*"

Decormis (d) after having said that "when the d vol. 2. peril ceases and the vessel has returned, maritime p. 810 interest ceases, *ipso facto* and legal interest com-mences," in which he speaks the language of the

---

per cent. upon the maritime interest and all costs of insu-rance, together with his pr ncipal. Of the same opinion is *Valin,* on art. 15. h. t. and Emerigon agrees with them provi-ded the non-performance of the voyage happen through the fault of the borrower. *vid infrà.*

The allowance of interest, as stated in the text, is an excep-t on from the general law of France, by which interest does not commence to run except from the t me of action brought, which alone constitutes a legal demand; or, as in some of the provinces, from the date of the judgment, unless the contrary be st pulated in the contract of the parties. *Ferriere, in verb, interest.*

law, adds, that "it is by relation only to that which is due upon the 'principal; and you cannot, by adding it to and merging it in the profits obtain interest upon the total sum."*

Julian (a) says, ex usu, debentur usura à die finiti periculi sine ullâ petitione; quia piotus ex societate, quàm ex mutuo debentur, ratione periculi quod creditor in se suscepit. Sed an usurarum quæ pro periculo debentur, aliæ usuræ debeantur? dubito quod sic: non tam usuræ, quàm pretium periculi dicuntur.

Notwithstanding the doubt which *Julian* entertains and the contrary opinion of *Decormis,* we have seen in the preceeding section that our decisions add common legal to the maritime interest, not only from the time of the demand, but from the time that the latter became due. The point is not now disputed: but I do not know whether it be not disputable.

In the first place, it is certain that the contract of maritime loan is not a partnership as I have before proved; *(b)* and there is no law which provides that maritime interest shall, *ipso jure,* carry common legal interest. Upon what authority, then, do our decisions rest? They say that maritime interest is the price of peril, *periculi pretium:* that it is an increase of the obligation, according to the words of the Law: *(c)* that it is an addition to the capital, according to the language of *Doumoulin:* that this interest being added to the principal, becomes identified with it and the two sums make one entire whole which ought to carry interest. To such sophistry are they reduced; and I cannot suppress my emoti-

b ch. 1. Sect. 4. §. 2.

c L. 5. §. 1. ff. de naut. fœn.

---

* Our law is different. When a verdict is rendered for the principal and interest and judgment is entered for the aggregate sum, the whole bears interest from the date of the judgment.

on when I behold them, in this manner, overwhelm an unfortunate debtor, who returns to his country to be imprisoned by his fellow citizens, after he has escaped from the hands of pirates and survived the perils of the sea !*

If, in contracts which flow from commerce the law has paid more regard to publick convenience than to personal liberty ;† we ought at least not to be more rigorous than it is, and enlarge by a new addition that which is, in truth, but an addition it-self. It would not be surprizing if this point in our jurisprudence should be one day overruled. It is supported by mere *apices juris.*

---

* The substance of the argument is this. The maritime in-terest is a reward for the risk which I have incurred. When the peril ceases I am entitled to this reward immediately. If it be withheld I am entitled a compensation for the use of my pro-perty, from which I might have derived an advantage, by len-ding it again, if I had received it when it became due. I see no reason for the pathetick lamentation which the authour makes. If the allowance here complained of were not made, lenders would calculate not only upon the perils of the sea but upon the danger of delay upon land, and increase the maritime inte-rest accordingly. The borrower might thus be injured by the very rule which was intended for his benefit.

† This alludes to imprisonment of the body; which, in France, is allowed only in cases of debts arising from commer-cial transactions.

CHAPTER IV.

Every person who has an interest in a ship or cargo, may borrow money at gross adventure as far as his interest is put at hazard, and every person who is capable of contracting may make such loans. *(a)* Masters of vessels may sometimes borrow upon maritime loan on account of their owners, whether it be in the port where the vessel is fitted out or in the course of the voyage. This gives rise to the *actio exercitoria;* of which I shall treat in this chapter.

a Emerig. des ass. ch. 4.

SECTION I.

General observations on the action against the owner for the acts of the master.

The genius of the Romans, their thirst for glory, their military education, the form of their government, every thing, in short, in their character, was unpropitious to the pursuits of commerce. When they did engage in it, it was under the name or through the medium of their slaves or freedmen. The agent in negociations on shore was called *institor*, (factor) and he who conducted their maritime speculations was denominated master and sometimes merchant:

Naviget, et mediis hyemet mercator in undis.
Hor. lib. 1. Ep. 16. v. 71.

§. 1. Of the Owner (Exercitor.) The owner of a ship, or he who hired her for the purpose of navigating her on his own account was called the *exercitor*, because he exercised or carried on this sort of commerce. *Exercitorem eum dicimus, ad quem obventiones et reditus omnes perveniunt: sive is dominus navis sit, sive à domino navem per aversionem conduxit, vel ad tempus, vel in perpetuum.* (a)

a L. 1 §. 14. ff. de exercit. actio.

It results from the laws of the same title, that they applied the term *exercitor* indiscriminately to slaves who represented their masters in the property of the ship and to those who acted for their own account, as if they were the owners. This arrange- ment was undoubtedly adopted by *Lentulus*, who had promised a place to *Cicero* in one of his vessels. *Lentulus navis suas pollicetur.* (b) By these artifi- ces the Patricians of Rome eluded the law which prohibited them from engaging in merchandize on their own account. (c)

b lib. 1. Epist. 5. ad Atti- cum.

c 1. Eme- rig. des assur. ch. 4. §. 1. p. 102.

He, to whom the vessel and cargo beyond sea was entrusted, was called the master of the ship; *magistrum navis accipere debemus, cui totius navis curæ mandata est.* (d) In the same manner as they carried on the land commerce by means of an agent, called *Institor*, they placed him on board the ship to manage their speculations there. *Datur institoria, ex negotiatione terrestri; sic exercitoria, de tantùm navali.* (e)

§. 2. of the Mas- ter.

d L. 1. §. 1. ff. de exercit. act.

e Dumou- lin C. de Inst. et Exerc. act.

Magistri imponuntur locandis navibus, vel ad mer- ces, vel vectoribus couducendis armamentisve emen- dis; set etiam si mercibus emendis, vel vendendis fuerit præpositus, etiam hoc nomine obligat exercitorem. (f) 29. Pauli at Edict. and on the Code, de institoria.

f L. 1. §. 3. ff. de exercit. act. Vid. Cujas on L. 5. ff. eod. lib.

During the voyage, this agent represented the owner and had, in general, the same powers, in eve- ry thing that concerned the vessel. (g)

g Tota lege. 1. ff. de exercit act.

It was of little consequence whether this agency was committed to a slave or a freedman; to a per-

I

son of full age or to a minor, under twenty five years of age. *Cujus autem conditionis sit, magister ipse, nihil interest, utrum liber an servus; et utrum exercitoris, an alienus; sed nec, cujus ætatus sit, intererit: sibi imputaturo, qui eum præposuit.* (*a*)

a. L. 1. §. 4. ff. eod.

When they projected an important voyage, they sometimes appointed many masters, *plures magistros*, in the same ship, that they might be a check on each other, or that each might perform the task which was assigned to him. (*b*)

b L. 1. §. 13. ff. eod.

The pilot, *navicularius*, was the person to whom the direction of the voyage and the conducting of the vessel safely into port, was entrusted. This appears from the L. 13. §. 3. ff. *locati,* and the laws of the code under the title *de naufragiis.*

With us these functions are separated when the owners place a supercargo on board, with power to demand freight, make all commercial operations and pay the necessary expenses. The captain is then, saving the rights of third persons, simply a pilot and the supercargo is the master.

c L. 13. §. 2. ff. locati. L. 1. §. 2. 13. ff. nautæ.
d Calvinus, in verbo, navicularius.
e Budœus, ad L. 1. ff. nautæ. pa. 146.

Among the Romans these trusts were sometimes united, as it appears from their laws. (*c*) This is the reason why our writers sometimes compare our masters or captains of vessels to the *navicularius* or pilot of the Romans, (*d*) and sometimes they assimilate the *magister* or master with a captain or master of a ship in the modern acceptation of the word. (*e*) The latter idea prevailed and was adopted by the Ordinance.

f On the L. 1. §. 1. ff. de exercit. act.
g part. 4. cap. 15. n. 128. p. 543.

Faber *(f)* and Stypmannus (*g*) appear to be surprized that several masters of vessels should be placed on board the same ship. *Malè enim regitur navis, ut et respublica, si non ab uno regatur.* Their

surprize would have been well founded if the mere
navigation of the ship had been entrusted to many :
but the laws (a) speak of many factors and super- *a* L. 1. ff.
cargoes with the title of masters, not for the go- §. 13. 14. de exer-
vernment of the ship, but to make bargains, de- cit. act.
mand freight and do other things relating to a maritime commerce. *Si plures sint magistri, non di-*
visis officiis, quodcumque cum uno gestum erit, ob-
ligabit exercitorem: si divisis, ut alter locando, al-
ter exigendo, pro cujusque officio obligabitur exer-
citor. Sed et si sic præposuit, ut plerùmque fa-
ciunt, ne alter sine altero quid gerat, qui contraxit
cum uno, sibi imputabit.

SECTION II.

It is a general rule, that the owner is bound
by the acts of the master.

Gothofredus* thinks that the Prœtor's Edict, by
which the *actio* exercitoria was established† was *b* On the
nearly in these words: (b) *Quod cum magistro navis* L. 1. ff. de exer-
gestum esse dicetur, in exercitorem qui eum præpo- cit. act.
suit, in solidum judicium dabo.

The utility of this edict is evident: because, *ex*
necessitate, we are obliged to contract with masters,
of whose character or situation we are ignorant;
and therefore, it is but equitable that the owner
should be bound by the acts of the person whom
he has appointed, in the same manner as a shop-kee-
per must abide by the acts of his clerk.

---

* Godefroy is called Gothofredus by the English civilians
and is best known by that name.
† The forms of action at Rome were established by Prœto-
rian edicts which had the force of laws.

It may be urged as a further reason that he who
contracts with a Clerk or Agent on shore has am-
ple means of obtaining information about him; but
with respect to a master of a vessel, the time, place
and other circumstances, often prevent us from de-
liberating. *In navis majistro non ità; nam inter-*
dùm locus, tempus non patitur plenius deliberandi
concilium. (*a*)

a L. 1. ff.
de exer-
cit. act.

This, therefore is the reason why the owner is
bound by the acts of the master, because those who
contract *bonâ fidê* with the latter are not to be de-
ceived. *Omnia facta magistri debet præstare qui*
eum præposuit; alinquio contrahentes deciperen-
tur. (*b*)

b L. 1. §.
20. ff. eod.

Another motive of this Edict is that navigation
is of essential consequence to the Republick: *quia*
ad summam Rempublicam navium exercitio perti-
net. (*c*)

c L. 1. §.
20. ff. eod.

Of a sub-
stituted
captain.

The owners are responsible, not merely for the
acts of the Captain appointed by themselves, but
also for those of any one, who, during the voyage,
may be substituted in his place, although a substi-
tution has been prohibited. A third person who
has acted *bonâ fidê* ought not to suffer; the owners
in that case, are left to their recourse against whom
it may concern. *Magistrum accipimus, non solum*
quem exercitor præposuit, sed et eum quem magis-
ter. Quid tamen, si sic magistrum præposuit, ne
alium ei liceret præponere? An adhuc Juliani sen-
tentiam admittimus, videndum est: finge enim et
nominatim eam prohibuisse, ne Titio magistro uta-
ris? Dicendum tamen erit eo usquè producendam
utilitatem navigantium. (*d*)

d L. 1 §.
5. ff. de
exercit.
act.

Such is the general doctrine. *(e)*

e Duare-
nus ibid.
pag 1297,
Vinnius
and Pe-
ckius, ibid pag. 83. Stypmannus part. 4. cap. 15. n. 118. pag. 543.
Kuricke quæst- 15. pag. 869. Roccus de navib. not. 5 Targa. cap. 12.
n. 25. p. 40. Cujas, Peresius and Corvenus on the title of the Code de
institoriâ actione.

We ought not to attend to the distinctions which are made by Casaregis. *(a)*
Emerig. des Assur. ch. 7. Sect. 3.

a disc. 71. n. 17. and disc. 115. Vid.

SECTION III.

Are the owners answerable for the contracts of the Captain, made in the place where they reside?

Pothier,*(b)* observes that "the owners are suppo-sed to appoint a master to transact the business of the ship, only in their absence, and to do those things which they could not conveniently do themselves." In fact the Captain only becomes the master when he has unfurled his sails. Until that time he is under the controul of the owners, who may even dismiss him at will. *(c)* *He cannot, then, do any thing of consequence, but with the approbation of the owners, when he is in the port where they reside. *(d)*
d Art. 5. tit. du Capitaine.

§. 1. A captain who bor-rows mo-ney on bottomry in the place where the owners reside.
b n. 55.
h. t.
c Art. 4. tit. des Proprie-taires.

The *Consolato del Mare*,† *(e)* decides, that, in the place of the owners' residence it is necessary the Captain should have his consent to purchase the necessary rigging of the vessel. *Se il patrone del-la nave sara in loco che vi siano compagni, li deb-ba dimandare di quella exarcia, innanzi che la compri.*

Text of the Laws.

e ch. 236.

The ancient Ordinance of the Hanse towns *(f)* explains it in this manner: "The master being in

f Art. 58.

---

* Bee's Adm. Rep. 131. 339. 345. Molloy b. 11. c. 11. s. 11. 12,

† I know not what edition of the *Consolato* is used by our authour. According to *Boucher's* translation which is said to be a copy of the first *printed* edition, the quotation, in the text, is from ch. 239. pl. 694.

his own country shall not take more upon bottomry than according to the proportion of his own interest in the ship; and if he exceed this limit, the
other share-holders are not bound, neither can he
take any freight without the knowledge and consent of his owners." In the New Ord. of the
Hanse Towns *(a)* we find this provision. *Naucle-*
a tit. 6. *ri non debebunt, illo in loca ubi exercitores illorum*
art. 1. *præstò sunt, pecuniam sunt sub fœnore nautico ac-*
cipere.

The Ordinance of 1584, *(b)* contains nearly the
b art 95. same provision.

e art. 17.   The Ordinance of 1681, *(c)* provides that "In
tit. du   the place of the owner's residence no person shall
Capi-   cause repairs to be made to a ship, purchase sails,
taine.   cordage or any other thing for her, nor borrow money on bottomry, without the consent of the ow-
ner, under penalty of being answerable for it himself."

Art. 8. h.   "Those who lend money upon bottomry to the
t.   master, at the place where the owner resides, without his consent shall not have any lien or privilege,
except only on the portion of interest, which the
Captain may have in the vessel and freight, even
although the contract was made for the purpose of
obtaining repairs or victuals for the vessel."

The part   It results from all these texts, that the contracts
owners   of bottomry, made by the captain in the place where
who do
not con-   the owner resides, without his consent, are not
sent, are   binding upon him, The lender is not entitled to
not
bound by   hypothecation or privilege, but upon the mas-
such   ter's share, which alone is liable. *(d)*
loans.
d Pothier gis, disc. 71. n. 24. 27. Stypmannus, part. 4. tit. 5. n. 95. pag. 416.
n. 55. h. t. Vinnius. ad L. 1. §. 7. ff. de exercit. act. pag. 94. Kuricke, tit. 6. art. 1.
Casare-   pag. 764. Loccenius lib. 2. cap. 6. n. 8. pag. 993.

Nevertheless, if the lender prove that the money was usefully employed about the vessel and for the benefit of the owners, he may have the action *de in rem verso*, against them. *(a)* cus, de navib. not. 17. Casaregis disc. 71. n. 10. (Vid. Boniface, tom. 4. pag. 501.

[margin: Action de in rem verso. a Vinnius ad. d. le- gem pag. 98. Roc-]

"The master is bound to follow the advice of the owners of the vessel, when he takes freight, either in whole or in part, in the place of their residence." But a third person who contracts, *bonâ fidê*, on this subject is not bound to enquire, whether the terms be conformable to the orders of the owners.* It suffices that the charter party has been reduced to writing and delivered by the merchant to the captain. *(b)* It is sufficient that the bill of lading be signed by the master, or the clerk of the vessel, in order to authorize the presumption that every thing has been done with the privity of the owners. *(c)*

[margin: §. 2. Ad- venture shipped by the Captain without the know- ledge of the own- ers. b Art. 1. tit. des Chartes- parties. c Art. 1. tit. des connois- semens.]

"The master shall be responsible for all the merchandize laden on board his vessel and he shall render an account agreeable to his bills of lading. *(d)*

[margin: d Art. 9. tit. du Capi- taine.]

The owners are equally bound although they abandon the vessel and freight. They would not be permitted to say that the bill of lading was executed without their knowledge. General convenience, the welfare of commerce and publick faith require that such objections should not operate to the prejudice of third persons.

The Mess. *Saisset* shipped a box of hats on board the *Ste. Anne*, capt. *Meynete*, bound on a voyage to the French West Indies. A bill of lading, with freight at 5 sols, was signed by the captain. The ship put into Malaga, where the captain, being in

[margin: Saisset v. Meynete.]

---

* Vid. Abbott 79. 80. and see liv. 1. tit. 14. *de la saisie des vaisseaux*, art. 16. and *Valin's* Commentary.

want of money to prosecute his voyage, sold the hats. The vessel afterwards arrived at Martinique and then returned to Marseilles.

On the 27 June 1780, the *Mess. Saisset* obtained a sentence in our Admiralty, against the Captain, by which he was condemned to pay for the hats, at the rate of what they would have produced at Martinique. Appraisers were appointed, who valued the hats at 1561 liv. of France. Their report was confirmed by another sentence of the 24 November following.

There was a third sentence on the 6th February 1781, in favour of the *Mess. Saisset*, by which execution was ordered to be issued against him and M. Toussaint Paul, the owner of the ship jointly.* The Parliament on an appeal, by Arrêt. of the 15th July 1782, upon the report of M. de Thorame, the Son, affirmed this sentence, with costs.

M. Paul pleaded that the case of hats had been put on board without his knowledge; that the two former sentences had not been rendered against him &c. But 1. The two former sentences having been rendered against the Captain, acting as such, they were, of right, executory against the owner.

---

* By the French law an owner is bound by a judgment rendered against the Captain *as such,* and execution may go against both.

The owner has a right of action against those who have contracted with the master, without an asignment. *Ingersoll's Roccus* n. 4. xv. Roccus quotes, the Dig. l b. 14. tit. 1. de exercit act. L. 18. §. *sed ex contrario,* (translated in our appendix,) but misapprehends it, and has therefore contradicted himself. see n. xxvii. His ingenious scholiast and translator has very properly corrected him, and rescued the imperial law from the imputation of an unjust principle. The captain is the mere *locum tenens* or representative of the owner, and the common maxim, *qui facit per alium* gives the latter the right of action on all contracts made by the former, in that capacity.

2. The Bill of Lading signed by the Captain con- stituted a legal title in favour of the *Mess. Saisset.* *a* Vid. in- *M. Verdet*, junr. and my brother were the Advo- fr̀ Sect. cates for the parties respectively. *(a)*

SECTION IV.

Of a part owner who refuses to furnish his proportion,

Marquardus, *(b)* and Straccha, *(c)* maintain, that *b* lib. 2. the owner who delays for four months to contribute cap. 5. n, 19. his proportion, loses his right to a distributive share. *c* de na- They derive this opinion from the Senatus-Consul- vib. n. 3. tum, promulgated under the Emperor Adrian, which is quoted in the L. 52. §. 4. ff. *pro Socio* and in the L. 4. C. *de edific. priv*, But this Sena- tus-Consultum was simply a municipal regulation, which has no relation to the present subject, it hav- ing been intended to promote the decoration of the city of Rome.

The *Consolate del Mare (d)* says that "the own- §. 2. Mo- ers of the ship ought to contribute to the fitting ney may be bor- out of the ship, according to their respective shares. rowed on If some of them are unwilling or unable to furnish maritime loan on their proportions, the captain may compel them ju- their ac- dicially to do what is right; and he may also bor- count. *d* ch. 46. row money on their account and pledge their pro- portions for the payment of the sum borrowed."

The ancient Teutonic Ordinance *(e)* says, that *e* Art. 11. " when a merchant delays furnishing his part, the captain may borrow money on maritime loan and pledge the part of the recusant." And in the 59th Article, it is said that "the captain may borrow at bottomry for those who are unable or unwilling

K

to contribute their proportions of the expense of fitting out the vessel."

a Art. 18. tit. du Capi- taine.   The Ordinance of 1681 *(a)* says, "if a vessel has been freighted with the consent of the owners and one of them refuse to contribute his proporti- on of the expense of preparing her for sea, the master may, in such case, borrow upon bottomry, for the account of the person refusing, after having given him twenty four hours notice to come for- ward and pay his proportion."

b Art. 9. h. t.   (*b*) "The parts and portions of those owners who have refused to contribute to the expenses incurred in preparing the vessel for sea, are bound for the sums borrowed by the captain for her equipment and provisions."

   1. The master cannot borrow on bottomry on the proportions of the recusants, until the expira- tion of twenty four hours after they have had a writ- ten notice to furnish their quotas. We ought then

c ch. 6. not.8.   to yield to the doctrine of Targa, (*c*) who, in com- menting on the *Consolato del Mare*, contends that a summon is not necessary: *perche la legge e quel- la che interpella;* [the law itself gives notice.]

d tom. 1. p. 415. and tom. 2. p. 19.   M. Valin, in commenting upon certain articles of the Ordinance, which he cites, *(d)* says, that a loan made twenty four hours after a simple sum- mon "would be two precipitate. It is necessary, first, that the captain or master should summon the recusant to appear before a judge in order that he may be condemned to pay his proporti- on, without delay and within twenty four hours at furthest. If the money be not then paid, the cap- tain would be at liberty to borrow on maritime loan, on account of the recusant, such a sum as would

e n. 55.   be equal to his proportion." M. Pothier, *(e)* is of the same opinion.

These authours speak according to what is commonly practised; but I believe that a decree from a Judge is not necessary, since the Ordinance speaks only of a mere notice, and the circumstances of the case are such as sometimes not to admit of the delay which would be occasioned by the forms of justice.

2. The Ordinance relates to a master, whom a majority of the owners have authorized to fit out the vessel and do every thing necessary to that end, which they themselves could do. For, as I have before observed, the captain does not become master in fact until he has hoisted his sails. From which it follows, that what is said in this place of the master applies to owners. They have a right *a* Valin to borrow on maritime loan for account of recusants. *(a)* dictis locis.

3. If he could not borrow on maritime loan by *b* L. 4. §. pledging the proportion of the recusant, he might 3. ff. commence a suit against him, to compel him to mun. divid. §. 3. contribute or abandon his interest, and then he inst. de would be directed by the rules of the common oblig. law. *(b)* quæ quasi ex contr. nius, Despeisses tom. 1. p. 125. n. 7. ibiq. Vin-

Nothing prevents a part owner from disposing of §. 3. Whe-his share. But can he demand a publick sale of ther the recusant the entire vessel? can demand a publick sale.

Art. 5. Tit. *des Propriétaires* says, that "the o- Opinion pinion of the majority shall be followed as to *every* of the majority *thing that regards the common interest of the owners;* and they shall be deemed to be the majority who hold the largest share of the vessel."

The majority has no right to sell the vessel. They have only a right to prescribe, for the vessel

and the voyage whatsoever shall appear to them proper, although they may be opposed by those part
owners who compose the minority. But the Ordinance permits a publick sale, if the owners be equally divided, respecting the choice of a captain, the
destination of the ship or any other important object. "No one shall compel his partner to dispose of
a Art. 6.
Tit. des
Proprié-
taires. a vessel held in common between them, unless
they are equally divided in opinion respecting the
propriety of undertaking a voyage." *(a)*

This question came before our Admiralty on the
20th July 1751. The owners of fifteen parts demanded a publick sale of the entire vessel. They
said that if an equal division of opinion would entitle
them to demand a publick sale, with much more reason would the concurrence of fifteen shares give
them the same right. But it was answered, that, as a
general rule, no one could be compelled to sell an interest which he had in an undivided thing——that this
rule ceased as to a ship held in common by many only
when there was an equal division of opinion, *quæ mutuo concursu se se impediunt:* that as the ship could
neither be divided, (for, *qui navem dividet, perdit*)
nor sail at the same time to two opposite ports, a publick sale became absolutely necessary; but that
when there was not an equal division of opinion,
the greater number had a right to direct the voyage as they pleased, and therefore the applicants
had no right to compel a sale: and thus this question was decided.

b L. 12. §.
1. ff. de
usuf. et
quemad.
c On the
Ordi-
nance of
the Hanse
Towns
art. 59.
pag. 211. In this case, if the owners of the fifteen shares
had refused to contribute to the common expenses,
the others might have borrowed money on maritime loan, on their account: for a vessel is made to
be navigated: *navis enim ad hoc paratur, ut naviget, (b)* Cleirac *(c)* says, that "if there be two
owners of a vessel and one would send her to sea
and the other opposes him, the former should pre-

vail", but under such restrictions as the circum- *a* Vid.
stances of time and place may render necessary.(*a*) Straccha, de navi-
2. n. 6. pag. 478. See the cases cited in Peters Adm. Rep. 288. bus, part.

SECTION V.

Of a Captain, who borrows money on bot-
tomry during the voyage.

In the title of the Digests *de exercit. act.* there is §. 1. Text of the
not a word about money borrowed to be employ- laws.
ed in maritime speculations. [*pecunia trajectitia*]
It is said, in general terms, that the owners are responsible for all the acts of the master, respecting
the ship and the voyage. This rule has been some-
what modified by subsequent laws.

The *Consolato del Mare*, (*b*) permits the captain *b* chap.
to borrow money during the voyage *for the neces-* 104. 105. 236.
sities of the ship.

"If after his departure, the master stand in need Laws of Oleron,
of money to meet the expenses of the ship, he may art. 1.
pledge any part of the tackle, with the advice of the
mariners."

"If the vessel, in the course of her voyage, en- Art. 22.
ter a port and remain there so long that the money is all expended, the master should immediate-
ly send to his own country for more or sell a part Laws of Wisbuy
of his cargo." If the master want victuals he may art. 13.
pledge his cable and cordage.

"If the master, being upon his voyage, want
money, he ought to send home for it,—In case ibid. art.
of great necessity he may sell a part of his car- 35.
go."

Art. 45.   " If the master be obliged to sell part of his merchandize or *to borrow money on bottomry*, he ought to pay it at the port where he shall arrive &c."

The Old Laws of the Hanse Towns. art. 60.   " The master being in a strange country, if there is a necessity for it and he cannot do better, may borrow money on bottomry and the owners shall be answerable for it."

The New Laws of the Hanse Towns tit. 6. art. 2.   *Si nauclerus in cæteris locis, ubi suorem excercitorem compos non est, probabile damnum in navi, aut instrumentis navis perceperit, ac isthic loci nullum cambium ad exercitores transmittendum obtinere queat, aut etiam in navi nulla bona habeat, quæ meliori cum commodo exercitorum, quam pecuniá sub fænora nautico acceptá, vendere possit; tum hoc in casu necessitatis, pro servandá navi et bonis, habeat potestatem, nomine universorum exercitorum, tantùm pecuniæ sub fænore nautico accipiendi, quantum ad reparationem damni et alios similes casus necessitatis opus habet; et quidquid taliter fænori accepit, universi exercitoris solvere tenebuntur.*

Le Guidon de la Mer. ch. 5. art. 35.   " After having weathered a tempest and suffered injury, the captain, in order to repair the ship, may borrow money on bottomry."

ch. 18. art. 4.   " The captain may bind the vessel after she has sailed.—The reason of this is that the owners have placed confidence in his discretion and ability; by constituting him master, they make him *possessor* and *governor* of the ship, and all that is incidental to it." *(a)*

a Ibiq. Cleirac p. 332.

Ordinance of Antwerp. art. 19.   " The master of a ship shall not borrow money on bottomry, unless he is in a strange country and in a case of necessity."

"In the course of the voyage, the captain may borrow money upon the body and keel of the ship for her repairs, victuals and other necessities. He may even pledge the tackle or sell his cargo on condition of accounting for it at the rate at which the rest may be sold. All this must be done with the advice of his mates and pilots, who shall state in the log book the necessity of the loan, and the sale and the manner in which the money was expended." Ordinance of 1681. art. 19. tit. du Capitaine.

The Ordinance of Antwerp, *(a)* directs that the captain shall bring a certificate of the necessity which constrained him to do it. But there is no explanation of this law nor does it say by whom the certificate shall be given. §. 2. Ought the Captain to be authorized, by the Magistrate of
the place to take up money on bottomry? *a* Art. 19.

The Maritime Ordinance, *(b)* directs that the borrowing should be made with the advice of the mate and pilot, who should certify the necessity of it, on the log book. But the Ordinance does not create any penalty for a neglect of this formality. M. Valin observes, upon this article, that in such a case, the captains generally draw up a *procès verbal*, which is signed by their officers, attesting the necessity of borrowing the money. Bnt, as the only effect of these formalities is to justify the captain as against the owners; whether they be observed or neglected, the rights of third persons are not impaired; for the mere engagement of the captains gives them a legal demand upon the owners for their principal and maritime interest. b Art. 19. du Capitaine.

The Declaration of the 21 Oct. 1727, *(c)* directs that "the captains, masters or patrons* and others c Art. 30.

---

* In France, those who command vessels of war or merchant ships on long voyages are called captains; masters or patrons are those who comand vessels which are employed in the coasting trade. I presume they are synonimous with our *skippers* or *bay-craft-men.*

who borrow money at bottomry in foreign countries as well for the purchase and building of vessels in those countries as for the victualling wages and voyage, cannot bind themselves but to a Frenchman, born in our kingdom: *and ¹the contract shall be registered in the chancery of the French consulate.* We declare all contracts of this nature, executed before notaries in foreign countries to be null and void and direct our courts and judges to pay no regard to them.''

But this Declaration only relates to vessels which trade to the coast of Italy, Spain, Barbary and the ports in the Levant. In every other voyage, the contracts of captains and lenders are to be observed with good faith.

Nevertheless, it is very much the custom of captains, in case of any extraordinary expense, whether it be for the ship or for the cargo, to go before a Judge, who, upon being satisfied of the truth of their allegations and having heard the advocate for the King, permits them to borrow money at bottomry, for the account and risk of the concerned. This is a wise precaution. I have known many examples of it.

§.1. Ought it to be a publick contract?

We, every day, admit contracts made under private signature by captains and patrons in the course of a voyage. I am convinced that they are liable to be abused: an unfaithful captain may easily fabricate a contract of bottomry or receive those which were made during a preceeding voyage. I will observe once more, that a publick contract, the date of which is unchangeable, was formerly required. Duperier, *(a)* recites an Arrêt of the Parliament of Aix, in these words: "The Patron of a ship does not bind the owners by contracts of loan under private signature. Thus decided by an

a tom. 2. pag. 522.

Arrêt at the sitting of the 2nd November 1632, in favour of the Mess. Marin."

But, since the ordinance of 1681, the contract of maritime loan, made under private signature, has had the same effect, even against third persons, as a publick contract. It was thus adjudged by an arrêt of the 26th June 1767, in favour of Anselmo Rousseau, of which I shall give a report hereafter. *(a)*

a infrà ch. 6. sect. 2. § 2.

It is necessary that the loan should be for the necessities of the ship; *(b)* for refitting, victualling and other necessities of the ship; *(c)* *in refectionem navis(d) ad armandum, instruendamve navem, vel nautas exhibendos.(e)* It is necessary that the captain borrowed, *quasi in navem impensurus,* and that the lender should believe that his money is to be employed in that manner :* *sciat ut in hoc se credere, cui rei magister præpositus est.(f)*

§ 4, It is necessary that the loan should be eo nomine on account of the necessities of the ship.

b art. 16. tit. de la saisie. *c* art. 19. tit. du Capitaine. *d* L. 7. ff. de exercit act. *e* L. 1. §. 7. ff. eod. *f* L. 7, ff. eod.

Whence it follows that if the instrument does not state it to be for the necessities of the ship, the lender has neither an action direct against the owners nor a lien upon the ship, even although his money may have been employed in a manner beneficial to the voyage. *Si magister navis pecuniam mutuatus, non cavit se recipere, in refectionem navis, non tenetur hâc actione exercitor, etiamsi pecunia in refectionem navis impensa sit.(g)*

g Vinnius, ad L. Lucius —Titius 7. ff. de exercit, act. page 184. Cujas, on the same law, tract. 8. ad Africanum,

In fact, when I do not take the precaution of declaring in the contract, that the money is lent to relieve the necessities of the ship, I do not lend to the ship itself. I cannot say in the words of law*(h)*

h L 5. §. 15. ff. de tribut act

---

* Molloy b. ii. c. 11. S. 11. 3. Mod. 244. Hob. 12. Salk. 35. 1. Mag. 27. Bee's Adm. Rep. 120. 131. 339. And the lender should inform himself whether such necessity exists. Bee 157, 350, 3. 1. Magens 329.

that I have taken the *thing* as my security, in preference to the person: *merci magis quàm ipsi
credidi.* The captain becomes my debtor, directly
and solely : *in creditum ei abii.(a)*

a d.
Lege 5.
§. 18.

It is true that by making use of the rights of the
captain I can sue the owners and claim a lien on the
vessel.*   But if it appear that there is nothing due
from them to him, I cannot maintain an action a-
gainst them or the vessel.

§ 5. Can
the cap-
tain bor-
row at
bottomry,
to com-
plete his
cargo?

b Casar-
gis, disc.
69. n. 15.

c L. 5. ff.
mandati.

d L 14. ff.
eod.

According to some authors, the captain may borrow money at bottomry to complete his cargo, and
thus avoid the necessity of returning empty.*(b)*
But if the speculation be not successful, he runs
the risk whether the owners will allow it in his account, and I advise every captain not to exceed his
instructions. *Diligenter fines mandati custodiendi
sunt. Nam qui excessit, aliud quid facere videtur.(c) Si is qui mandatum suscepit, egressus
fuerit mandatum, ipsi quidem mandati judicium
non competit : at ei qui mandaverit, adversus eum
competit.(d)* Savery says that, he who exceeds
his orders, does it at his own risk.

SECTION VI.

*Various questions relating to the points which have
been treated in the three preceeding sections.*

§ 1. What
is under-
stood by
the
words,
residence
of the

According to the laws of the Oleron(c) and of
Wisbury,(d) the captain, cannot, in the course of
his voyage, borrow money at bottomry, but in case
it is not possible to send home speedily for it.
owners. *c* art. 22. *d* art. 35.

---

* In order to understand this passage, it is necessary to know
that the lender may sue the captain by attachment, and by this
process become entitled to his rights and actions against the
owners as well as others. In this manner he becomes possessed
of the captain's lien, if he have any.

By the late ordinance of the Hanse Towns(*a*) ^{a tit. 6. art. 2.} the captain, being in a strange place could not receive the necessary succour from his owners: *in cæteris locis, ubi suorum exercitorum compos non est.*

Our ordinance is limited to the prohibition of the captain from borrowing, in the place where the owners reside, without their consent: and it recognizes loans made *bonâ fidê*, where the owners do not reside even without their consent.

I believe that the word *residence* ought to be understood according to the common law. A vessel was at Antibes. The owners, living in neighbouring villages had paid their proportions. The master, before he set sail, borrowed money at bottomry. The vessel arrived at Marseilles, where she was seized at the instance of the lenders. Being consulted by them, I answered that a person is held to be *present, where he is domiciliated* in the same bailiwick; (which is the opinion of Brodeau, of Duplessis and Fevriere on the custom of Paris, art. 116.) and consequently the totality of the vessel was not affected by the loan. ^{Residence in the same county.}

But it is a different thing if the loan has been made in another district, no matter how near it is. A vessel sailed from Toulon and went to Marseilles to take in a cargo. She belonged to three owners; of whom two were at Marseilles and the third lived at Toulon. The captain borrowed money at bottomry from *Francis Boule,* and the two owners at Marseilles consented to it. In the course of her voyage, the vessel was declared to be not sea worthy. The nett sales of the rigging, amounting to 360 dollars, was deposited in the consulate of France, at Tripoli. *Boule* claimed this sum, in payment of his contract. The owner who resided at Toulon ^{Residence, not in the same county.}

objected as to his proportion, because in the commencement he had furnished his proportion of the
expences. Sentence was rendered August 9, 1748,
in favour of *Boule*, in conformity to the art. 8. h.
t. I shall report hereafter(*a*) an arrêt, which decides the question in the same manner.

a infra
ch. 6.
sect. 2.
§. 2.

§. 2. May
the cap-
tain bor-
row mo-
ney in the
port
where the
vessel is
fitted out,
without
the con-
sent of
the own-
ers domi-
ciliated
else-
where?

b Laws of
Wisbuy
art. 25.

c Guidon
de la Mer.
ch. 18.
art. 4.

d First
ordinance
of the
Hanse
Towns,
art. 60,
&c.

According to the ancient laws, the captain could
not borrow money at bottomry, on account of the
owners, but when *on his voyage*,(*b*) *when he has
hoisted sail*,(*c*) *or when he is in a strange country*.(*d*)
Upon this point, our ordinance has left a cloud
which is not very clear. In art 17,(*e*) it is said that
the captain shall not borrow money on bottomry,
in *the place where the owners reside, without their
consent.* The same rule is repeated in the 8th article,(*f*) where it is said, that those who lend
money at bottomry to the captain, in *the place where
the owners reside,* without their consent, shall have
no hypothecation or lien but on the master's proportion. Whence it follows, that the captain has an
indefinite power to borrow money at bottomry in
every place where the owners do *not reside*, even
though the voyage has not been commenced. But
the 19th art.(*g*) in denying to the master the power
of borrowing at bottomry, without the consent of
the owners, seems to require that it should be *in
the course of the voyage.*

e tit. du Capitaine. *f* tit. des Contrats à la grosse. *g* tit. du Capitaine.

In order that the whole of the vessel should be
bound for the payment of money borrowed by the
captain, is it necessary that it should not only be
borrowed in the course of the voyage, but at a
place where the owners do not reside? Or, is it
sufficient that it be not at the place of residence,
although at the place where the vessel is fitted out?

h Valin
art. 8. h.t.

" It is only during the voyage,"(*h*) or *when a
vessel is equipped at a place where the owners are*

not domiciliated (or their correspondents) that a master is allowed to pledge the whole of the vessel and
the freight by borrowing at bottomry, for refitting
and victualling. He then binds all the owners by
his act, with a saving of their remedy against him,
if he make an improper use of the money."

I adopt this commentary as the most consonant
with the Ordinance and the least subject to litigation. The absent owners are supposed to have given to the captain a power to equip the vessel where
she lies and to make such contracts on the subject
as are necessary.

M. Valin, in the place above cited and also on
the *9th art. h. t.* says, that the Captain is permitted to pledge the whole of the ship when he is in a
place where the owners have neither a domicil *nor*
correspondents. From which it follows that if there
be correspondents at the port, the Captain should
do nothing without their consent. §. 3. If the own-ers or their Cor-respon-dents be on the spot?

But if the third person who has furnished an unfaithful captain with provisions, was ignorant that
the owners have correspondents on the spot, he has
an action against the whole of the vessel, because
he has acted *bonâ fidê.* The Captain had a legal
authority. It is necessary then that this third person should have notice that this *legal authority* has
been revoked, or at least that the knowledge of it
was publick in the place. As to the rest, the difficulties which may arise from the subject, ought to
be decided by the rules of the common law.*(a) *a* L. 11. §. 2. ff. de Inst. act. L. 12. §. 2. L. 34. §. 3. L. 51. ff. de solution. L. 11. ff. depositi. § 10. inst. de man-dato.

See the next Section.

---

* When the French writers use this term, they are to be
understood as alluding to the *civil law,* which is the common
law of France. What changes may have been made in it,
by the Napoleon Code, must be learned by a reference to that
work, which has but recently been promulgated.

SECTION VII.

Of an unfaithful Captain.

§. 1. The owners are bound by those acts only, of the Captain which relate to the voyage.

The law does not give, against the owners, an indefinite right of action on account of the acts of the Captain, whatever they may be : *non autem ex omni causâ prætor dat in exercitorem, actionem; The right is restricted to those acts which are necessary for the purposes of navigation and which result from his situation or character of master : sed ejus rei nomine, cujus ibi præpositus fuerit.* *

So that if the Captain has borrowed money, without stating in the contract, that is for the necessities of the ship, or if he has done any act which does not flow from his situation as master, the owners are not bound. *Quid, si mutuam pecuniam sumpserit? An ejus rei nomine videatur gestum?*

a L. 1. §. 8. ff. de exercit. act.

Et Pegasus existimat si ad usum ejus rei, in quâ præpositus est, fuerit mutuatus, dandam actionem ; quam sententiam puto veram.(a)

§. 2. Penalties against an unfaithful Captain.

If the money which was borrowed for the purposes of commerce, be squandered by the Captain, he deserves to be severely punished.

Ordinance of 1681. tit. du Capitaine, art. 20.

" The Captain who has borrowed money without necessity at bottomry for the victualling or refitting of the ship, sold the cargo, pledged the tackle or made false entries in his journal of charges and expences, shall be bound in his proper person, declared unworthy of the privelege of a burgher and also be banished from the port where he commonly resides."

---

* Abbott, 77.

The 29th Article prohibits Captains from borrowing " for the voyage, more money than shall be necessary for their lading, under penalty of being deprived of their burgher-ship and forfeiting their share of the profits."

Si præter hæc, nauclerus in aliis peregrinis locis absque necessitate fraudulento modo pecuniam sub fænore nautico mutuò acceperit, solus damnum refundere, et pro qualitate rei capitaliter puniri debet. *(a)*

ricke, tit. 6 art. 3. pag. 766.

Jus Hanseat. tit. 6. art. 3. *a* Stypmannus, part. 4. cap. 5. n. 134. pag. 419. Ku-

But the infidelity of the captain shall not prejudice third persons who have made contracts with him *bonâ fidê*. These third persons are not the less entitled to an action against the owners and a lien on the ship, because the contract was entered into for the promotion of the voyage. *Undè quærit, Ofilius, si ad reficiendam navem mutuatus nummos in suos usus converterit, an in exercitorem detur actio? Et ait, si hâc lege accepit quasi in navem impensurus, mox mutavit voluntatem, teneri exercitorem, imputaturum cur talem proposuerit.* *(b)*
exercit. act. Vinnius ad. L. 7. ff. eod. pag. 182. 184. Stypmannus, part. 4 cap. 15. n. 144. pag. 545. Marquardus lib. 2. cap. 5. n. 27. Locceni-us lib. 3. cap. 7. n. 7. 8. pag. 1032. Valin, art. 19. tit. des Capitaines, pag. 416.

§. 3. The infidelity of the Captain who has squanlered the money shall not prejudice a third person who has contracted with him bonâ fidê. *b* L. 1. §. 9. ff. de

It follows, from this principle, that he who, in the course of the voyage, has lent money to the Captain for the necessities of the ship, is not obliged to follow this money, nor prove that it was usefully employed.* It is evident that he believed the Captain to be honest; and, moreover, it is necessary that he should be one of that profession or trade in order to enable him to judge of the expediency and the nature of the disbursements made or to be made on any particular occasion. *Non*

§. 4. The lender is not obliged to prove that the money was usefully employed.

---

* Dg. 14. 1. 7. 2. Abbott, 104, Marshall 639.

a L. 7. ff.
de exercit
act. Ibiq.
Glosa,
Cujas
Gothofre-
dus Sco- *oportet creditorem ad hoc adstringi, ut ipse refici-*
endæ navis curam suscipiat, et negotium domini
gerat; quod certè futurum sit, si necesse habeat
probare pecuniam in refectionem errogatam esse.(a)
tauus, ff. eod. pag. 322. Casaregis, disc. 71. n. 1.

SECTION VIII.

Of an imprudent Lender.

b Lucius
Titus 7.
ff. de ex-
ercit. act. The law *(b)* directs that he who has lent money
to a faithless Captain should at least use some dili-
gence to recover it from him. *In summâ, aliquam*
diligentiam in eâ creditorem præstare.

§. 1. Is it
necessary
that at
the time
of the
loan, the
necessity
should ac-
tually ex-
ist? The creditor, says this law, shall have an action against the owners, if, at the time when the
loan is made, the ship really requiring refitting:
Creditorem utiliter acturum, si non pecunia crede-
retur, navis in eâ causâ fuisset, ut refici deberet.
It is necessary, according to the text, not only that
the loan should be for the use of the ship, but also that the person should know that it is required
for that purpose. *Si illud quoque sciverit necessa-*
riam refectioni pecuniam esse. Whence it follows, according to the text, that if the necessity
was but imaginary, the owners would not be responsible.*

c See the
Ordi-
nance. I believe that it is the *necessity* of the case which
gave rise to the action *exercitoria;* but, by our
Ordinance "the master who shall have borrowed
money at bottomry, without *necessity,* shall be
personally bound to repay it, forfeit his burgership
and be banished from the port where he resides."(c)

---

* Marshall, 639.

If the contract be in due form and the creditor was not cognizant of the fraud it shall not be less good against the vessel. Such is our law, as appears from the decisions already cited. (a)

a Suprà Sect. 5.

The same law, 7. adds, that if one lend to the Captain more than is necessary, he shall not have an action against the owners for the excess. *Si in ed causâ fuerit navis ut refici deberet, multò tamen major pecunia credita fuerit, quàm ad eam rem esset necessaria, non deberet in solidum adversùs dominum navis, actionem dari.* But this is only the law in cases where the lender knew the Captain did not require so large a sum. For if the lender have acted *bonâ fide*, his right of action against the owners still remains: *Sed et si in pretiis rerum empturum fefellit magister, exercitores erit damnum, non creditoris. (b)*

§. 2. If the loan be excessive.

b L. 1. §. 10 ff. de exercit., act in. nius. ibid. pag. 186. Stypman nus, d. loeis.

The same law 7. *ff. de exercit. act.* prohibits any action against the owners if money has been lent to the Captain in a place where he could not make use of it. *Interdùm etiam illud æstimandum, an in eo loco pecunia credita sit, in quo id, propter quod credebatur, comparari poterit.* But if it cannot be employed in that place, it is sufficient if it can be used in another, and that the lender, whose title is in due form, should not be cognizant of fraud, in order to entitle him to his action against the owners, notwithstanding the inability to employ it.

If the Captain be in a place where the money cannot be used.

If the power of borrowing at bottomry has been expressly prohibited, are those persons who furnish the captain with money entitled to an action against the owners? from borrowing.

§. 3. Of a Captain who has been prohibited

It seems at first view in this case that all actions between lenders and owners for money which has not been employed, ought to be prohibited: *qui cum alio contrahit, vel est, vel debet esse, non ig-narus conditionis ejus.* (*a*)   There are several texts which confirm this doctrine

a L. 19.
ff. de reg.
jur.

L. 7. ff.
exercit.
act.

Sciat ut in hoc se credere, cui rei magister quis sit præpositus.

L. 1. §, 7.
ff. eod.

Non autem ex omni cansâ prætor dat in exerci-torem actionem, sed ejus rei nomine cujus ibi præ-positus fuerit.

D. Lege.
§. 12.

Præpositio certam legem dat contrahentibus, modum egressus non obligabit exercitorem.

b D. Lege.
1. §. 14.

Si sic præposuit, ne alter sine altero quid ge-rat, qui contraxit cum uno, sibi imputabit. (*b*)

All this is true, if the lender knew how far the Captain was restricted; but if he was ignorant of the prohibition, his right of action against the own-ers still exists, for the perservation of good faith. Every Captain is presumed to be a master, and to be at liberty to exercise all the priveleges attached to that character.   Those who contract with him in a strange country, are not obliged to demand his authority and he could easily deceive them. The §. 5. of the law above cited, after having de-cided that a contract entered into with one whom the captain has substituted in his place, is binding on the owners, adds, that it shall be so, although they had actually prohibited the Captain from sub-stituting another.   *Dicendum erit eò usquè produ-cendam utilitatem navigantium.*

I admit that there is a great difference between him who embarks in a ship or who puts merchan-dize on board, and him who lends money to the Captain.   But the intention of the law, founded upon a common error, should be regarded in every case.

I believe then, that, notwithstanding the prohibition to the Captain to borrow money at bottomry during the voyage, those who have lent money to him, *bonâ fidê* have not the less right of action against the owners and their lien on the ship is not impaired. It is necessary that they should have notice of the prohibition, or, at least, that it has been publickly given in the place where the contract is made. (a)

a L. 11. 17. ff. de inst. act. Vide. Stypmannus part. 4. cap. 15. n. 135. pag. 543. Locceni- us. lib. 3. tit. 7. n. 9. pag.

Vinnius, pag. 88. 103. 111. Roccus de navib. not. 12. Casaregis, disc. 71. n. 8. Pothier, des Obligations, n. 79. tom. 1. pag. 39.

1033 Pec- kius and

Duarenus, (b) explaining the law of Lucius Titius, says, that it is sufficient if he who lends money to a faithless captain, should conduct himself with some diligence, in order to avoid the suspicion of any fraud, *satis est eum adhibere aliquam diligentiam, ut non appareat eum malo animo mutuam pecuniam dedidisse.* Whence it follows, that if the negligence be extreme, and he is much in fault, he may forfeit all right of action against the owners: *gravis culpa dolo equiparatur.*

§. 4. We may, ac- cording to circum- stances, adopt the excepti- ons estab- lished by the law Lucius- Titius.

b ff. de exercit. act. pag. 1297.

M. Valin, (c) repeats the provisions of this law of *Lucius-Titius.* "But all this" says he, "has been rejected in the usage of merchants, as too nice and punctilious, and affording too much room for chicanery: and in order to give the lender a right of action against the owner, it is sufficient if he have lent, *bonâ fidê*, a sum of money to the Captain; that is, that there is neither proof *nor reasonable presumption of any collusion between him and the Captain.*"

c Art. 19. tit. du Capi- taine pag. 417.

This authour does not exclude those reasonable presumptions of collusion, which arise out of the

transaction itself and which are innumerably various. He who is desirous to embark himself or to
lade a vessel, has not often the choice of a vessel.
He is obliged, *propter navigandi necessitatem*, to
take the first which offers. But he who lends
money to a Captain does it voluntarily and without any constraint; the motive of the Prætor's E-
dict is not applicable to him.

a Vide
Cujas
Vinnius,
Faber,
and other
It is then just that he should use common pru-
dence: *aliquam diligentiam.* (*a*)
Civilians upon the law of Lucius-Titius, 7. ff. de exercit. act. Stypman-
nus part. 4. cap. 6. n. 124. cap. 15. n. 154. pag. 418. 544. Pothier, des
Obligations, n. 448. tom. 1. pag. 231.

SECTION IX.

*Of a Captain who sells part of his cargo,
during the voyage.*

b Art. 68.
The Ordinance of Wisbuy, (*b*) contains a singular provision. " In case of necessity, the master may dispose of a part of his cargo in order to
raise money, if he has need of it for the vessel;
and if the ship be afterwards lost, the master shall
be obliged nevertheless, to pay the merchant for
the goods sold."

c Art. 14
tit. du
fret. pag.
621.
M. Valin, (*c*) cites the provision of the Ordinance of Wisbuy, and contends that the owner of
the ship ought to pay the value of the goods sold,
during the voyage, for the necessities of the vessel,
independently of the subsequent hazard of the ship;
in the same manner as if, instead of selling merchandize, the master had borrowed of another, a
certain sum, for which he had drawn a bill of Exchange upon him.

M. Pothier, *(a)* informs us that, " persons of experience on the subject of maritime jurisprudence, whom he has consulted respecting his treatise, were of opinion that the owners of merchandize, sold to supply the necessities of a ship, could demand nothing, if the vessel should, afterwards be lost.....But," says he, "I should have some difficulty in making such a decision and I think the Ordinance of Wisbuy and the opinion of M. Valin more consanant with law.....It is a sort of *compulsary loan* of which the Owner of the goods has made to the master for the necessities of the ship. From this loan arises an Obligation, that the master contracts with him, to return the money so lent. The owner of the goods sold has also his action against the proprietors of the ship, for the price of his merchandize, They cannot defend themselves under the 2nd. article, *(b)* which applies only to those obligations of the master, for which there would not be allowed any recourse against the owners for indemnification.....The ill success of a transaction which was ordered, when it does not proceed from the acts of the agent, does not release the principal from his obligation to pay the expenses which have accrued and the contracts which the agent has made in the execution of his orders &c.".

Con-tts nri-nes, n. 5 and 7

bit. des pprie-tes.

Kuricke, (c) *and Cleirac, (d)* follow the Ordinance of Wisbuy.
d pag. 88. n. 2.

lit. 6. t. 2. g. 765.

But the *Consolato del Mare, (e)* decides that, if, in the course of a voyage, the Captain connot find a person who will lend him money to provide for the necessities of the ship, he may dispose of a part of his cargo, according to the sum which he requires; and the owners of the merchandize have no more than a mere lien and preference upon the ship.

ch. 105,

a Art. 2   The laws of Oleron, (*a*) do not admit any action, on this subject, against the master, until the ship has arrived at her place of discharge.

b Art. 1   The Ordinance of Antwerp, *(b)* says, that the master of the ship, "shall neither sell nor pledge any merchandize as long as he can raise money by way of bottomry. He may, in the last extremity, sell a part of his cargo, for which the merchant shall be paid *at the rate at which the remainder shall have been sold*" This is all; so if the remainder of the merchandize be lost by shipwreck, the lot of all will be the same.

c Art. 1 tit. du C pitaine. art. 14. tit. du Fret. *d* Vid. Traité des Assurances, ch. 12. Sect. 4. §. 5. *e* Cleira pag. 88. n. 4. in-frà, ch. 12. Sect. 4.   The goods thus disposed of are supposed to have been always on board. This is the reason why freight is due and likewise the part sold to raise money must be paid for at the rate at which the rest may be sold at the port of discharge.(*c*) We find the same law in the 69th art. of the laws of Wisbuy. (*d*) These goods must contribute to a gross average. The privilege which belongs to the owners of them is similar to that which is allowed to lenders at bottomry. (*e*)

It is then evident, that if the ship perish, neither the Captain nor the owners are subject on that account, to any personal Obligation. It is here a sort of compulsory maritime loan.

f ch. 12. Sect. 41. §. 4. pag 616. and Sect. 43. §. 1. pag. 653. Vid. infrà Sect. 12. § 2   It is a question whether the goods saved ought to contribute to the payment of those which have been previously sold? I believe that they must, and I derive my opinion from the rule which is established respecting goods thrown overboard to lighten the vessel, of which I have spoken in my treatise on Assurance, *(f)* For it is immaterial whether the goods be cast away or sold for the common benefit. I admit that if the ship arrive in port, the owners are obliged to pay the value of the goods Suprà ect. 3. 2. sold in the course of the voyage for the necessities of the ship, without power, excepting the case of right, to institute the action of gross average ;(*a*) But if the vessel be lost and part of the cargo be saved, the action of gross average is the only means of establishing an equality among the freighters and regulating the contributions of the parties respectively.

In the 11th section of this chapter, we shall find, as a general rule, that the owners who abandon ship and freight, are not obliged to pay those bills which the captain may have drawn upon them in the course of the voyage, without having a special authority to do so. The captain is not, in every respect, the agent of the owners. He has no power legally beyond that which is given to him by the Ordinance. If he borrow money at bottomry or sell goods for the necessities of a voyage already commenced, he does not, properly, bind any thing more than the vessel itself; and if it perish, the obligations attached to the vessel are cancelled by the shipwreck, saving the lien upon the wreck and the freight.

A question has been started, whether the Captain should dispose of a part of his cargo in preference to adventures. The Ordinance is silent on the subject, and the question appears idle in this case as well as in that of Jettison. (*b*) Emer. Insurance, C. 12, Sect. 40, § 4.

I ought to observe in this place, that this sale is one of the perils of the sea for which the assurers are liable. An adventure which I have ensured is sold in the course of a voyage: from that time, I have a lien upon the ship and freight for the price of my goods. If the vessel afterwards perish or become not sea-worthy the assurers are obliged to pay me, saving their right to the things preserved. If the adventure thus sold should belong to one who has borrowed money by way of maritime loan, the produce should be for the benefit of the lender.

SECTION X.

*Of the several kinds of actions called principal, ac-
cessary and contrary.*

In order to understand the nature of these different actions, it is necessary to revert again to the
principles of the Roman laws.

§ 1. Ro-man Law. — The Masters of vessels were Factors, of a particular class. In every thing that concerned maritime
commerce, they acted as real *masters*. It was with
them principally and directly that persons contracted.
It was then proper that they should be personally
bound to third persons who had acted upon their
credit.

The action a-gainst the owner was ad-ded to that against the mas-ter. — The exercitory action [*actio exercitoria*] was only
introduced to give more stability to their contracts
and to inspire those who dealt with them with greater
confidence, by adding to their own personal obligation, that of the owner; *non transfertur actio, sed
adjicitur.(a)* The principal action then combines
that against the master and that against the owner.

a Law 5. ff. de ex-ercit. act. — *Obligatio quâ tenetur magister navis, est principalis ; ea autem qua tenetur exercitor, est accessoria.*

b Duaren-nus, de exercir. act. pag. 299. — *Non enim ex suâ personâ tenetur exercitor, sed
ex personâ magistri.(b)*

It is op-tional to sue either the mas-ter or owner. — Nevertheless we have the choice of suing either the
master or owner; *est nobis electio, utrum exercito-
rem, an magistrum convenire velimus.(c)* Cujas,(d)
says, *hæ actiones sunt accessoriæ : nam principalis*

c L. 1. § 17. ff. cod.   *d* on the title of the code, de exercit. et inst. act.

actio datur in institorem aut magistrum. Potest tamen etiam in exercitorem agi, in eum qui præposuit, quasi in principalem.

But the principal action against the master is not affected, either by the *addition* of a right of action against the owner, nor by the election of suing the one or the other. *Nec prætor eâ mente introduxit exercitoriam, ut perimeret eam, quæ ex contractu in magistrum competit, et quasi novatione factâ hanc in illam transferret; sed ut civili actioni honorariam adjiceret; atque itâ ei, qui cum magistro contraxit, pleniùs consuleret.(a)* part. 4. cap. 15. n 231. pag. 550. Duarenus, pag. 1299. {This choice does not make any change in the principal action against the master. a Stypmannus}

This was the law only when the master was a free man. If he was a slave there was no right of action but against the owner.(b) For a slave could not appear in judgment. *Cum servo nulla actio est.(c)* act. lib. 29. Pauli ad edictum. Vinnius at Leg. 1. §. 17. ff. eod. pag. 129. Stypmannus dicto loco, n. 224. Dumoulin, Peresius. Corvinus, C. de institut. c. L. 107. ff. de regul. jur. L. 6. C. de judiciis. {What, if the master was a slave? b Cujas on Law 5. ff de exercit.}

In this last case, if the person elect to sue the owner, setting aside the master who was a free man, the action which was, in its nature accessary, becomes principal or *quasi-principal.* {If the person elect to sue the owner, the action would be principal.}

The owner was bound for the whole of the debt; without being allowed to abandon the *peculium* of his slave or of his son not emancipated, who had been appointed master. *Si voluntate domini vel patris exerceant, in solidum tenebuntur,* [father or master.](d) Duarenus pag. 1297. Corvinus, C. de inst, pag, 198. {It was in solidum and for the whole. d L. 1. §. 22. ff. de exercit. act. Ibiq.}

Although the exercitory action arose from the edict of a prætor, it was nevertheless perpetual, in order to favour commerce. It remained in favour of or against heirs. *Hæ actiones perpetuò et in hæredibus et hære des dabuntur.(e)* act. Ibiq. Duarenus, pag. 1299. Cujas C de inst. {The exercitory action was perpetual. e L. 4. §. 4. ff. de exercit.}

§. 2. New Law. Does the Captain cease to be master when the voyage is aidded?

a Sect. 3.
b ch. 18. art. 4.

I have said before, *(a)* that in the place where the owners reside, the captain cannot do any thing of consequence without their consent; and that he does not become *master, possessor and governor of the vessel,* to use the language of the *Guidon de la Mer,* (*b*) until she has set sail, &c. Whence it seems that the *master* should cease as soon as the voyage terminates. Nevertheless, after the return of the vessel, he preserves some vestige of his former authority, as we shall presently see.

Can we commence actions against him?

c Vinnius ad Leg. 1. §. 18. ff. de exercit act. pag. 128.
d Valin. art. 2. tit. des Proprietaires, tom. 1. pag. 537.

The *oblique actions* established by the Roman law, of which I have before spoken, are scarcely known in practice. *Hodiè obliquæ istæ actiones, seu potiùs actionum adjectiones, usum non habent. Sed directò ex contractibus institorum nostrorum, aut aliàs præpositorum tenemur.*(*c*) Those who have contracted with the captain have the choice of proceeding directly against the owners, or the captain, or against both at the same time.(*d*) Every day, among us, we see sailors proceeding against their captains to procure the payment of their wages.

The judgment obtained against the master may be executed against the owners.

e Art. 2. tit. des proprié-taires, ib.

But the judgment which has been obtained against the captain may be executed against the owners although they may not have been joined in the action. M. Valin, *(e)* says, "that there is no direct action and executory condemnation against the master, but when the engagement with him is proper and personal; as to oblige him to fulfil his bills of lading, to answer for his own acts, his faults or offences. All other judgments against him, can only be executed on the owners, or, which is the same thing, if they be against him, they cannot be but in a qualified manner, as the representative of the owners, according to the amount which he may have in hand belonging to them."

A captain was sued by his sailors, whose wages were to depend upon the profits, for an account of the profits and freight of a voyage——Our Admiralty appointed persons of experience to adjust the account between them; and in consequence, a sentence was rendered, by which the proportion of each sailor was fixed at 27 livres. The same sailors filed a petition praying that the sentence might be declared to be common and executory against *Paschal Zino,* the owner of the ship. He moved to set aside the report which established the shares of the sailors. It was objected to him that he was not entitled to make that motion, because final sentence had passed against the captain, by which he was bound in the same manner as if he had been a party to the suit.

Sentence was rendered 24th April 1750, which without regard to the prayer of Zino ordered a joint execution. The owner could not have had any other resource than that of an appeal. The same question was decided in a similar manner in favour of M. Saisset, by an Arrêt. *(a)*

a Supra Sect. 3. §. 2. See also Sect. 8. 9. and 11. of this chapter and Roccus, de navibus not. 27.

According to the Roman law, he who contracted with the captain was entitled to an action *in solidum* against each of the owners. *Si plures navem exerceant, cum quolibet eorum in solidum agi potest, ne in plures adversarios distringatur, qui cum uno contraxerit. (b)* And he who contracts with one of the owners, has no right of action against the others, unless that one has been appointed master of the ship. *(c)* This doctrine is very little in use among us. *(d)*

Action in solidum against each of the Owners. *b* L. 1, §. 25. and L. 2. ff. de exercit. act. *c* L. 4. ff. eod. L. 7. ff. nautæ. *d* Infrà Sect. 11.

According to the Roman Law the *actio Contraria* was not given to the Owners against those who had contracted with the Master. They could only

An Essay on

a L. 1. §.
18. ff. de
exercit
act. (Ibiq.
Duarenus
pag. 1299.
and Fa-
ber. Pere-
sius, C.
de Inst.
act. Styp-
mannus
institute the action *locati* against them, in order to
compel them to account. *Exercenti navem adver-*
sus eos, qui cum magistro contraxerunt, actio non
pollicetur, quia non eodem auxilio indigebat. Sed,
aut ex locato, cum magistro, si mercede operam ei
exhibet; aut, si gratuitam, mandati agere po-
test. (a)
part. 4. cap. 15. n. 242. pag. 550. Loccenius lib. 3. cap. 7. n. 15. pag.
1036. Straccha, de nautis, part. 6. n. 4. pag. 455.

b Vinnius.
ibid. pag.
132. Sco-
tanus,
pag. 323.

c Casare-
gis, disc.
1. n. 187.
and disc.
91. n. 18.
Brodeau
Cout. de
Paris,
tom. 1.
pag. 43.
Laroche
This rule was liable to one exception as to the
transportation of provisions intended for the publick
service. But the action, which was granted in
such case to the owner against the merchant was
extraordinary: *dictâ lege primâ*, §. 18. Our authours convert this exception into a rule. (*b*) With
so much the greater reason that among us, the creditor is suffered to carry on the actions of his debt-
or, even without any conveyance from him, *ad evi-*
tandum circulum. (c)
and Graverol, pag. 19. 159. 501. Vedel, tom. 2. pag. 107. Boutaric,
inst. pag. 467. &c.

It is then lawful for the owners, themselves to
demand the freight, average and hypothecation and
to pursue the execution of every contract which
concerns the ship. In a word, the captain can do
nothing without their advice, in the place of unlading and of their residence.

Do the
powers of
the Cap-
tain cease
upon the
loss of
the ship ?
d Sen-
tence re-
ported in-
frà Sect.
11. §. 6.
Do the powers of the captain in his quality of
master cease by the loss of the vessel? This question was discussed in the case of the owners of the
ship *le Prince de Lamballe. (d)* I contended, for the
shippers, that in case of wreck, the captain ought
not to forget *to save all that he can*, of the ship
and cargo, beginning with the most precious
things. *(e)*
e Art. 27. tit. du Capitaine.

This Obligation is imposed upon him in his capacity of governor of the ship. The freight of the

things saved belongs to him in his quality of mas- *a* Art. 21. ter. (*a*) This character even obliges him to seek $\frac{\text{tit du}}{\text{fret.}}$ another vessel in order to convey the things saved to their port of destination. (*b*) It is certain then that shipwreck does not absolve the captain, either from the shippers or the owners; and that so far from releasing him from the care of the thing *b* Art. 22. wrecked it imposes further obligations upon him. $\frac{\text{tit. du}}{\text{fret.}}$ Thus, since the wreck does not terminate the prior contract against the owners, who profit by the freight of the things saved, it follows that they must answer for the errors and faults committed by their agent, in all his operations which relate to the salvage, which necessarily result from his situation as the master.

It follows, from these principles, that if the cap- *c* Emerig. tain requires money to effect the salvage of the des ass. ship, he may borrow it and pledge the freight of $\frac{\text{ch. 21.}}{\text{sect. 21.}}$ the things saved. In case of capture, he may ransom the ship and draw upon his owners. (*c*)

SECTION XI.

Abandonment, by the owners, in order to avoid being bound by the acts of the Master.

The owners are bound *in solidum* by every thing §. 1. Are which the captain does in the course of the voyage the own-ers bound for the promotion of the voyage. *Omnia facta* in soli-*magistri debet præstare qui eum præposuit...Sed* $\frac{\text{dum for}}{\text{the acts}}$ *ejus rei nomine cujus præpositus fuerit...Si plures* of the *navem exerceant, cum quolibet eorum in solidum* master? *agi potest. (d)*
d L. 1. §. 5. 7. 25. ff. de exercit. act.

But this action *in solidum* does not exist against the owners, further than according to the interest

a Consu-
lato del
Mare, ch.
33. and
236. Clei-
rac, tit.
des Ri-
vieres,
art. 15.
pag. 595.
Statut. de
Ham-
burg, ci-
ted by
Kuricke,
on the
Hansia-
tic law, which they have in the body of the ship; hence,
if the ship perish or they abandon their interest
they are no longer liable for any thing. It is thus
that the maritime laws of the middle age have directed. *(a)* Such is the law which is observed in
the north. *(b)* And such is the regulation of our
Ordinance. *(c)* "The owners of the ship are responsible for the acts of the master, but they may
discharge themselves from it, by abandoning the
ship and freight."

tit. 6. art. 2. pag. 766. *b* Grotius lib. 2 cap. 11. §. 13. Stypmannus,
part. 4. cap. 15. n. 190. pag. 547. Kuricke, question 20. pag. 886. Loccenius lib. 3. cap. 7. n. 10. pag. 1033. Vinnius, ad Leg. 4. de exercit.
act. pag. 155. Scotanus ibid. pag. 321. *c* tit. des proprietaires art. 2.

§. 2. The
obligation
of the
owners
for the
acts of
the mas-
ter is
more of a
real than
a personal
nature.

It appears, from what has been said, that the
Obligations of the owners to guarantee the acts of
the master, is more of a real than a personal nature. During the course of the voyage, the captain may borrow money at bottomry for the necessities of the vessel, pledge the tackle or dispose
of a part of his cargo. *(d)* This is all——His legal power does not extend beyond the limits of the
ship of which he is master or *manager*. He cannot bind the property of his owners other than the
ship, cargo and freights, unless he has been thereto
authorized, in a special manner.

d Art. 19.
tit. du Ca-
pitaine.

ch. 33.

The *Consolato del Mare*, *(e)* after having said
that the interest of the owners is pledged for the
payment of debts contracted by the captain in the
course of the voyage, adds, that neither the person
nor the other property of the owners are bound,
unless they had given a sufficient power for that
purpose. *Ma li detti compagni, ne altri lor boni,
non sono obligati, se il detto patrono non ha avuto
procura, o altro poder sufficienti de obligarli.* In
chapter 236, it is said that if the ship perish, it is
sufficient that this loss be borne by the owners;
che il compagno assay perde.

The Ordinance, (*a*) speaks of a captain, simply as the conductor of the ship and to whom the transportation of the cargo has been entrusted. The owners, by abandoning the ship and cargo are discharged from contracts made by the captain, because his orders were limited to the mere navigation and did not extend further. It is otherwise of a captain who is likewise appointed to the money concerns of the cargo. The owners are bound by his acts, not only to the amount of the value of the ship and freight, but even to the value of the merchandize entrusted to his care and the returns which it way produce.

§. 3. Of a Captain who is al, so Super-cargo.

a Art. 2. tit. des proprie-taires.

We find ourselves then, as to certain respects, within the provisions af the *actio institoria.** *

But, 1. by this action, the constituent is bound to third persons by the acts of his agent, (*b*) provided they were necessary to the transportation of the goods delivered to him. (*c*) The constituent is bound even by the faults of the agent which may be committed in the exercise of his trust. *(d)*

b L. 1. f. de inst. act.

c L. 5. §. 11. ff. eod.
L. 5. §. 8.
ff. de ex-ercit. act.
L. 31. ff.

10. C. de procur. *d* Cujas. on the Law 58. ff. de procurratoribus lib. 71. Pauli ad edictum. Pothier, des obligations, n. 453.

negot. gest. L.

2. By the same action, the person advancing money acquires, in right of what he has advanced, a lien upon the thing purchased or preserved in consequence of his assistance. *(e)*

e L. 80. ff. de pro-curatori-bus. Ca-saregis,

ses, tom. 1. pag. 159. 162. Valin, Cout. de la Rochelle, tom. 3. pag. 368. Pothier, Traité du mandat, n. 59. 86. Bezieux, pag. 138.

disc. 22. n. 12.
Despeis.

It follows from these principles, that if the owners refuse to comply with the engagement contracted by a captain-supercargo, they ought to abandon

---

* The *actio instoria* of the Romans was that which arose from the acts of factors engaged in the land trade. D. lib. xiv. Tit. 1. Law vii. §. 2.

the ship and cargo, as well the outward as inward, or at least to render an account thereof; (for a formal abandonment not having been prescribed in this case, they are not held rigorously to it;) It suffices that they have not profited by the engage-

a L. L. 10. and 17. ff. de inst. act. ments of their Captain and that their fortune at land will not be encreased thereby. This is relative to the provisions of the Roman law. *(a)* *Nota.* When I speak of a case where the owners abandon

b Vid. in-frà §. 5. the ship and freight, I consider the captain merely as the *master* and not as an agent for the sale of the goods. This latter quality modifies the provisions of the Ordinance. *(b)*

§. 4. If the own-ers aban-don the vessel and freight? If the owners abandon the ship and freight, do the engagements which the captain has contracted in the course of the voyage, in his own name, still exist against him, in favour of third persons? Art. 2. tit. *des proprietaires* seems to decide this question in the affirmative: but it must be understood with the exceptions which I shall make in the next section of this chapter. Kuricke, *(c)* speaks of a case

c Tit. 6. art. 2. pag. 766. where a captain, in the course of a voyage, had borrowed money at bottomry, beyond the value of the ship and freight and he decides, according to the *Statut de Hamburg*, that the captain shall answer such engagements in his own proper person, as far as they exceed the value of the ship and freight. *Sed, quid si nauclerus in locis exteris tantùm pecuniæ trajectitiæ seu nauticæ in carinam recipiat, ut illi excsolvendæ nec navis, nec naulum, nec vectura, nec armamenta navalia sufficiant? Eo in casu, secundùm statutum Hamburg, exercitores non sunt obligati pecuniam hanc reddere; sed qui pecuniam suam in carinam crediderunt, nauclerum, ejusque bona tantummodò obligata habebunt.* This

d infrà Sect. 12. is sound doctrine, if the captain has been guilty of fraud or has bound himself in his individual name.

If the ship perish during the voyage the contract of maritime loan becomes extinct.* The shippers, whose goods have been sold for the necessities of the vessel, can claim nothing; because if they had remained on board they would have been *a* tit. du involved in the same disaster. This is the spirit of capitaine. the 19th art. (a) and for this reason we should re- *b* art. 68. ject the provisions of the *Ordinance of Wisbuy*, (b) as I observed in the preceeding section.

I observed before that the title of the Digest, §. 5. May *de exercit. act.* does not say a single word on the the captain bor- subject of *pecunia trajectitia;* and that the Edict row mo- of the Prætor authorized masters to have recourse ney to be repaid at to simple loans, in the course of the voyage, to a fixed supply the necessities of the ship: *si fuerit mutu-* day, or draw bills *atus, dandam actionem. (c)* of ex- c L. 1. §. 7, and 8. ff. eod. (Loccenius lib. 3. cap. 7. n. 6. Vinnius change. pag 94. and 183. Targa, pag. 29.)

The Ordinance of Antwerp, (d) did not permit *d* art. 19. the Captain to borrow money at bottomry but when he could not obtain it by drawing bills.

By the *New ordinance of the Hanse Towns, (e)* *e* tit. 6. if the Captain want money during the voyage, and art. 2. cannot draw upon his owners, *si nullum cambium ad exercitores transmittendum obtinere queat*, and it would not be advantageous to sell a part of his cargo, he may borrow money at bottomry. *Tunc, in*

* Property found derelict at sea, will be restored after any length of time on payment of salvage, unless there be proof of an intention to abandon wholly. Bee's Adm. Rep. 82. In such cases, generally,¹ one half should be allowed as salvage, ib. 195. In cases of salvage monition issues to the owner to show cause: it is not a proceeding *in rem*. 3 Rob. 177. *Am. Edit.* The courts look not merely to the exact *quantum* of service performed in the case itself, but to the general interest of commerce. *ib.* 287. A vessel with *slaves* on board but no white person considered as derelict, in *South Carolina*. Bee's Adm. Rep. 82.

O

hoc casu necessitatis, habeat potestatem tantùm pe-
cuniæ sub fœnore nautico accipiendi, quantùm opus
habet.

a pag.
765.

Kuricke, on this article, *(a)* observes, that in a strange country the captain may borrow money at bottomry, 1st. if he has need of it: 2nd. if he cannot draw upon his owners: *si isthic loci, cambio sub fide exercitorum, pecuniam ab exercitoribus solven-dam comparare non queat;* 3rd. if the sale of his merchandize would be more prejudicial than paying maritime interest. Stypmannus, *(b)* holds the same language, and says that in the last case the captain should draw upon his owners, *pecuniam collybo pa-rare, quam exercitores solvant,* rather than borrow money at a considerable interest.

b part 4.
cap. 5. n.
107. pag.
417.

But our ordinance has restricted the power of the captain, during the voyage, to borrowing money at bottomry, pledging his tackle or disposing of the goods in his charge for the necessities of the ves-sel. If he draw upon his owners, this engage-ment, although it be expressly in his name as cap-tain, becomes personal, because he has exceeded his legal authority. He ought not to contract any obligation which is not inherent in the vessel itself, and which does not depend on the success of the voyage. It is only whilst he keeps within proper limits that the authority of a master is delegated to him; (unless his articles with the owners, or the common law in certain cases, should give him a more extensive authority.)

The following are remarkable decisions on this subject.

1. Captain *Pierre—Joseph Babin* commanding the ship called *the Raphael,* being at Cape François was in want of money for provisions, custom-house fees, and for the replacement of his crew. He drew

upon *Francis Raphael* two bills of Exchange for
1000 and 750 liv. *value received in shipbread, flour
and* in money for insuring the vessel on her return
home. He set sail. He met an English privateer,
with which he engaged. His ship took fire and he
was blown up.

The two bills were protested for non acceptance
and non payment. *M. Pelisseur,* the holder, sued
Raphael, in our Admiralty court and filed his petition against the guardian of the children of captain *Babin,* as parties to the cause and in order to
obtain a personal condemnation. *Pelisseur* and the
guardian pleaded that the money had been borrowed for the urgent necessities of the vessel; that the
captain was not able to borrow at bottomry: that
he could not sell the rigging which was necessary
to him; that he could not dispose of the merchandize, but upon very disadvantageous conditions;
that *Raphael* would derive a great advantage from
the insurance upon the return cargo, that if he refused to pay the bills he ought at least to abandon
his claim upon the underwriters; that this injustice
would be the more odious as it would be ruinous
to two children whose father had sacrificed himself
in the discharge of his duty, &c. &c.

Raphael answered, that if captains were authorized to draw upon their owners, their fortunes
would never be certain. The Ordinance has cir-
cumscribed the power of the captain, during the
voyage, within the limits of the vessel. The captain can hypothecate no more than the vessel, the
freight and those things which are under his direction, and not the policies, to which he is a stranger and which belong to the general estate of the
owners. It is essential to commerce that a merchant should be allowed to place limits on his risks,
and that when he despatches a vessel, he should be

allowed by a wise precaution, to moderate the hazards, to which he is exposed: instead of which, by admitting the contrary doctrine, owners might be overwhelmed at once by accidents and ruinous contracts. He added that nothing remained at Cape François of the outward cargo.

An Arrêt was rendered 20th June 1760, by the Parliament of Aix, on the report of M. de Montvallon, which, correcting the sentence of our Admiralty, condemned the heirs of Babin to pay the amount of the bills of exchange.

2. In 1759 *Dominique Pauquet* fitted out the barque, called *St. Jean Baptiste*, commanded by *André Gabriel Jauffret*, for a voyage to Grenada and back to Marseilles. The captain was appointed supercargo. The vessel arrived in safety at Grenada. Part of the cargo was converted into bills of exchange upon Copenhagen, drawn to the order of Pauquet, who received the amount. The remainder of the proceeds was invested in produce and shipped on board the barque. The captain, being in want of money to enable him to clear out the vessel, borrowed on the spot, for that purpose 12000 *liv.* and accordingly drew bills upon his owners in these terms: "You will please to pay the sum of——value received, on account, of——for the return voyage of the barque, payment of duties and sailors wages, without which I could not have departed from the port." The bills were presented to *Pauquet* who said he would accept them, payable one month after the safe arrival of the *Jean Baptiste*, at Marseilles.

On her return voyage, the vessel was taken by the English. The holder of the bills, *Jean Baptiste Rey* filed a petition against *Pauquet*, the owner of the barque, and captain *Jauffret*. The cap-

tain also filed a petition against *Pauquet* claiming
a guaranty against *Rey*.* *Pauquet* pleaded *that*
the captain had embezzled or secreted various funds
which would have been amply sufficient to supply
the necessities of the ship at Grenada. In opposition to the demand of *Rey* he contended that in
no case had a captain a right to draw upon his owners. On the 15th January 1760 a sentence was
rendered by our Admiralty, by which *Pauquet* was
condemned to pay the money to the holder of the
Bill. The Arrêt of the court of Appeals which
was given on the report of *M. de Boutassy*, reversing this sentence, was to the following effect:

The court reversed the judgment of the Admiralty Tribunal, and proceeding to a new judgment,
nonsuited both the holder of the Bill and the captain, as against the owner of the Barque, and condemned the captain to pay the amount of the two
Bills in the first instance; but directed his accounts
with his owner to be investigated by another Tribunal, in order that it might appear whether he was
entitled to claim from him the reimbursement of
the amount of the Bills.

The case was deliberated in Parliament 18th
May 1761. *M. Pazery* was of counsel for *Pau-*
quet and I was opposed to him. These two arrêts
compelled our tribunal to correct its former principle, which had been eulogized by M. Valin. (*a*)
taine, pag. 417. and art. 2. des Proprietaires, pag. 536,

a Art. 5
tit. des
Prescrip-
tions,
pag. 297.
art. 19.
tit. du
Capi.

3. In 1760 the ship *St. Joseph* capt Michel Talon
was at Grenada. The captain died. Captain *Don-*

---

* This proceeding is analogous to the *voucher to warranty*
at Common Law—The captain who had made himself liable
to the holder of the Bill, merely for the benefit of his owner,
claimed his guaranty, or in other words *vouched him to war-*
ranty against the said Bill holder.

de, who happened to be on the Island, took the command and drew upon *M. Jean Pierre Talon,* the owner, a bill for 4000 liv. tournois, to *provide for the equipment of the St. Joseph.* The ship left Grenada and was driven into the Canary isles, where she was declared unseaworthy. The wreck and the freight were absorbed by the wages and other expenses.

M. Talon received the amount insured from the underwriters, and suffered the Bill drawn at Grenada, to be protested.

In 1764, captain *Donde* having returned to Grenada, which then belonged to the English, was sued on the Bill and was released from the proceeds of the court by the English Judge, who thought the Bill should be paid by the owner.

Eight years afterwards, the holder of the Bill proceeded, in our Admiralty, against *M. Talon,* who pleaded that he had abandoned the ship and freight; Sentence was given in his favour on the 19th November 1772. I appeared for *M. Talon.*

It follows, from these determinations that, 1st. As a general rule, the captain, during the voyage, has no authority to draw upon his owners, and that in case of a protest he is obliged to pay the bill himself, because he has exceeded the power which is vested in him by the ordinance. 2nd. That if he has incurred necessary expense, either for the ship or the cargo, he has a lien upon the one or the other, from which he may reimburse himself: 3rd. that if, notwithstanding a capture or wreck, the owners have received a part of the freight or other returns, they are obliged to honour the Bills of the captain, as far as they have funds of this kind.

From this it appears that it is very wrong in masters to draw upon their owners, without a special authority to that effect. Nevertheless nothing is more common and the masters become the victims of their own imprudence.

4. In 1779 the ship Nymph, captain Mouries arrived at Boston. The captain remained there in order to dispose of his cargo and he gave the command of his ship, which he loaded with planks, staves and drugs, to *Thomas Louis Roux*, his mate. When he arrived at Martinique, captain *Roux*, disposed of his cargo for sugar and coffee. He filled up the hold with merchandize on freight. He sailed under the convoy of M. le Comte d'Estaing and reached Cape François where he was obliged to remain one month. It became necessary to procure provisions. The captain called together his principal officers and by a *verbal process* of the 10th August 1779, it was agreed that *in order to obtain provisions, they should borrow money and draw upon M. Lazare Peyrier, the owner*. The next morning, the captain presented a petition to the Judge at the Cape, representing his situation and praying to be authorized to draw upon his owners for 3000 liv. money of the Islands, inasmuch as it was impossible to dispose of his goods, as they lay quite at the bottom of the vessel having been first shipped——and he having completed his cargo with merchandize on freight."

A decree was passed, with the advice of the Kings attorney " authorizing captain Roux to borrow the sum of 3000 liv. money of the colony for the victualling of the ship; and that he might effect this he was permitted to draw upon his owners, on the best terms that he could sell his bills."

If this Judge had been acquainted with our re-cent decisions he would have directed the captain to borrow at bottomry or to sell a part of his car-go and not expose himself to the danger of a pro-test, which would fall upon him, if any accident happened.

In consequence of the decree of the Judge, Cap-tain *Roux* drew upon *M. Lazere Peyrier* a bill for 2000 *liv. tournois*, payable to the order of Jour-dan, brothers and Jubelin, value received in 3000 liv. money of the colony, for the purpose of pro-viding victuals for the *Nymph*.

Upon leaving the cape, the vessel was captured by the English. The Bill of Exchange was pro-tested for non-acceptance and non-payment.

Louis Jubelin, the holder of the Bill, came to consult me. I told him that according to our pre-sent decisions, he had no right of personal action against the owner, but he had an action *in rem* against what remained of the cargo at Boston or that which was sent to France.

On the 20th December 1780, a sentence was rendered by our Admiralty which "rejected, at once the petition of *Louis Jubellin* against *Lazare Peyrier;* which condemned captain *Thomas Louis Roux* to pay to *Jubellin* 2000 *liv. tournois* the va-lue of the said Bill of Exchange; and, having re-gard to the incidental petition of *captain Roux*, gave him a lien on that part of the cargo which had been left at Boston and Martinique, or the pro-duce thereof, to the full amount of the principal, interest and damages. And for this purpose the said *Lazare Peyrier* was enjoined to render him an account of the state and value of these goods or the returns which he might have received: to the concurrence of the amount of the said Bill.

It is very desirable that this question should be settled by an ordinance, that might serve as a guide to captains and also to the colonial Tribunals, which are ignorant of our decisions and are led astray by the opinion of M. Valin. (*a*)

a Vid. in-
frà ch. 12.
Sect. 8.
§. 2

The Ordinance says, the owners shall be released from their responsibility for the acts of the master, *by abandoning the vessel and freight.*
the owners, to avoid being bound by the acts of the captain.

§. 6. Form
of the a-
bandon-
ment
made by

But it does not direct any form of abandonment. It may, therefore be made in any manner. It does not prescribe any time; the person therefore may make it at any stage of the cause. If the owners cannot otherwise avoid their liability to the acts of the master, and are sued on that account they ought to be condemned to guaranty him and pay the costs, until they have abandoned the ship and freight: it is just at the same time that they should be permitted to make this abandonment, by the judgment itself which pronounces the decision prayed against them.

So it was decided, 4th April 1770, in the case of captain P—— master of the *Prince de Lamballe*, who was accused of theft and barratry. "The judgment pronounced against the Captain was declared to be common and executory *in solidum* for principal, interest and costs against those interested in the vessel, who had not abandoned, *unless*, said the sentence, they shall *elect to abandon*, in which case they shall so declare it within two months after notice of this decree, and in this case they shall be released from the execution pronounced against them, in common with the others and shall pay only those costs which they themselves have incurred. In default of making this declaration within the aforesaid time, and that term being passed, they

P

shall forfeit their right of election, without any further judgment, from that time forward. And as
the other persons concerned in the vessel have
agreed to abandon their interest, we have discharg-
ged them from the process of the court issued at
the instance of the owners of the Spanish Dollars,
but condemn them, nevertheless, to pay the costs
which they have occasioned, up to the day of the
abandonment."

§, 7. Mo-
ney paid
for ran-
som, an
excepti-
on.
Nothing that I have said in this section applies
to the case of money borrowed to procure the release of a *hostage* for the ransom of a vessel. In
favour of liberty such a person is protected against
the rigour of general rules. *(a)*

a Vid. E-
merig.
Traité des assurances, ch. 12. Sect. 21. §. 7. and Sect. 41. §. 9.

SECTION XII.

*Is the Captain bound, personally, for contracts
made by him in that capacity?*

§. 1. Is he
who con-
tracts in
the quali-
ty of an
agent
personal-
ly bound?
In general the delegate who promises, who stipu-
lates, who acts in the capacity of an agent, does
not bind himself in his own proper name. He is
simply the representative of another person. He is
bound only to exhibit his authority. *(b)* The Guardian who acts *tutorio nomine*, does not contract any
personal obligation. *(c)*

b Emerig
des Ass.
ch. 5.
sect. 3.
c L. 43. §. 1. ff. de Adm. tut. L. 15. C. eod. L. 12. ff. de his qui ut
indign. L. 30, §. 1. ff. de inoff. test. L. 5. §. 1. ff. quandò ex facto.

d L. 4. ff.
de soluti-
onib. Ca-
saregis,
disc. 78.
n. 8. and
seq. disc.
199. n. 31.
D'Argen-
treé, art.
But the agent who contracts in his own name,
binds himself, without any destinction with respect
to third persons with whom he contracts, because
they are ignorant of his quality and he is rather
believed to act for himself than for another. *Potiùs meo nomine quàm pro alio. (d)*
96. 2. n. 3. Ansaldus, disc. 30. n. 32. Despeisses, tom. 1. pag. 51. n.
25. Maortica, de tacitis, lib. 7. tit. 18.

There is a case mentioned in *L.* 20. *ff. de inst.* Where an agent mentions his quality or the person dealing with him is not ignorant of it.
act. which I shall mention. As the agent of *Oc-*
tavius Felix, rem agens Octavii Felicis, I have received from you a thousand crowns, which I am
to return *quos numerare debebo,* within a specified
time. I am not bound in my own proper name,
because I have signed the obligation in the capacity of an agent, *institoris officio.*

He who acts in a contract as an agent is only a L. 15.
bound as such. *Frustrà vereris, ne ex eâ inter-* C. de admin. tut.
cessione quâ signasti ut curator, conveniri possis.(a) L. 43 §.
In a word, the agent who designates his quality in 1. ff. eod.
the contract, whatever it may be, whether that of b Dumoulin, cout.
a Guardian, Proctor, Father, Husband, Syndic,* de Paris,
Factor or Tenant, is not personally bound. (*b*) It is gl. 1. n. 31 pag.
sufficient if his quality be designated in the act, (*c*) 61. D'Ar-
or that it has been designated in a preceeding act, gentré art. 96.
of which the second is a consequence. (*d*) The not. 2. n.
quality of an agent may even be implied against 4. Des-peisses,
third persons, if the act could not otherwise have tom. 1.
been done. *In dubio videtur celebrari actus in il-* pag. 158. n. 3. Mor-
lâ qualitate, in quâ subsistere potest. (*e*) nac, ad
eo. Mey**n**ard liv. 4. ch. 15. c D'Argentré, d. loco. d Bezieux, pag. 276. Leg .7. C.
e Dumoulin, dicto loco. § 1. gl. 1. n. 31. and 32. pag. 61. quod cum

The contract of an agent who binds himself in Whether he may be personally bound notwith-standing the de-
his own name, is valid against him, although he de-
signates his quality. *Si subscripsisti quasi fide-*
jussor, conveniri potes. (*f*)
signation of his quality. *f* L. 15. C. de admin. tut.

Si dixeris: fiet tibi satis aut à me, aut ab alio, g Nov. 115. cap. 6. §. 4.
integrum cogeris persolvere. (g)

---

* Those who have permission to form a company or corpo-
ration, have also their rights, their privileges, their goods,
their affairs ; and all the members not having leisure to attend
at the same time the business of the community, they may
appoint persons to take care of it, who are called *Syndicks* or
by some other names. L. 1. §. 1. ff. quod cui un. dom. lib. 2.
Tit. 3. Sect. I.

a Albert, pag. 314. Bautaric, inst. pag. 482. Despeisses, tom. 1. pag. 51. n. 25. Faber, def. 6. n. 2. C. de evict. Cujas, ad L. 31. ff. de neg. gest. lib. 2. resp. Papiniani.

The *L. 67. ff. Procurat.* decides that the agent who pledges his faith to a purchaser, cannot, in case of eviction from the thing sold, be released from the contract which he has made. *Procurator, qui pro evictione prædiorum quæ vendidit, fidem suam adstrinxit: obligationis onere, prætoris auxilio, non levabitur. Nam Procurator, qui pro domino vinculum obligationis suscepit, onus ejus frustrà recusat.* The same provision is to be found in *L. 27 C. de evict.* and it is so held by all our authours. *(a)*

b L. 12. C. de fidejus. §. 1. inst. de verb. oblig.

There is no particular form for entering into security. The parties may couch their contract in what terms they please, provided the intention is not expressed in an equivocal manner. *(b)* He who binds his own goods for another necessarily becomes his security; for hypothecation "does not exist alone. It supposes a principal obligation, to which it is only accessory* and for the security of which it is intervened. *Pignus est contractus accessorius, qui principalem obligationem suponit, cujus vinculum est, et confirmatio."(c)* The argument which derives hypothecation from surety is valid.

c Ferriere, inst. quib. modis re contrah. tom. 4. pag. 350.

Valet argumentum à causâ pignoris, ad causam fidejussoriæ obligationis. Merlinus, de pign. pag. 504. lib. 4. tit. 5. quest. 126.

§. 2. Usage of merchants.

d ch. 5. Sect. 3. 4. and 5.

In my treatise on Insurance *(d)* I have observed that, by the custom of merchants, every merchant who effects an insurance, or who subscribes a policy, or freights a ship, is personally bound to fulfil his contract, although in the instrument it be expressly said to be done *for account* of another.

Is the law the same in the case of a captain who borrows money by maritime loan, whether it be be-

---

* *L. 50. ff. de fidejus. hi qui accessionis.*

fore his departure, for account of those owners who refuse to contribute, or during the voyage to supply the necessities of the ship, if on his return the owners abandon the ship and freight and the whole is not sufficient to discharge the debts which he has *bonâ fidê* contracted and for a lawful cause?

I believe we ought to make a distinction here. 1. If, in the contract the master has bound *his own person and property*, (of which I have seen a thousand instances,) he is personally bound, although the quality in which he acts be expressly mentioned : because he became the guarantee of the contract and the lenders acted on his credit. It suffices, then, that the ship shall safely arrive, in order to compel him to discharge the principal and maritime interest which he has promised, in his own name, to pay.

2. But if he entered into the contract in the capacity of a captain, exclusively, the lenders, notwithstanding the safe return of the vessel, are restricted to their action against the ship and freight without the right of suing either the owners who have abandoned, or the captain, who having contracted in a qualified manner, ought not to be responsible for the ill success of the voyage. The Ordinance does not compel the captain to pay money borrowed at bottomry, but when he effected [a] the loan in the place where the owners reside, without their assent, or in cases where the borrowing was without necessity. (*a*)

 a Art. 17. and 20. tit. du Capitaine.

3. If the Captain draw a bill of Exchange, he must pay it, because he exceeds his legal authority, as we have before seen. (*b*)

b Sect. 11.

4. Instead of borrowing at bottomry, if the captain, for a legal cause, dispose of a portion of his

cargo, and, on the return of the vessel, the vessel and freight (increased by the latter engagement and the seaman's wages) be insufficient to pay for the goods sold, this loss should be borne *pro ratâ* by the rest of the cargo, which, at the time of the forced sale, was on board and afterwards reached the port of destination: to which loss the value of the goods sold would have been equally subject to contribution.

a Vid. Suprà Sect. 9. He who lends money at bottomry to a Captain may take such precautions as he thinks proper; but he whose goods are sold during a voyage for the necessities of the ship, has no power to prevent it or to obtain any particular remedy against the captain. It then becomes just, that when the vessel and freight, being abandoned by the owner, are not sufficient he should be indemnified by all the owners, whose situation was similar.*(a)*

SECTION XIII.

Stipulated penalty against a Captain who violates his contract.

§. 1. The conventional penalty is of rigour. Conventional penalties are of rigour. Those who have agreed to them, ought to be condemned, if they have violated their contract. *(b)*

b §. 7. inst. de verb. oblig. L. 11. ff. de stipul. prætor. Pothier, des obligations. n. 345.

---

* Though the master of a vessel be also lessee of it, by agreement with the owners, for a term of years, under covenants on their parts that he shall have the sole management of the ship and employ her for his own sole benefit &c. And on his part, that he shall repair her at his own sole cost and charge &c. The owners are still liable for necessaries furnished for the ship by order of the master, though without their knowledge or without their being known to the person who supplied

1. On the 9th October 1743. *M. Raphel,* shipped for Martinique, certain merchandize, on board the *St. Mathew,* at a stipulated freight, "on condition, that if the vessel should not sail during the month of November following *the said merchandize should go free of freight.*" The vessel did not sail within the time mentioned, although the wind was favourable and other vessels in port had put to sea.

M. Raphel filed his petition in our Admiralty against the captain and demanded that the bills of lading should be signed *free of freight.* The captain and *M. Mathew Lée,* his owner, in order to gain time, pleaded that the court could not hold jurisdiction of the cause. In this they were overruled by a sentence rendered 18th January 1744, and this sentence was confirmed by an arrêt of the 14th May following.

The ship, whose departure had been retarded because the cargo was not ready, at length set sail and arrived at Martinique. The correspondent of *M. Raphel* required that the merchandize addressed to him, should be delivered free of freight. A sentence was given by the Judge of St. Pierre ordering that the goods should be delivered to the correspondent, upon his giving security to pay the freight if it should be so determined by our Admiralty.

The ship returned to Marseilles. The owner sued *Raphel* for the freight and filed his incidental petition for the annulling of the penalty contained in the charter party.

---

them. Cowp. 686. He who furnishes a ship with necessaries has a treble security ; 1. The person of the master. 2. The specific Ship. 3. The persons of the owners. ib. 639. which may be enforced in the Adm'ralty. Bee's Adm. dec. 78.

A sentence was rendered, on my report, in September 1752 discharging *Raphel* from the payment of the penalty demanded and ordering that the agreement entered into on the subject, before the Judge of the Admiralty of Martinique, should be cancelled.

2. Capt. *Pierre Lambert*, commander of the *Ste. Anne* freighted his vessel to *M. Jean Baptiste Gautier*, the Elder, to go to the Levant and bring a cargo of wheat to Marseilles. It was agreed that "the *captain* should not in his outward nor inward voyage take any merchandize from individuals on freight——nor even receive letters without the express consent in writing of the owners; *under penalty of forfeiting one half of the freight.*"

The *captain* put a small adventure on board on his own account, consisting of sugar, cocoa and liquors. He set sail and touched at Smyrna. He went next to the Gulf of Volo (in Thessaly) where he took a cargo of wheat, and returned to Marseilles.

M. Guatier contended for the forfeiture of one half of the freight, because, after his departure from Marseilles, the *captain* had put merchandize on board clandestinely, as well on his own account as for that of others. He added that at Smyrna the *captain* had taken goods on freight by which the vessel was retarded.

A Sentence was rendered on the 21 November 1752 on the report of M. le Lieutenant Gerin Ricaud, by which after hearing the pleadings and conclusions of the parties, it was ordered, that *Guatier* should adduce proof that the *captain* had, in the first instance, put merchandize on board for account of individuals, and that at Smyrna he had taken merchandize on freight.

This interlocutory judgment, to which the parties submitted, decided the principal question.

It was considered that the prohibitory clause did not relate to adventures of the *captain: quia in generali sermoni, persona loquentis non comprehenditur,* but that he was only obliged to pay freight for them. It is not allowed to extend the conventional penalty from one case to another, nor from one person to another. *Pœna conventionalis non egreditur personam expressam in conventionem,* says Mantica.(*a*)

a de tacitis, lib. 27. tit. 6. n. 36.

3. *Jerome Bourre,* owner of the ship, *L'Esperance,* captain *Benet,* freighted her to *Antoine Paul,* for a voyage to the French Islands; and by the charter-party it was agreed, that "the captain should not, in going or returning, take on board any merchandize, effects, nor specie from individuals, without the consent, in writing, of the freighter or of his correspondent, *under pain of forfeiting one half of the freight.*"

The ship arrived at St. Domingo, from which port she returned to Marseilles. *M. Paul,* knowing that the contract had been violated and desirous of obtaining proof of the fact, filed a petition in our admiralty, in which he accused the captain of having purloined a part of the cargo. He summoned the mate. All the papers of the ship were seized and deposited in the office. From these papers it was discovered that the captain, in conjunction with *Bourre,* his owner, had put goods on board for different people, but the captain was acquitted of the embezzlement, or any appearance of it.

He filed a petition for damages as on a malicious prosecution.

Q

Bourre, the owner, made himself party to the suit and filed a petition against *Paul* for the payment of 18511 livres, the amount of the freight. *Paul* exhibited the charter-party and prayed that the freight might be reduced to one half the amount claimed.

The cause was adjudged on my report. All the parties found themselves in fault. *Benet* and *Bourre* had violated the contract, which prohibited the lading of any thing without the consent, in writing, of *Paul*, under penalty of forfeiting one half of the freight. It was inexcusable in *Paul* to have commenced a criminal action against *Benet* and to have defamed him by a charge of embezzlement. It is true that the captain had violated the contract; but this violation, the proof of which *Paul* had obtained by the invocation of papers which he had prayed, was not, properly speaking, a crime, which deserved the *eclât* of an extraordinary manner of proceeding. The merits on each side being thus balanced, we were of opinion that captain *Benet* should be compensated for the damage done to his reputation, by the moiety of the freight which he deserved to forfeit by his breach of the charter-party.

Accordingly a sentence was given 20th March 1756, by which *Benet* was released from the process of the court and *Paul* was condemned to pay the whole freight and costs. By an Arrêt, in June 1758, on the report of M. de Boutassy, this sentence was affirmed. *Illi debet permitti pœnam petere, qui in illam non incidit.(a)*

a L. 154. §. 1. ff. de regul. juris.

Agreement that the freighter may demand the penalty

In a great many charter-parties I have seen a stipulation that in case of a violation of the agreement the captain should forfeit *half the freight, with damages and interest*. But the conventional penalty agreed upon, with damages and interest.

is in compensation of damages, of which it forms a kind of liquidation. *Ne quantitas stipulationis in incerto sit, ac necesse sit actori probare quid ejus intersit.(a)* The freighter who complains that the contract has not been executed, cannot demand, both an indemnification of the damage suffered and the conventional penalty. He ought to choose one or the other.*(b)*

a §. 7. inst. de verb. oblig.

b Pothier, des oblig. n. 342.

He should not be prevented from making this election, because the penalty has been stipulated for his benefit and he cannot be hindered from claiming a common right.

This conventional penalty cannot operate to the prejudice of the lien or privilege, to which the sailors and those who lend money at bottomry are entitled on the body of the ship. ed by the conventional penalty in question.

Whether the lien of seamen and lenders at bottomry be affect-

1. The seamen and lenders at bottomry have acted on the credit of the ship itself. They are ignorant of any agreements between the captain and the merchant.

2. The privilege granted to mariners and lenders at bottomry is of publick right: It is of consequence to the country, that seamen should not be defrauded of their wages and that the faith of maritime loans should not be impaired.

3. The ordinance,*(c)* places merchant shippers after sailors and lenders, on account of the necessities of the ship. From which it follows that lenders and seamen have a right to enforce their liens upon the ship and freight affected to them, before the freight be absolutely absorbed or diminished by a conventional penalty, to which they were utter strangers: without prejudice to the right of the freighter to pursue the goods and person of a captain who has committed any fault.

c 16th art. tit. de la saisie.

CHAPTER V.

What things may be pledged in a Maritime Loan.

In general, every thing which can be insured may be the subject of a contract of a maritime loan, provided that the maritime risque and the subject of it be real on both sides and that there be nothing repugnant to the nature of the contract.

In this chapter I shall treat of the manner in which the thing should be described upon which money is lent at maritime interest; what are the subjects on which it may be lent, and whether it be legal to lend any other thing than money in a contract of gross adventure.

SECTION I.

Maritime Loan on the Vessel or the Cargo.

§. 1.
Loan on the Cargo.

a ch. 19. pag. 337.

b ch. 18. art. 1.

The *Guidon de la Mer,*(*a*) says that "the masters, owners or shippers, may borrow on interest, as much money as will enable them to furnish their quota of the victualling and repairs, *in which the value of the ship must not be taken into consideration : because, if they fear to hazard her, they may cause insurance to be made on her value at a premium which will be less than the profit which they will derive from the money which they may borrow."* Hereis a proof, not that they were restricted from borrowing on the vessel, but that it was customary only to borrow for the victualling and repairs, as appears from the *Guidon.*(*b*)

But to remove every doubt upon this point, the ordinance(*a*) decides, that " money may be lent at bottomry on the body and keel of the vessel, her rigging and apparel, jointly or separately." *a* Art. 2. h. 2.

At present we make no distinction between the equipment and the body, excepting in Royal vessels, which private individuals sometimes are permitted to fit out for their own account; but as to merchant vessels, the distinction of which the ordinance speaks, is scarcely ever made. The *body* of the vessel comprehends all its parts. It is sufficient if the money be lent *on the body*, to give a lien upon the rigging, arms and victualling.*(b)* There is nothing to prevent you from expressing, in the contract the value of the vessel. The contract is as valid against lenders, as againt insurers.*(c)* *b* Valin, art.2. h.t. Traité des assurances, ch. 10. sect. 1. *c* Emerig des ass. ch. 9. sect 4.

The ordinance *(d)* says, that the money shall be lent *on the whole or part of the cargo.* According to the custom if the money be lent on the *cargo*, the contract will embrace all the interest which the borrower has, as well in the cargo, properly so called, as in the small adventures. But if a person borrow *on the cargo* and also on *the small adventures*, they will constitute two distinct liens. So it was decided by an Arrêt of the Parliament d'Aix,(*e*) on the report of M. Pazery de Thorame, in favour of Beaussier, the elder and Felix Gravier. They had made a loan *on a small adventure* shipped by Jean-Pierre C...in the brigantine *le Bienfaisant*, capt. Paul, The returns of this package were adjudged to them to the exclusion of those who had made loans on the cargo of the same ship. §. 2. Loan on the cargo. *d* Art. 2. h. t. *e* 21 July, 1779.

It is not necessary that the borrower should give notice that his adventure consists of articles subject to leakage, because the lender does not contribute to simple average.*(f)* It is equally unnecessary to *f* Infra ch. 7. sect. 1

give a specification in detail of the merchandize bought or to be bought; it is enough if the subject of the risque be on board.

The contract on maritime loan on the cargo affects, not only the goods on board, at the time of departure, but all which may be taken on board for account of the borrower, during the voyage. If the contract be for the outward and inward voyage, it covers the returns for account of the borrower, as will appear from an *arrêt* which I shall quote hereafter.*(a)*

a Infrà ch. 12. sect. 2. § 3,

But the lien does not attach upon merchandize which the borrower voluntarily, and without being compelled by necessity, ships in another vessel. To the risk of this merchandize the lender is a stranger, even though it be the returns of the first cargo.*(b)*

b Infrà ch. 8. sect. 4.

It is enough that the subject of the risk be on board at the time of the accident. If it be not, the borrower is not released from his personal obligation by the loss.*(c)*

c Infrà ch. 12, sect. 2. § 3.

Nota. If I borrow money at maritime risque, on *a part of the shipment,* for instance, a moiety, or half of my cargo or adventure, the lender would have a lien only upon this moiety, for which in case of wreck, the effects saved would be obliged to contribute.*(d)*

d Vid. Infrà ch. 11. sect. 2. §. 2.

The 2d. art. h. t. seems to be equivocal. " Money may be lent at bottomry on the body and keel, the rigging and apparel, arms and victuals, *jointly* or *separately*, and upon the whole or part of the cargo, for the entire voyage or for a limited term." It seems that the words *jointly* or *separately* should be placed at the end of the article ; because nothing prevents a person from borrowing *jointly* on the ship and cargo, if he has an interest in them. *Quan-*

§. 3. a loan on the vessel & goods.

do il Capitano, ò essercitori imbarcano robbe, e mer-
ci di proprio conto, puonno prender danari à cambio
maritimo sopra corpo e merci giontamente, perche
hanno la dispositione dell' una, et l'altra materia;
et chi la dà, hà hipoteca più amplia.(*a*)* The ac- a Targa
tion of the lender in such case is *in solidum*, against cap. 32.
the ship and cargo.(*b*) b Infrà ch. 12. sect. 2. §. 4.

In general the words, *per denari dati a cambio* §. 4.'
sopra la nave† apply only to the body of the ship. What if
Nevertheless they may, according to the circum- it be ex-
stances of the contract and the presumptive inten- upon a
tion of the parties, be equally applied to the cargo. certain
The captain of a vessel borrowed money at bottom- out going
ry at Venice, *sopra la detta Tartana*‡ for a voy- further.
age which he was about to undertake. The len-
der caused insurance to be made at Genoa, *super*
dicto cambrio maritimo.§ The vessel and cargo perished. The body of the vessel was inferior in value to the money lent. The assurer refused to pay
the entire loss. They said that the containing clause
would not embrace the contents: *appellatione con-*
tinentis propriè non comprehenditur contentum; that
according to the clause in their policy they had assured the money lent upon the cargo, whilst the contract of bottomry upon which that policy was affected, applied only to the body.

Casaregis,(*c*) says, that their refusal was unjust. c disc.
It is undoubtedly true that the *container* does not 127.
signify the *contents*: *in dubio sub continente non*
comprehenditur contentum. But 1. the sum bor-

---

* When the captain or owners ship goods and merchandize
for their own account, they may take up money at maritime
risque, on the vessel and goods jointly, because they have the
disposal of both, and the lender thereby has a more extensive
lien.

† For money lent at bottomry on the ship.

‡ On the said vessel.

§ On the said maritime loan.

rowed was relative to the value of the ship ʼand the cargo, from which it may be presumed that the master intended to pledge both of them. 2. The law, *cùm tabernam,* (*a*) decides that he who hypothecates his magazine or store, is presumed to hypothecate what is contained in them. 3. A master who makes a voyage with his own vessel and goods considers the whole together as forming the indivisible object of his commercial adventure. 4. If his intention was merely to borrow upon the body, he would have said that he borrowed, on the *body, rigging, furniture and freight of his vessel.* 5. Finally, the bottomry contract was executed according to the custom of Venice; whence it follows that the policy effected at Genoa, ought to be construed in the same manner as that contract.

a 34. ff.
de pigno-
rib.

In another place (*b*) Cassaregis observes that according to the case, the word *ship,* ought to be understood as referring either to the containing or the contained : *expressio navis dupliciter potest interpretari, scilicet pro continente, aliquandò pro contento, ac etiam pro mercibus.** And he adds, that the judges ought to interpret the contract according to the intention of the parties.

b disc.
63. n. 11.

This question came before our admiralty under the following circumstances : By a contract of maritime loan, 2d July, 1743. *Ravel* acknowledged that he had received from *Refay,* the sum of 400 liv. " which he lends *on the return from a voyage,* that I am about to go, in quality of lieutenant on board the St. Joseph, *Captain Pierre Giraud*———

---

* This construction seems to be principally derived from the idiom of the Latin language, See Ingersoll's Roccus on Insur. p. 93. not. 16. In our language, and by our law a pledging or hypothecation of a ship could never be construed to extend to the cargo, if the word " ship" only was used.

which sum I take for the term of three months and so *pro rata* for a greater time, to the end of one year from the day of our departure from Marseilles, at a maritime interest of two and a half per cent. a month : declaring that in case of a war with England or Holland, I am to pay interest on the said sum at the rate which may be paid, in consequence of that event, in this place. In consideration of which the said *Refay* is to bear all the risques and perils of the sea."

The vessel was captured by the English. *Refay* claimed his money and pleaded that this was not a contract of bottomry, because the instrument did not express that the money had been loaned on the vessel or the cargo. *Ravel* replied, that the ordinance did not make it absolutely necessary that the contract should expressly specify, whether the money was lent on the ship or the cargo, or both, that the law applied it, of right, to the interest of the borrower——to whom in the present instance twelve shares of the ship belonged : that the lender should have explained these things better : that when any doubt arises on a contract, it must be so explained *ut valeret, et in favorem debitoris.*

A sentence was rendered on the 11th January, 1746, in favour of *Refay* and condemning *Ravel* to pay 400 liv. with interest from the time of the demand. This sentence was however reversed by an Arrêt, 24th January, 1748, on the report of M. Pazery de Thorame : and by a new judgment, the petition of *Refay* was dismissed with costs. M. Valin,*(a)* mentions this Arrêt, of which I very cheerfully mentioned the circumstances. The vessel and the cargo having both become the prey of the enemy, it was of little consequence whether the interest of the borrower was in the one or the other. It was evident that *Ravel* had borrow-

a Art. 2. h. t. pag. 5

R

a Emerig. des ass. ch. 10 sect. 1. §. 3. ed at maritime risque upon the effective interest which he had in the ship, and that, in case of her safe arrival, he would have had no idea of proposing to him any diminution of the rate of interest.(a)

SECTION II.

Contract of Bottomry upon freight, profits or wages.

§. 1. Upon the freight.

b Art. 4. h. t.

c dicto loco. To borrow money at maritime risque on freight to be earned by the ship is forbidden. (b) M. Valin observes, (c) that the lender would be at the mercy of the borrower who would make no exertions to obtain freight, when it could yield no advantage to him. He adds that it is lawful to borrow on freight *already earned*: that is to say, to borrow for the purpose of paying a stipulated freight which is to be paid at all events, whether it be for the transportation of merchandize or for a mere passage.

But may an owner borrow at maritime risque on freight already due to himself? For instance: I have a vessel ready to sail for the West Indies, worth 50,000 liv. I freight her to you for 50,000 liv. which you are to pay *at all events*. I borrow from another person 50,000 liv. at bottomry on the hull. The ship perishes, without having incurred any intermediate expense. May I demand from you the 50,000 *freight earned* and keep the sum borrowed at bottomry. Is the gain of 50,000 liv. which I make by this operation lawful? I think not; but that notwithstanding the loss of the ship, the sum borrowed should be returned, with legal interest. *Nota.* I take the most easy manner of calculating, and the most perspicuous to develop my ideas. It is of no consequence whether the sum borrowed be great or small : the principle is the same.*(a)* aEmerig. des ass.

ch. 8. sect. 8. ch. 17. sect. 9.

To borrow money on profits expected to result from an adventure is not permitted because the profit is uncertain and has no physical existence, nor is it lodged in the ship.*(b)* § On the profits. b Art. 4. h. t. Poth. n.

14. Emerig des. ass. ch. 8. sect. 9. [Sed vide p. 39. ante.]

The Guidon de la Mer *(c)* permitted the master " to take up as much money as the amount of the primage, and that money which was promised to him in the charter-party, in consideration of the advances which he may make to the crew. The advances to seamen is one of the expenses of equipment and outfit. It may therefore be the subject of insurance, and of a contract of maritime loan for the benefit of those who fit out and equip the vessel." §. 2. on the wages. c ch. 19. art. 7.

The ordinance of 1584, *(d)* says, that " no one shall lend at maritime risque to seamen, more *money* than is necessary to them for the voyage. This is forbidden as well in the case of the lender as the borrower, under pain of losing the money and forfeiting thirty livres, one half to the informer and the other to the Admiral. Nor shall such loan be made but in the presence and with the consent of the captain and principal owner, who shall record it, for future information, if it should become necessary.*(e)* d Art. 95 e Clerac, pag. 476.

But this ordinance does not say that the seamen may borrow at maritime risque upon their wages. It permits them to borrow only *such sum as may be necessary to them for the voyage :* by whic h it is only intended to allow them to borrow as much money as will enable them to purchase the quantity of merchandize, which, in those days, each one was allowed to ship, free of freight. *(f)* f Consulat. de la Mer, ch. 128, 129. Juge-mens d'Oleron, art. 16. Ibiq. Clerac, pag. 46. 73. Ordi-nance

de Wisbuy. art. 30. Ancienne Ordonnance Teutonique art. 55. Nou-velle Ordonnance Teutonique, tit. 13 art 6.

It was just to allow them to borrow what would enable them to enjoy a privilege that belonged to them. The law even permitted " the fishermen going to Newfoundland, to borrow a reasonable sum at maritime risque upon their shares of the voyage in order *that they might leave a support for their wives and children during their absence*." (*a*)   But that was a bad law.

a Clerac. on the Guidon de la Mer, ch. 19. art. 8. pag. 339.

At present, (*b*) " the sailors cannot put on board any merchandize on their own account under pretence of *privilege* or otherwise, without paying freight, unless there be a clause to that effect in their contract."

b Art. 2. tit. de l' engagement.

The seamen undoubtedly are at liberty to borrow on merchandize laden for their own account, because they are considered *pro hac vicé* as owners. Here they do not require permission from any person. But as mariners are restricted from insuring their wages, (*c*) so they may not borrow money at maritime risque on that fund. The reasons of this law, flow from the necessity of securing their attention to the safety of the ship, and they apply, with equal force to both contracts.

c Emerig. des ass. ch. 8. sect. 10.

Nevertheless the ordinance of 1681 (*d*) permitted sailors to borrow money *on their wages, to the amount of less than a moiety in the presence and with the consent of the master.* (*e*)

d Art. 4. h. t.

e Infra ch. 6.

But 1. how shall we ascertain this moiety as to sailors engaged by the month or for a proportion of the profits? 2. By custom, the seamen receive two months pay in advance before they embark, with which they purchase cloathes; and during the voyage, in case of necessity, they sometimes receive money on account of their wages which is paid to them with the approbation of the Commissary* of the port, or of the French Consul.

3. If they borrow at maritime risque upon their moiety of their wages, the whole wages would be soon absorbed by the principal and the enormous rate of maritime interest which they would be obliged to pay on their return.

For these reasons, this part of the Ordinance of 1681 is not in use. I never saw a contract of maritime loan on wages. Such a commerce would be ruinous, it would be the prey of innkeepers and people of that sort who engross the substance of the poor sailors. The wages are meant as a support to the family of the seaman; they are the pledges for bread furnished to his wife and children. By a *Regulation†* of the 1st. of November

---

* *Du Commissaire de la Marine ou des autres Officiers chargcs du detail des classes.* In France all who exercise the profession of seamen, are *classed*, that is to say registered as such in a book kept in every Sea Port by an officer who is styled *Commissary of the Navy*, and are liable to be called at any time from the Merchant's into the publick Service. When a Merchant Vessel is ready to sail, the conditions of the Mariners Agreement with the captain or owners are stated in an instrument called the *Role d'Equipage*, which is agreed upon by the parties in presence of that officer. It contains the names and the surnames, places of birth and residence, day of hiring, amount of monthly wages of each seamen, and every thing else which with us is inserted in what we call the *Seamen's Articles.* When the vessel returns, the Commissary from that document states the amount due to each mariner, which (unless he can show good cause to the contrary) the owner is obliged to pay before the vessel can be permitted to sail again. No money can be paid to a seamen on account of his wages, but in the presence of such a Commissary or of a French Consul, who endorses every such payment on the *Role d'Equipage.*

† *Reglement*—is a specie of Ordinance which has the force of Law—The Laws which in France before the Revolution emanated solely from the Royal authority, were called *Ordinances*, when they were general and comprehensive, and took

1745 "His Majesty forbids all private persons and inhabitants of maritime towns, who pretend to be creditors of seamen to commence any action or demand on account of their said debts, against the produce of the pay which the seamen have earned on board of merchant vessels, unless the said debts shall be due by the seaman or their families for house-rent, subsistence or cloathing, which have been furnished with the consent of the Commissary of Marine or his Deputies and unless they are noted by the said officer on the *role* in which Seamen are registered. In default of which the said creditors, shall not, under any pretext, attach the wages, but shall have only the common remedy against their goods and effects."

This Regulation and all the others which have been made on the subject, since the year 1681, are incompatible with the permission which was given, by the Marine Ordinance to seamen, to contract a maritime loan on the moiety of their wages. (Nota. The remarks which I made, *suprà ch.* 1. *Sect.* 4. *pag.* 397. *n.* 6, related to the ancient practice.)

§. 3. Penalties inflicted by the ordinance for the violation of the provisions here treated of. The 4th art h. t. prohibits the loan of money at maritime risque, upon freight to be earned by the ship or upon expected profits, under penalty of being obliged to pay *the whole sum borrowed, notwithstanding the loss or capture of the vessel.*

The 5th art. h. t. "forbids all persons from lending money at maritime risque to seamen upon their wages or the voyage, but in the presence and with the consent of the master, under penalty of

---

up an entire subject of Legislation—They were called *Reglemens or Regulations,* when their object was partial, or temporary, or of inferior moment, or explanatory of a former Law.

forfeiting the sum lent and of being fined 50 *liv.*"

The 6th art. adds, " the master shall be liable in his own name for money borrowed with his consent, if it exceed the moiety of the wages, notwithstanding the loss or capture of the vessel."

It is certain then 1. That in every case the contract would not be valid as a contract of maritime loan; and that the loss or safe arrival of the vessel would have no influence upon the fate of the parties. *(a)* 2. The forfeiture of the sum lent, was suffered by those who lent money to the seamen upon their wages without the consent of the master; but this penalty is not inflicted upon those who lent money on freight to be earned or profits to be made. They would be entitled to an action for the return of the principal. 3. They could not recover any maritime interest, because they would not have encountered the perils of the sea. The 3rd and 6th art. h. t. give them no more than the sum lent without any interest. *(b)* 4. They could not claim common legal Interest, but from the time of a legal demand* because the thing cannot be the subject of a contract of maritime loan.

a Pothier n. 14.

b Pothier n. 14.

SECTION III.

Contract of maritime loan upon a thing already at risk.

Money procures those things which we wish to send out or carry to sea, and without that neces-

---

* By the general law of France common debts, even though evidenced by writing, and though a day of payment be fixed, do not bear interest except from 'the day of action brought, unless it be otherwise expressly stipulated in the Contract.

sary article, a vessel could not leave her port. This is the reason why privileges, so extensive, are given to maritime loans. But when the vessel has put to sea, the publick interest is subserved and it is not necessary to grant particular privileges to an enterprize already executed.

a Emerig. Traité des ass. ch. 8. Sect. 6.

Our Ordinance, which admits Insurance *before or during the voyage (a)* does not contain the same provisions on the subject of maritime loans. So far from it, the lien given by the 7th art. h. t. is not allowed *on the hull,* but to those who have lent their money *for the necessities of the voyage;* and it is not allowed *on the cargo* but to those who have furnished *funds to purchase it.* According to the 10th art.* h. t. the money lent for a former voyage and left outstanding does not come into concurrence with money actually lent for the last voyage.——We might revert here to all the texts before cited. (*b*)

b Suprà ch. 4. Sect. 5.

c On the 16th art. tit. de la saisse, tom. 1. pag. 346.

But M. Valin, (*c*) says that it is of no consequence whether the loan be made before or after the sailing, because, he adds, the presumption is, either that it has been usefully employed for the thing at hazard or that it has been applied to the payment of debts contracted on the same account. But this presumption would go too far. It effects the interest of third persons and those privileges are not to be extended by construction.

---

* The tenth Article here referred to is in these words : " The monies left by way of renewal or Continuation" [that is to say the monies lent for a former voyage even tho' they should be included in a new contract of Maritime Loan] " shall not be paid concurrently with the monies actually furnished for the last voyage."

The reason of this law, say the commentators, is that it was the money last supplied which enabled the vessel to perform the last voyage and therefore preserved the pledge of the former lenders.

I am of opinion therefore that the third person would be at liberty to oppose the payment by pre ference or even *pari passu* of a lender, whose con- tract was posterior to the commencement of the risk.*

Such was the principal ground of an arrêt, of which I shall relate the circumstances. B. and L. equipped the ship *l'Amitié*, capt. V. They pur- chased the cargo on credit and borrowed the mo- ney necessary for the equipment by maritime loan. In order to raise funds, they made captain V. and B. the lieutenant, sign respondentia bonds to the amount of 27000 liv. without mentioning the names of the lenders, which were left in blank. After the departure of the vessel B. and L. negoti- ated these bonds and then became bankrupts. An arrêt was pronounced on the 23d June, 1769, which "declared these bills null, saving and reser- ving to the holders and indorsers the right of in- demnifying themselves against the bonds thus can- celled, in such manner and against whomsoever they might find solvent." (a)

After the departure of the vessel nothing pre- vents the borrower from contracting to pay the mo- ney borrowed out of the interest which he has at stake; but this indication of a particular fund does not give the creditor, any lien upon the fund thus pointed out. The money cannot truly be termed *trajectitia* but when it has been employed in the ac- tual purchase of the goods shipped or has enabled the borrower to purchase them. *Trajectitia ea pecu- nia est, quæ transmare vehitur. Sed videndum, an merces ex eâ pecuniâ comparitatæ in eâ causâ habe- antur; et interest, utrum etiam ipsæ periculo credi-*

a Infrà
ch. 6.
Sect. 3.

---

* *Marshall* thinks Emerigon's reasoning is plausible. but that of Valin is more satisfactory. vid. p. 645.

S

a L. 1. ff. *toris navigent : tunc enim trajectitia pecunia fit. (a)*
de nautic. But money borrowed subsequent to the sailing of
fœn. the vessel, did not contribute to the purchase of
goods already at hazard : *merces ex eâ pecuniâ
comparitatæ (non fuerunt.)* This money *non erit
trajectitia.*

b Infrà,   The presumption of which M. Valin speaks is
ch. 6.   contrary to the text of the law ; it would create an
sect. 3.   opening for great abuses. (We do not here treat of
and ch.   money lent at bottomry during the voyage, for in-
12. sect.   termediate necessities. (*b*)
4. and 5.

SECTION IV.

*Whether it be lawful to lend any other article than
money at maritime risque.*

§.1.What   There is no doubt that merchandize or
may be other effects, may be the subject of a maritime
lent at loan instead of money. The civilians require
maritime
risque. only that the effects lent should be designated
by weight, number or measure ; and that that
should be of such a nature, according to the custom of the place that they may be consumed, or be
intended for sale by the borrower, who becomes
c Styp- the owner on condition of paying the price and a
mannus, maritime interest in case of the safe return of the
part 4.
cap. 2. n. vessel. *(c)*
18.

d n. 8.h.t.   Pothier, *(d)* says, " in order to form a contract
of maritime loan, there should be a sum of money
borrowed by one from another, on conditions specified in the contract. It is not meant that nothing
but money may be the subject of this contract ; for
this contract includes that of *mutuum,** to which is

---

* The contract of *mutuum,* or loan of things to be restored
in kind, as it is termed in our legal language, is a covenant by

added an agreement, by which the lender takes upon himself the risks : he may require all those obligations which are contained in the contract of *mutuum*, that is, of all those *quæ pondere, numero et mensurâ constant, et quæ usu con-umuntur.(a)* But it is not usual to lend any thing except money, in a maritime loan." ^{a L. 2. §. 1. ff. de reb. cred.}

I have mentioned already, *(b)* an Arrêt concerning six dozen skins of Morocco Leather which were lent in this manner. They were estimated at 270 liv. This valuation would operate as a sale against the borrower, who, by this means, would be considered as having borrowed 270 liv. upon merchandize purchased by him. ^{b ch. 3 sect. 3. dec. 6.}

We are now prevented from modifying this contract by particular agreements or even from uniting others with it of a different kind. *In contractu mutui, citrà ullum labem usurariam, concurrere vel accumulari possunt alii contractus, seu paacta, dummodò justa et licita sunt. Et pro-ut similiter sequitur in cambio maritimo, &c.(c)* ^{§. 2. Unio on between the contract of maritime loan and those of a different species.}

c Casaregis, dis. 201. n. 3. (Suprà ch. 1. sect. 6.)

In the year 1756, the widow *Floret & Sons*, owners of the ship *la Marseill-ise*, *Capt. Eydin*, sent her on a voyage to St. Domingo With a cargo also belonging to them. Previous to her departure, the captain and his officers subscribed an instrument of writing to this effect. " We acknowledge to have received from *Floret & Sons*, owners of the ship *la Marseill-ise*, the sum of 11,000 liv, in a fifth part of the cargo of the said ship which they cede to us, amounting to 55,000 liv. by the invoice.

---

which one gives to another a certain quantity of the k nd of things that is given by number, weight and measure ; such as money, corn, wine, &c. on condition that the borrower shall restore, not the same individual thing he borrowed, but as much of the same kind, and of the like quality. Vid. inst. quib. mod re contr. obl. l. 2. §. 1, & 2. ff. de reb. cred.

And in case of our safe return we agree that they shall pay themselves out of the returns of the said cargo, as well the said sum of 11,000 liv. as the further sum of 9000 liv. which we are to pay as maritime interest. In consideration of which the said *Floret & Sons* take upon themselves the perils of the sea, and for the performance of this our contract of maritime loan, we bind ourselves *in solidum* each for the other."

The ship arrived at Jacquemel, whence she went to the cape. The outward cargo produced 178496 liv. Agreeably to the orders of his owners, the *captain* shipped the greater part of the returns in 15 French vessels. In his own vessel he shipped sugar and indigo to the amount of 49795 liv. He set sail and arrived at Marseilles. Of the 15 vessels, in which the remainder of the returns had been shipped, only two arrived in France. The others were captured by the English. The cargo of the Marseilloise produced . . . £. 77340

Of which, 1-5 for the captain and
officers . . . . £. 15468
They (the captain and sailors consented to allow for the *pro rata* on the 20,000 liv. capital and maritime interest due from them. £. 5579

And they demanded payment of
the difference. . . . £. 9889

They proposed the same mode of adjustment as to the other two ships which had arrived in port: and they said that the loss occasioned by captures ought to be borne equally between them as partners in proportion to their respective interests.

Floret & Sons contended that the *Marseilloise*, having returned safe, the capital and interest became due and that therefore they were entitled to retain the 15468 liv. already paid on account of the 20,000 due to them.

On an arbitration, an award was made by M. Bres and myself, March 11, 1760, which, " considering the demand of *Capt. Eydin* and his officers as legal, decided that the risk of the 11,000 liv. which were the consideration of interest transferred, as well as the maritime interest thereon was to be apportioned between the *Marseilloise* and the other fifteen vessels. The whole in proportion to the merchandize shipped on board of them for the joint account of *Floret & Sons* and those interested with them, according to a proportional account to be settled between them, having regard to the money lent, and the maritime interest, on the one side, and to the value of the return cargoes of all the ships, on the other." An arrêt, confirming the award with costs, was pronounced by the Parliament of Aix, in February 1762.

In this case, if the contract of maritime loan had been simple and unmixed, the capital of 11,000 liv. and the maritime interest would have been due to *Floret & Sons,* upon the arrival of the *Marseilloise,* although all the returns had not been laden on board of that ship. But here was a contract of maritime loan subordinate to a real contract of partnership between the owners and the officers, in consequence of which it ought to be regulated by the rules which are applicable to both species of contracts.

It follows, from this case, 1st. That every thing may be lent in a maritime loan as well as money. 2d. That this contract may be united with another, and that it is susceptible of any modifications which the parties may think proper to make. *(a)* (*a* Vid. Infrà, ch. 12. sect. 9. §. 4.)

Jean Joseph Marseille, Innkeeper, furnished for the use of the state room and kitchen of the king's ship, *Notre Dame de Santé*, Capt. Contrepont, divers utensils which were estimated at 1043 liv. A list and valuation thereof were made, at the foot of which *Pierre Pinel armateur** of the vessel, who signed an agreement in these words : " On the arrival of the vessel, I promise to return the above mentioned articles to M. Marseille, (and pay him 110 *per cent.* on 1043 liv ; the valuation thereof, two months after the ship shall be unladen, at which time the risk shall cease) he shall receive the said articles in the state in which they may then be, I obliging myself to pay for those only which may be lost, at the valuation and in consideration of the said interest of 110 *per cent.* payable in two months after the discharge of the ship, the said *Marseille* takes upon himself all the perils of the sea." Mess. Guis and Remuzat insured 800 liv. on the utensils by the order of *Marseille* and for his account. On the 15th April 1761 the ship departed from Toulon. Being pursued by the English she was obliged to run in to Oran, and afterwards into Carthagena, whence, after a long absence she returned to Toulon.

Marseille filed a petition against *Pinel*, praying the restitution of the utensils and plate, the use of

---

* *Armateur.* This French word is synonimous with the Latin word *Exercitor* so frequently met with in the books of the civil law, and means the person who fits out and equips a vessel, whether he be the obsolute or qualified owner, or even a mere agent. In English we sometimes use the word " *ships husband*" but it is generally to designate and distinguish from among several part owners of a ship, the one who has the immediate care and management of her. In the present case *Pinel* appears to have been a qualified or temporary owner, which may appear strange, as the vessel is denominated a king's ship, but it often happened in France before the late revolution, that the government let out ships of war to be employed for a time in the merchant's service, sometimes also they were sold, when thought no longer fit for warlike use, which may perhaps have been the case in the instance before us.

which had been lent at maritime risque and also the stipulated maritime interest. *Pinal* declared that the voyage had been broken up by *vis major* and abandoned. *Marseille* filed a petion against *Laval*, his assurer *en assistance de cause**——to the end that, if the abandonment, made by *Pinel*, should be admitted, *Laval* should be condemned to pay the amount insured. *Laval* replied that there was no ground for abandonment and claimed a return premium from *Marseille* and from Guis and Remuzat who had effected the insurance.†

On the 22nd December 1764 a sentence was rendered, which "considering the petition of *Jean Joseph Marseille* as legal, condemned *Pierre Pinel* to restore within 24 hours to *Marseille* all the utensils and plate, which *Marseille* had lent him at maritime risque and which had been enumerated at the commencement of the suit. Otherwise and in default of returning the aforesaid articles, henceforward and without another judgment being passed, he should stand condemned to pay 1043 liv. 3. s. the price of the aforesaid articles, or the price

---

* These words taken according to their *literal signification*, imply a proceeding similar or anologous to *aid prayer* at common Law, but the preceeding which they designate might be more aptly compared to that of *Voucher to Warranty*, or perhaps might be in some measure assimilated to what is called a *Bill of interpleader* in Equity. In this case it was making the Insurer a party to the cause between the lender and the borrower at maritime risque, on the ground that the lender, who promoted the suit, was entitled to satisfaction from the one or the other, and that the court might decide who was to make it. It was bringing before the Judges at one view all the contending parties and their respective claims on the same subject that they might be enabled to do full and final justice between all concerned.

† That is to say from them or some one of them, or that they might be condemned to pay the return premium jointly and severally.

of such of them as should not have been returned, at the rate agreed upon in the inventory and the said *Pinel* was also condemned to pay the sum of 1247 liv. 6. s. 6. d. the amount of maritime interest and also common legal interest since the delay, with costs, with execution against his body, after the expiration of eight days. And with regard to the petition of *Laval*, of the 26 July and 1st October 1762, *Marseille* was condemned to pay two thirds of the premium of the Insurance made on the return voyage, with interest and costs, and execution against his body after the expiration of eight days; and further declared this part of the sentence common and executory against Guis and Remuzal, for the principal and interest, with execution against their bodies after the expiration of eight days. And with regard to the petition of Marseille 9th April 1762 in aid of the cause, the said *Laval* is dismissed the Court and *Pinel* is condemned to pay the costs."

Appeals and cross appeals were interposed from this sentence to the Parliament of Aix, who, on the 28th of June 1765, rendered an *Arrêt*, on the report of M. de Mons, by which the judgment rendered below was rescinded, and by a new judgment the Court decreeing on the petition of Marseilles of the 17th of May 1762 ordered that no other maritime interest or premium should be paid to him by *Pinel* but the amount of the premium of insurance which *Marseilles* was adjudged to pay to *Laval* by the first sentence—Each party as to this part of the cause, to pay his own costs—As to the appeals by *Pinal* against *Marseilles*, and by *Marseilles* against *Laval*, the court dismissed them, and affirmed the sentence of the court below, condemning *Marseilles* to pay the usual fine for appealing without cause. And lastly decreeing on the petition of *Laval* of the 22nd March 1765 calling him in aid of the cause, the court ordered this arrêt to have its effect against Remusat and Guis, jointly and severally, and condemned Pinal to pay the costs of that part of the suit.

We find from this arrêt the principles of which I shall endeavour to develop hereafter (a) that any other article than money may be the subject of a maritime loan: and that it is even permitted to stipulate that the lender shall continue to be the owner of the articles lent and at his risk. This last case embraces two contracts, which being united, form a *hiring at maritime risque.* My brother was the advocate of Jean Joseph Marseille.

a infrà ch. II. sect. 3. §. 2.

CHAPTER VI.

Of cases in which maritime interest is not due.

a ch. 1.
sect. 3. Maritime risk is the essence of the contract of maritime loan, as we have before seen, (*a*) It is necessary then that the money should be actually applied to the purpose for which it was borrowed. If it be not so employed, there is no risk; the contract can have no existence as a maritime loan; it is *ipso facto rescinded, causâ non sequutâ.* The non-departure of the ship gives an equal right, according to circumstances, to the rescinding of the contract; but the risk being once commenced, the contract should have every effect which the circumstances will warrant.

SECTION I.

Of a return in consequence of there being no risk.

§. 1. If
there be
no risk,
it is not a
maritime
loan, The maritime interest is the price of the risk: *periculi pretium.* If there has been no risk, it is evident that no maritime interest is due to the lender.* M. Pothier, (*b*) says, "suppose there has been no risk in consequence of the voyage having been broken up? in this case the borrower would b n. 38.
h. t. be obliged to return the money lent to him; but he would not be obliged also to pay the sum which he had promised, by way of maritime interest. For the maritime interest being the price of the risk which the lender ought to encounter, he would not be entitled to maritime interest for the effects upon

---

* Marshall 647,

which the loan was made, if they never had been
at hazard: and he cannot be entitled to the price of
a risk, who never has incurred it. The condition
that there shall be risks to be encountered, is one
that is necessarily included in a contract by which
the borrower has agreed to pay the price of a risk:
tacitè inest ex naturâ rei in obligationem deductæ."

The Italian authours do not admit the non payment of maritime interest except in cases where
the voyage has been broken up by *vis major* before
the commencement of the risk. *Se per sorte il re-*
cevitore non potesse, per alcuno accidente forzoso,
far impiego alcuno, overo navigare, non è dovuto
l'utile accordato; perche si accordo à quelle contem-
plationi. (a)

§. 2. It is of no consequence that the borrower is unable, or unwilling to lade the goods

a Targa, cap. 33. not. 3. pag 141.

Casaregis, (*b*) after having said that the borrower,
who voluntarily neglects to employ money borrowed, owes the stipulated interest, excepts cases
where the employment has been prevented by an
unforeseen obstacle: *hoc non procedit in casu, quo*
cambiatarius propter aliquod justum impedimen-
tum à se ipso minime dependens, merces onerare
non potuiset. Tunc enim non potest cogi ad solven-
dum cambia maritima. This relates to the clause *volo*
per pieno, for which, see *antc.* ch. 1. sect. 3. §. 3.

b disc. 62 n. 4.

With us it is different, excepting in cases of
fraud, of which I shall treat in the next section;
and it is certain that, in the same manner as the
assured, the borrower may retract and release himself from the obligation, without the consent of the
lender, either *by breaking up the voyage before*
the departure of the vessel or by not putting any
thing on board. There not being any peril, the
contract cannot exist as a maritime loan. The
borrower has a right to say to the lender, I had a
design to send my vessel to sea, or to load her

The borrower may retract and rescind the contract by his own act.

with merchandize: To enable me to do this I borrowed money of you. I have changed my deter-
mination: I shall not send my vessel to sea, or,
I shall not load any thing: here is your money.
I have borrowed from you a certain sum for a voyage; this voyage, for which your money was to
have been employed, never will take place; I will
satisfy you. *Si eodem loci consumatur, non erit
trajectitia. (a)*

a L. 1. ff. de naut. fœn. [suprà, ch. 1. sect. 3.]

"We do not make any difference between the
borrower in a maritime loan, who has had it in
his power to load the ship and him who could
not do it. Let the lender have acted with ever so
much good faith, we must always recur to principles, for the solution of any question on the subject: for the nature of the contract is such that the
lender could not be entitled to any maritime profit, but as far as he has incurred the risks to which
the contract is subject. In the case of not lading
the vessel, he has run no risk: and therefore no
maritime profit can have been earned. Whether
the borrower was *able* to ship is of no consequence." (*b*)

b Valin, art. 15. h. t. pag. 16.

M. Pothier, (*c*) holds the same language. "The
maritime profit," he says "is not due to the lender, even in cases where the voyage has been broken up by the act of the borrower. For, let the
cause be what it may, it is enough that the voyage
was broken up; the lender has run no risk, for
which he would be entitled to a maritime interest:
and cannot demand the price of a risk which he
never encountered."

c n. 39.

The 15th art. *h. t.* speaks of a borrower who
has not shipped *to the value of the money borrowed*, and leaves to the common law the disposition
of a case where the borrower, having changed his
intention, relinquishes a projected voyage. M.

Valin, (a) considers this article as if it had said; c d. loco. If he who has borrowed at maritime risque shall not have shipped goods to the amount &c.*

It follows from this principle that where the bor- §. 3. The contract rower is unable or unwilling "to ship goods to is only a the value of the sum borrowed, the contract, in maritime case of loss, shall be diminished in proportion to loan as far as in- the goods shipped, and shall only be valid as to terest ap- the surplus, for which the borrower shall pay in- pears. terest according to the custom of the place where it was executed, together with the principal: if the ship arrive safe, there shall be no more due than b Art. 15. common interest and not maritime interest on the h. t. [Va- excess above the value of the goods shipped." (b) lin 15.]

---

* In order to understand this passage, recurrence must be had to the 15th Art. of the ordinance quoted by Valin, and to the 14th which immediately precedes it. They are as follows.

Art. 14.—The shipper who shall have borrowed on his goods at maritime risque, shall not be liberated by the loss of the vessel or of her cargo, if he does not prove that he had goods on board to the amount of the sum borrowed.

Art. 15.— If however, he who has borrowed money at maritime risque, shall prove *that it was not in his power* to ship goods to the amount of the sum borrowed, the contract, in case of loss, shall be reduced in proportion to the value of the effects shipped, &c.

Valin, and with him Emerigon, contend that the words of the Ordinance *that it was not in his power to ship* must be construed *that he has not shipped*, whether the omission was occasioned by a superior force or by his own caprice or neglect. But the anonymous commentator on the Ordinance, who wrote after Valin, and whose work was printed at Marseilles in 1780 in two duodecimo Volumes maintains against him that the text ought to be taken literally, and that Valin's construction militates with the clear and express terms of the law. From this it would seem to follow that the doctrine of Valin and Emerigon on this point is an ingenious theory of their own, but that the ordinance of France is conformable to the principles of the Italian writers, which they so strongly disapprove.

Here we find that the contract is only considered as a maritime loan as far as there has been a maritime risk: for example, I have borrowed 6000 liv. by maritime loan at 10 *per cent.* I ship no more than a moiety of this sum. If the ship perish, the lender will lose 3000 liv. the value of the goods shipped, and I owe him the balance, with legal interest.   If she arrive safe I shall be obliged to pay the whole principal.   -   -   £. 6000

Maritime interest on the moiety   -   £.   300
And if the loan had been made a
    year ago I should be obliged to
    pay him legal interest according
    to the custom of the place, for
    the other moiety.   -   -   -   £.   180

a n. 39. M. Pothier, (*a*) says that if the voyage be broken up before the commencement of the risk, without the fault of the borrower, he ought not to pay legal interest but from the time of a demand for the money to be returned. But this opinion is at variance with the text of the 15th art. which particularly mentions the case where a borrower *justifies by his inability to load* and which, notwithstanding this circumstance, compels him to pay interest according to the custom of the place.

The one half per cent to the underwriter, As to the legal interest, M. Valin* "would add a half per cent on the premium against a borrower, in a case where the lender had insured his

* The passage in Valin, to which our authour refers is as follows. " If the shipment has not been made, the contract of maritime loan is *pleno jure* rescinded, *ob causam finalem non secutam*, saving the damages and interest due to the lender, which consists, on the terms of this article (15th) in the interest or exchange for the sum at the rate of the place, from the day of the loan to final payment; *to which I would add, the one*

capital and the borrower had failed to load *by his own fault.*" This is just. But if the vessel was prevented from being laden by *vis major*, it is sufficient if the borrower return the capital, with legal interest, from the date of the loan.

SECTION II.

Of a fraudulent Borrower.

" **Too** much money (says the *Guidon*) being borrowed by maritime loan excites a violent presumption against the master of the ship that he has been instrumental in her loss or capture : for, as in every business, whether by land or sea, the object and end of traffick is profit and gain, he could not undertake a voyage with an expectation of gain, who became a debtor before the commencement of it ; It is therfore necessarily to be inferred, that he might contemplate some accident that would release him from those debts, which, by acting honestly, he could not pay upon his safe return. Such being the facility of abuse, we may attribute more of the ruin and loss of vessels, and the pillage or capture of merchandize to this cause, than to the perils of the sea. This presumption, with the slightest proof that can be adduced, shall subject the guilty to death.* *(a)*

§.1. Whe= ther fraud is presu- med a- gainst the person who bor- rows be- yond his interest.

a Guidon de la Mer, ch. 19. art. 10

---

half per cent on the premium (of insurance) against the borrower who should not have shipped the goods through his own fault or neglect, in case the lender had caused his principal to be insured, as the Ordinance permits him to do ; for it is easy to understand, that the Insurance having failed the Underwriters would in that case only be entitled to one half per cent for his signature." 2. Valin 17.

* This is carrying very far the doctrine of *semi plena probatio*.

Cúm Capitaneus ad cambium receperit longè ma-
jorem pecuniæ summam, quàm fuerit risicum super
navi existens; præsumi debet, sinistrum fuisse dolo-
sum.(a)

a Casare-gis, disc. 62. n. 7.

Our ordinance is conformable, precisely, to the above.   Art. 15. h. t. directs that he who has borrowed money and pleads inability in justification of his not having shipped to the amount borrowed, &c. It follows from this that he who has borrowed beyond his interest, must rebut the presumption of fraud and prove his innocence.

b n. 12.   M. Pothier,(b) says that fraud is not to be presumed; that "the borrower should be heard willingly in his justification, and we should be satisfied if he allege any thing plausible in his defence." As a general rule it is true that fraud is not to be presumed, but in this case the right of presumption is established by the ordinance itself, which requires that the borrower should justify himself.

He is justified, if instead of equipping, and before the departure of the ship, he declare that the plan is relinquished, (in whole or in part;) but if he wait until the ship be returning before he propose to return the money, it is very suspicious and his justification ought to be very complete, in order to excuse him.

§ 2. Punishment of a fraudulent borrower.   The 3rd art. h. t. "forbids persons to borrow by maritime loan upon the hull and keel of the ship or upon the cargo, beyond their value, under pain of being obliged, in case of fraud, to pay the whole sum, notwithstanding the loss or capture of the vessel."

He must restore the money not-   According to the text, he who has fraudulently borrowed money, by maritime loan beyond the va-withstanding the loss of the ship.

lue of the thing at risk must repay the whole sum borrowed, notwithstanding any accident.

The action of the lender, in this case, is confined to the demand of the sum lent, without a claim of maritime interest, because he is not affected by the loss, and he has not encountered any risk of which maritime interest is the price. Such is the opinion of M. Valin, *ibid.* Must he pay maritime interest?

This authour contends that this being the case of a penal law, which is always to be construed strictly and never to be extended by implication, it is sufficient if the fraudulent borrower restore the sum borrowed, even without legal interest; because he is sufficiently punished by the loss of the effects beyond *the value* which he had borrowed. I do not agree with him. The contract being declared to be null in consequence of the fraud of the borrower, it comes then under the provisions of the common law, which allows legal interest.(a) Or legal interest? *a* vid. decisions before cited ch. 3. sect. 3. and Emerig. Traite des assurances ch. 18. sect. 5.

Captain Francis, of Goa, was the owner of six *shares* of a vessel called the St. John Baptiste. He borrowed 3,300 livres on the hull, in the place where the other owners resided. The ship was wrecked. The lenders demanded their money because the captain had borrowed more than the amount of his interest. A sentence was rendered on the 31st January 1755, which condemned the captain to pay the 3,300 livres, *with legal interest from the time it was furnished and costs.*

If the ship arrive in safety the fraudulent borrower cannot avoid the payment of legal interest. His deceit imposes silence upon him and he is not allowed to demand that the contract be rescinded.(b) If the ship arrive, is a fraudulent borrower to pay maritime interest? *b* Emerig. Traite des assurances ch. 16, sect, 5.

In such a case the owners would be obliged to pay the money with maritime interest for sums bor-

U

rowed by the captain at maritime risque in the
course of the voyage, because they are responsible
for his acts and they represent him at least until
they abandon the ship and freight.

Durand
v.
Rousseau
1767.

a sect. 5.
§. 2. and
sect. 6.
§. 1.

In the 4th chapter(*a*) I cited an Arrêt in the case
of *Rousseau.* The circumstances were these. The
St. Jacques, armed at Arles by the owners domiciliated there, and commanded by captain Durand,
sailed a short cruise in the waters of Languedoc and
Provence. On the 13th September 1765, she arrived at Marseilles. The captain borrowed at bottomry according to the rate of interest of the place,
200 livres from Anselme Rousseau. *This was for
the rigging, armament and victualling of the vessel,*
on a voyage about to be undertaken thence to Arles
or elsewhere and return to Marseilles. The vessel
left Marseilles and arrived at Arles. The affairs of
Durand being deranged, he was dismissed from
the ship by the owners.

Rousseau filed a petition in the admiralty of
Arles against *Durand* claiming the 200 livres with
maritime interest of two per. cent. a month, and
legal interest, if the captain would not immediately
put to sea for Marseilles and end his voyage. He
also prayed that the execution of the judgment
which might be rendered, should be declared to be
jointly against the owners also.

On the 20th December, 1765, a sentence was
passed, which condemned *Durand* to pay the 200
livres borrowed by him, with one half of the maritime interest of the place and interest since the
demand and costs. This sentence was declared to
be common and executory against the owners, as
such, but to be executed on the ship only or its
proceeds.*

---

* That is to say, that the sentence was given against the
captain and owners, merely as such, and the subject matter

The owners appealed from this sentence. They contended 1. That the bottomry bond being secret, it could not effect them, according to the Arrêt reported by Duperier, (*a*) 2. That all the victuals and every necessary expense had been furnished by themselves. 3. That the captain had not taken the advice of his officers.

a tom. 2, pag. 521.

On the report of M. Descrottes, an arrêt passed the 26th June 1767 which confirmed this sentence. By this arrêt it was decided: 1. That a secret bottomry bond executed by the captain, and in the course of the voyage was not less binding upon the owners than if it were publick, because it was occasioned by the necessities of the ship. 2. That the consultation of the officers is a domestick form, in which third persons take no part. 3. That the owners should pay not only the principal, but maritime interest.

Nota. The whole maritime interest would perhaps have been adjudged to *Rousseau* if he had entered a cross appeal from the sentence. The question on the subject of legal interest was not agitated, nor even started, on account of the smallness of the sum.

I shall remark hereafter that this sentence was irregular, *inasmuch, as it condemned the owners merely as such, and awarded execution against the ship only*, or because as they had not abandoned the vessel and freight they were personally and absolutely bound by the acts of the master; but *Rousseau*, who had the whole ship as a fund of payment, was not very anxious to correct errors, which did not operate to his prejudice.

being a bottomry, the sentence of course, could be only executed upon the ship, though nominally, it was against the owners and master.

SECTION III.

Proof of the Shipment.

§. 1. In case of the loss of the ship, the borrower must prove the lading.

a Art. 14. h. t.

"The person who shall have borrowed money by maritime loan on goods, shall not be released from his contract by the loss of the ship, unless he prove that he had goods on board to the amount of the sum borrowed."(*a*) M. Valin,)(*b*) observes that in such a case, the proof of property should be the same as in cases of Insurance. (*c)*

b ibid. *c* Emerig. Traité des assurances ch. 11.

Ought the borrower to run the risk of the tenth part. (*)

d ch. 33. not. 16. pag. 148.

It suffices if the borrower prove property on board to the amount of the sum borrowed, without being obliged to run the risk of the tenth part; for borrowers frequently are men of no fortune and have nothing but their industry to depend upon. We must not, then, be misled, by the opinion of Targa,(*d*) who says that the borrower should run the risk of a third part of the thing borrowed.

If the borrower carry the money with him?

It is not necessary that the borrower should expend the money, which he has borrowed, in merchandize, at the place where the contract was made. He may carry it with him, in order to make a more advantageous use of it during the voyage.

This was the most common manner, among the Romans, of using the money. They exported very little merchandize from Rome; but they imported a great deal into that vortex of the world. It is sufficient if he prove that the money was expos-

---

* By the 18th art. of the *Ordinance de la Marine title des assurances* it is provided: that the assured shall always run the risque of one tenth of the goods which they shall have shipped, unless there be in the policy an express stipulation to the contrary. It is to this article that our authour refers, and enquires whether it is to extend to maritime loans.

ed to the perils of the sea, to make the maritime interest due; and on the other hand, the borrower will be released from his bond by proving the property to have been on board at the time of the loss.

Nor is it necessary to show the particular manner in which the money was employed. It is enough to prove that at the time of the loss he had property on board to the value of the sum borrowed. *(a)* *Non est necesse probationem fieri in specie, videlicet quòd pecuniam sibi ad cambium datam cambiatarius oneraverit in eâdem specie, aut quod eâ fuerit imposita in emptionem talium, et talium mercium per eum deindè oneratarum in navi. Sufficit enim, si ille constare tantùm faciet risicum in navi extitisse, sive hoc fuerit majus, sive saltem correspondens sorti ad cambium datæ. Et hoc communiter practicatur absque ullâ controversiâ. (b)*

Must he prove the special employment of the money?

a D. art. 14.

b Casaregis disc. 62. n. 13.

From this, it has often been contended that it is lawful to borrow when the thing is already at risk, and that in case of accident, it is sufficient to prove that the subject of the risk was on board when the loss happened. It is so as to Insurers, but not as to lenders at maritime risque, who cannot be considered in that character, unless they have made a loan to effect the equipment, to purchase the cargo or to supply the necessities of the ship during her voyage. The nature of the contract and good faith will not allow that the interest of third persons should be injured without a good and lawful cause, such, for instance, as those of the lenders for the equipment of the ship and furnishing of the cargo, which would be thus injured by a concurrent and not equally meritorious claim and those

Must he prove that the money was furnished before the risk commenced?

of the Insurers, who in case of loss would be deprived by an intruder of this proportion of the effects saved. *(a)*

a suprà ch. 6. sect. 3.

§. 2. The proof of the application of the money does not lie upon the lender.

The proof of the application of money lent at maritime risk is never thrown upon the lender. It is sufficient for him to exhibit his contract to the person who has received his money or his agent. *Sola probatio traditionis pecuniæ ad cambium, absque probationis illius oneratione, sufficit. (b)*

b Casaregis, disc. 1. n. 37. Pothier. n. 52. [Suprà ch. 4. sect. 7. §. 3. 4. and sect. 8.

CHAPTER VII.

Of the risks.

Cleirac, *(a)* says that the contract of maritime loan is subject to the same risks as the policy of Insurance. Valin, *(b)* and Pothier, *(c)* adopt this rule, admitting the exceptions to which it is liable. [a] Notes on le Guidon de la mer. ch. 18. art 2. pag. 331.

b art. 11. h. t. and art. 6. tit. des assurances. *c* n. 16. h. t.

In the present chapter I shall endeavour to make some general observations respecting those risks which are borne by the lender in a maritime loan, and I shall reserve for the 11th chapter those which relate to the annulling or extinction of the contract. In that chapter, I shall also treat the question of abandonment of the thing upon which the money has been borrowed.

SECTION I.

Losses and average occasioned by the perils of the sea.

The *Guidon de la Mer*, *(d)* decides that maritime money does not contribute to any particular average. [§. 1. Simple average.]

d ch. 19. art. 5.

This decision has been adopted by the ordinance.*(e)* "The lenders at maritime risque, *shall not contribute to any simple average* or particular damage which may happen to the merchandize, *unless there is a stipulation to the contrary.* *

a Vid.
Emerig
Traité
des assu-
rances ch.
12. sect.
39. 40.

Thus, in order to charge the lender with particular average, there must be an express agreement to that effect, whilst the insurer is obliged to contribute, if he have not protected himself by a special clause to the contrary. *(a)*

b n. 42.
and 47.

Pothier*(b)* endeavours to illustrate the meaning of this difference. He says that "the insurers bind themselves to indemnify the insured, against every loss and injury which their property may suffer from the perils of the sea; but, in a maritime loan, the lender enters into no obligation to the borrower." We may add that the safe arrival of the vessel is the essential and characteristick condition of the latter contract. Now, simple average has no influence on the accomplishment of this condition. The lender, therefore, is a stranger to it, unless he has made himself liable by a special agreement.

c d. loco.

M. Valin,*(c)* appears to be surprized at this provision of the ordinance. He observes that "maritime loans would have been abolished if the 16th article had not permitted persons to stipulate that the lender should contribute to simple averages. Therefore, says he, we see no borrowers who do not provide against the effect of this article, and who do not take care to insert a precise clause, by which the lender takes upon himself all the risks and perils of the sea, in the same manner as an insurer. I have never seen such a clause among us; and the lenders do not contribute to simple aver-

---

* By the law of England, there is neither average nor salvage upon a bottomry bond. *Joyce and Williamson* reported in Park 421 and Marshall 652. This point as far as it relates to average is adopted by Lord Kenyon in *Walpole v. Emer.* Marshall 660. Park 423. See, particularly, Marshall's observations on these cases.

ges. Excepting in those cases, where the aver- *a* Vid. age being occasioned by the unseaworthiness or infrà ch. 11. sect. stranding of the ship, the borrower is thereby 1. §. 5. prevented from fulfilling his engagements.(*a*)

The *Guidon de la Mer*,(*b*) says that "bottomry §. 2. gross average. money must contribute to ransoms, compositions *b* ch 19. and jettisons made for the safety of the whole, and art. 5. for the release or avoiding of dangers."

The ordinance,(*c*) also decides that "the len- *c* art. 16. ders shall contribute, in acquittance of borrowers, h. t. to gross averages, such as ransoms, compositions, jettisons, masts and cordage cut away for the com- mon safety of the ship and cargo."

What is the reason of this difference between simple and gross average as to the lender? I have already explained it. It is because simple average which is occasioned by accident and without the fault of man, contributes nothing to the fulfilment of the contract and the safe arrival of the vessel: on the *d* §. 1. inst de contrary, without the aid of ransom or jettison the oblig. ship would never return. If, then, a person has quæ quasi ex con- incurred an expense or voluntarily suffered an in- tract. L. jury to save your contract and to make it advanta- 2. et 9. ff. de negot. geous to you, it is but just that you should contri- gest. L. bute towards his indemnification. If you refuse to 3. et 5. ff. de in rem submit to the action *negotiorum gestorum* impetrat- verso. 1. ed against you, expose your vessel once more to Domat [civil law the rapacity of pirates or the impetuosity of the lib. 1. tit. hurricane. *Qui utiliter gessit negotia, dominum* 9.] *habet obligatum negotiorum gestorum.(d)*

M. Prevot de la Jaunes,(*e*) says "the lenders *e* Princi- pes de la ought to contribute to discharge the borrowers from jur:spru- gross averages, such as ransoms, compositions, dence Francoise jettisons for the common safety of the vessel and tit. 20. n̄ cargo; for it is no more than a loss that they suffer 556.

W

for the preservation of their money, which, without this might have perished with the vessel."*

§. 3. free of average.

It is evident that the words *if there is no stipulation to the contrary*, relate only to the second part of the 16th article, in which simple average is spoken of. From which it follows, that a lender is not allowed to stipulate that he shall be exempt

a dicto loco.

from gross average. This is the opinion of Valin,(*a*) and of Pothier.(*b*) Such an agreement is absolutely

b n. 46.

void and ought to be rejected, because it is contrary to natural equity and even to the interest of the lender, to whom every thing would be lost, if the vessel perish.

The same reasoning would not apply to the insurer, because he is a *fidejussor* who is only responsible for risks embraced by his contract and to whom such an exception cannot be otherwise than favourable.†

In 1776 captain *Jean Baptiste Joseph Reyne*, commanding the *Heureux Joseph* borrowed at maritime risque from *Jean Baptiste Scipion Febre*, 16000 livres. It was cumulatively on the vessel and goods on a voyage out and home from the French West-India Islands, at the rate of 15 *per cent. free of average*. He borrowed 4000 livres of *M. André*

---

* Where repairs are ordered by the underwriters, for the payment of which a bottomry bond is given, and they refuse to pay it on the arrival of the vessel, in consequence of which she is sold, they are liable for all the damage which occurs to the owner in consequence of that refusal. Where a ship has been repaired, the underwriters are not entitled to the usual deduction of one third, new for old, unless the ship has been put into the free possession of the owners again. Where a ship is obliged to put into port for the benefit of the whole concern, the charges of loading and unloading the cargo and taking care of it, and the wages and provisions of the workmen hired for the repairs, become general average. *Da Costa* v. *Newnham*, 2. T. R. 407.

† Marshall 658.

Vaille, on the hull and goods of the same ship, out and home, at 15 *per cent. free of average and a-bandonment in case of innavigability.* He insured his ship and cargo, with a clause *free of average,* &c.

The ship arrived in safety at Martinique. He set sail to return to Marseilles. On the 29th of September 1777, he met with a tempest, in which the masts were cut away and several other things thrown overboard. He put in at Cape Francois where the ship was declared innavigable. The cargo was put on board another vessel and arrived at Marseilles.

Captain *Reyne* filed a petition against the owners and consignees of the cargo, the assurers and the lenders at risque, praying that they might contri. bute to a common average. *Fabre* and *Vaille* filed their petitions against the captain, praying a condemnation against him for the sums lent at risque, with maritime interest and charges.

There was a considerable argument whether the clause *free of average* was lawful against lenders, and further whether it was lawful in *Vaille* to sti-pulate against *abandonment in case of innavigabi-lity.*

An interlocutory order was made on the 15th May, 1778, which without prejudice, " to the rights of the parties directed that the papers and vouchers should within three days be lodged with the register, in order to proceed to the adjustment of the average, if necessary, but that in the mean while the sums due to *Fabre* and *Vaille* should be paid without delay, with maritime and legal interest. To this payment captain *Reyne* to be bound, under pain of execution against his body."

A definitive sentence was rendered August 3, 1779, which "without regarding the petition of captain *Reyne* as to the insurers on the goods, discharges them from the process of the court with costs, and considering the other parts of the petition as just, decrees, 1st. The lenders are to contribute *pro ratâ*, to a general average, as well on the cargo as the vessel the *Heureux Joseph*, to the relief of captain *Reyne*, with costs. 2d. The insurers on the hull are to contribute to the gross and also the simple average, with costs, in consequence of the abandonment made at the Cape, by the captain 13th November 1777, notice of which was given 27th July 1778. The decision of the former sentence in favour of *Fabre and Vaille*, for the amount of the sum lent with maritime and legal interest, is pronounced to be definitive."

M. Pazery being consulted upon this sentence, by the lenders, replied, that the clauses *free from average and abandonment in case of innavigability* were void and contrary to the ordinance. In consequence of this opinion, the lenders submitted to the sentence   The Insurers on the hull, against whom the abandonment had not been prosecuted, also acquiesced.

§ 4 Agreement that the lender shall only bear certain risks. In my treatise on Insurance *(a)* we have seen that Insurers are permitted to specify the risks which they will bear, and to exclude others, for which they will not be responsible. The Italians admit a similar clause in their bottomry bonds. *(b)*

a ch. 12 sect. 1.   *b* Casaregis, disc. 62 n. 2. disc. 64. n. 1. et seq

c ch. 32 s. 27. and 2 137.

d n. 24 h. t.

Targa *(c)* disapproves of this agreement; and it would not be allowed by us, notwithstanding the opinion of Pothier, *(d)* to the contrary. He says that "the lenders bear all the risks which are specified by the ordinance, *saving those which are added or excepted by express agreement.*"

I have already observed that the safe arrival of
the vessel is the essential condition and characteristick feature of the contract of maritime loan.
Consequently it should be preserved scrupulously.
To make the contract lawful the money must be
used at the risk of the creditor. *Periculo creditoris naviget. (a)* If the ship perish before she ar- ª L. 1. ff.
rive in port or previous to the expiration of the li- de naut.
mited time, the condition has not been performed fœn.
and consequently the expectations of the lender
vanish. This is the reason why the 11th *art. h. t.*
decides generally and without exception that "every contract of maritime loan shall become void by
the entire loss of the thing pledged in the loan,
provided that it happens within the time and place
of the risk."

It is sufficient then that the entire loss shall happen within the time and place of the risk in order
to render the contract void. It would be intolera-
ble if the borrower, after having lost his property,
by an accident, within the time and place agreed
upon, should be obliged to pay the whole principal
with maritime interest, under pretence of an agreement which was radically void and usurious. According to those principles the sentence of a 3rd.
August 1779, which I just cited, paid no attention to the stipulation of *André Vaille*, which made
him *free from average and abandonment in case of
innavigability.*

Assurance is a species of fidejussory security.
The Insurer, therefore, may specify the risks which
he is willing to bear; but the lender could only claim ᵇ Vid. in-
his principal in case of the safe return of the ves- frª, ch.
sel or of her safety during a certain specified 11 sect.
time. *(b)* 3.

M. Valin, *(c)* observes that the contribution does §. 5. In
not become, *ipso jure*, chargeable on the money what
manner
lender contribute to ransoms and gross average? c art. 16. pag. 19. shall the

lent, to the diminution of the maritime interest. The deduction is only chargeable from the day that the lender has refused to pay the contribution. This authour adds, that it is necessary to say how much of the contribution ought to be paid in the other cases mentioned in the 16th article and he quotes a sentence rendered on my report in 1750, the circumstances of which I have before related *(a)*. I shall treat, of a contribution between the borrower and lender hereafter. (*b*)

a Suprà ch. 3. sect. 3.
b infrà ch. 11. sect.1 §. 2. and sect. 2. §. 2.

SECTION II.

In general, the lenders only bear the risks of the sea.

§. 1. The lenders only bear the risks of the sea.

The 11th art. h. t. decides that the contract shall become void upon the entire loss of the thing, which is the pledge in the loan, *provided it happens, by accident, within the time and places of the risks.*

c Roccus, de navib. not. 51.

It is then certain, that the lender bears no other risks than those of the sea. *Creditor subit periculum navigationis, in casibus fortuitis tantùm.* (*b*)

c 12th art. h. t.

To illustrate this matter the ordinance adds that, (*c*) "nothing shall be termed, an *accident*, which happens through the internal defect of the thing, or the act of the owners, master or shippers, if it is not otherwise agreed in the contract."

§ 2. Internal defect.

The lender is not responsible for accidents which may happen from the internal defect of the thing: as if the commodities rot, if the liquors leak out of the casks, if, from length of time, dry goods get heated, or if the vessel become innavigable by age.

M. Valin, (*a*) seems to disapprove of the clause *a* ibid.
by which the lenders make themselves responsible
for the internal defect of the thing;* but there is
nothing to prevent them from bearing the risk of
a defect to which the thing may be liable in the
course of a voyage. It is allowed by the 12th and
16th art. h. t. (all that I have said in my *Traité
des assurances*, ch. 12. sect. 9. and 38. may be
applied here.)†

According to the 12th art. h. t. the lender is not $.3. A
responsible for any accidents which happen through $\substack{\text{loss hap-}\\\text{pening}}$
the acts of the owners of the vessel, the master by the act
and mariners or shippers. It is not, then, a peril of man-
of the sea at the risk of the lender, if the voyage
be changed by order of the owner, or a loss has
happened by barratry or the fault of the merchant:
si infortunium, vel naufragium ex culpâ debitoris $\substack{b \text{ Roccus,}\\\text{de navib.}}$
processerit, tunc creditor non tenetur de periculo et de navib.
damno in quod incurritur exculpâ vehentis, aut al- not. 51.
terius. (*b*) But, according to circumstances, these
general rules cease to operate, *if it be otherwise
provided by the contract.*‡

If the effects be forfeited in consequence of their $\substack{\text{Contra-}\\\text{band.}}$
being contraband, in which the lender has not par- c4L. 3. C.
ticipated or of which he was ignorant, he does not de naut.
suffer from this accident, because it is not a peril $\substack{\text{fœn.}\\\text{(Styp-}}$
of the sea: *non ex marinæ tempestatis discrimine,* mannus,
sed ex præcepiti avaritiâ et incivili debitoris auda- $\substack{\text{part. 4.}\\\text{cap.}}$
tiâ. (*c*) $\substack{\text{2. n. 105.}}$
pag. 385. Casaregis disc. 64.)

---

* Marshall, lib. 2. ch. v. p. 651.

† Where a ship's bottom is injured by worms in the course
of the voyage, so that in consequence thereof she is incapable
of completing the voyage, and is condemned, it has been held
that the loss is not a loss " by perils of the seas." 1. Esp. N.
P. C. 444.

‡ Marshall, 654.

a Kuricke
tit. 6
pag 762.
Valin,
ibid.
But if the design of smuggling or trading in contraband was evident from the contract, the loss would fall upon the lender. *Si sciente et consentiente illo fiat, consen us jus facit.* (*a*)

Observations up-
on the
text of   the 12th art, h. t.
The text of the 12th art. h. t. appears to be equivocal.

1. By the word *owners*, M. Valin understands the owners of the thing upon which the money was lent. But this interpretation is inconsistent with the remainder of the text, which speaks of owners, master or shippers. We must then take these terms as synonimous, which is not admissible, or distinguish the word, *owners*, on which the doubt arises, from the term, *sh ppers*. It is evident that the 12th art. speaks of owners of the ship. *That which happens by their acts*, it says, *shall not be esteemed an accident.* The lenders are not answerable.

b tit. des
assuran-
ces.
2. By the word *master*, Valin properly understands the captain of the ship. Even this term also comprehends *mar ners*, as we find in the 28th art. (*b*) Whatever happens through the acts of the captain or mariners shall not be esteemed an accident. The lenders do not answer for them.

2 By the word *shippers* I believe that the Ordinance means those who have put merchandize on board which is hypothecated in a maritime loan. Whatever happens through their acts is not esteemed an accident. The lenders are not answerable for them; at least unless there has been smuggling in the lading, with their consent. But, as a general rule, I cannot agree with any one, that he shall be charged with the faults which I shall commit. This stipulation, says Valin, *should be rejected as deceptive and fraudulent.*

4. If any other shipper, than the borrower, be the occasion of an accident by his own act, without the borrower being able to prevent or repair it, this would be a *vis major* and an accident at the risk of the lender, provided it occurred at sea and was not the subject of particular average.

5. We should take this article in connection with the 27th, 28th, and 29th, *tit. des assurances.*

The Insurers are not answerable for losses which happen through the acts of the shippers: that is to say, by the act of those who have borrowed at maritime risque, unless they were employed in a smuggling trade, in which the Insurers or the lenders have concurred.

The Insurers or lenders are not answerable for any accident which happens by the acts or fault of the owners of the ship, the master and mariners, unless there is an express stipulation to the contrary.

Neither are the Insurers or lenders answerable for the internal defect of the thing, unless there is an agreement to that effect. (What I have said in the *Traité des assurances* ch. 12. sect. 1. 2. 3. 4. 5. 6. and 7. applies here.)

If the goods remain unsold at the place where they are exported; if they be sold under the limited price or to an insolvent person, or if they be pillaged, burnt &c. the lender is not affected by such accidents, because they are perils of the land. *Quandò post existentem conditionem, cùm navis salva pervenerit, res admittitur, tunc periculum nequit dici marinum. (a)*

§. 4. Dangers by land.

a Styp- mannus part 4. cap. 2. n. 104. pag. 585.

X

CHAPTER VIII.

Time and place of the risk.

Among the Romans, *pecunia trajectitia* or money lent on maritime interest and risk, was given either for the whole voyage, that is, out and home, or only out, or only on the return voyage, or for a limited time.

a L. 122.
§. 1. ff de
verb, ob-
lig. (su-
prà ch. 1.
sect. 1.)
b L. 3. C.
de naut.
fœn.
c L. 1. C.
de naut.
fœn.
To go and return, for example, *from Beritus to Brundusium and from Brundusium back to Beritus.* (*a*) To go, only: *from Beritus to Africa.* (*b*) For the return, only. (*c*) For a limited time. *(d)* These different cases are comprized, by implication within the 2nd. *art. h. t.* which permits persons to borrow at gross adventure, *for an entire voyage or for a limited time.*

d L. 4· and 6. ff. eod. [vid. Styp. part. 4. cap. 2. n. 33. et. seq. pag. 379. Kur. tit. 6. pag. 762. Locc. lib. 2. cap. 6. n. 7. pag. 993.]

SECTION I.

Of the contract of maritime loan, for an entire voyage.

§.1. What
is to be
under-
stood by
an entire
voyage?
The 13 art. h. t. says that if "the time of the risk be not stipulated in the contract, it shall commence, as to the vessel, when she hoists sail, and continue *until she drops anchor in her port of destination;* and, as to the cargo, as soon as it should be laden on board of the ship or of the lighters to be carried thither and continue *until it be delivered on shore.** According to this article, the voyage

---

* Marshall 656.

which the vessel makes from her departure until her arrival at the port of destination, whether it be out or home, constitutes, what is called, the *entire voyage*, to distinguish it from the voyage for a limitted term.

The voyage *out and home* which is spoken of in the title *des assurances (a)* is yet more full than the preceeding and appears to be more analogous with the nature of a contract of maritime loan, which, on that account, we sometimes denominate a contract of *return voyage (à retour de voyage.)* (b)*

a Art. 6, and 7.

b Emerig Traité des assurances ch. 13.

It is very common among us to borrow money at gross adventure for the voyage *out and home* whether it be on the vessel or the goods. In this case, the risk commences at the place of equipment or lading, and does not end until the vessel has returned to the same place: the whole, according to the provisions of the 13th art. *h. t. (c)*

Contract out and home.

c Pothier. n. 34.

According to the 13th art. if the time of the risk be not regulated by the contract, it appears that we ought to presume the money to have been lent only for the outward voyage; *M. Pothier, (d)* believes, not without reason, that in doubtful cases, we should adopt the contrary presumption, which, in effect, is analogous with the nature of a contract as we often term it of *return voyage* and also with the daily practice.

In case of doubt, it is presumed that the money was lent, out and home *d* n. 32

From the same article, we must not be surprized that the ordinance has omitted to provide for the case where a ship, which was the thing pledged, does not return to her port of outfit. Per-

§. 2. If the ship do not return.

---

* Because in most cases the maritime money is to be repaid on the safe return of the vessel to her port of outfit.

haps it was thought that no one would lend but
on the outward voyage. But, whatever ground
there may be for this conjecture, our tribunals
have adjudged the whole maritime interest, although
the vessel has not returned. *(a)*

It would not be wonderful, if a jurisprudence
so injurious to poor shippers of small adventures,
should be changed. It may be said that if the ordinance had foreseen the custom now in use, of
borrowing money at gross adventure for the voyage out and home, it would have established the
same reduction of the maritime interest in case of
the vessel not returning as it has prescribed with
respect to a premium.

This deduction is so proper, that it was admitted by our consulate Tribunal, not long ago. But
"justice ought to be so uniform in her decissions,
that the law should be but one rule and not depend
on time and place; as it is her chief praise to be
ignorant of persons."

This point, as well as many others, requires the
decision of the sovereign. The title respecting maritime loans contains only eighteen articles, whilst
that which relates to Insurance includes seventy
four. Many of these articles are expressed in am-
biguous terms. It is frequently difficult to distinguish between the rule and the exception. Hence
arises the uncertainty of decisions and the multi-
plicity of suits with which commerce is harrassed.
The knowledge which has been acquired since the
year 1681, the extension of our commerce and
the experience of more than a century, all con-
spire to demand a new marine ordinance, which,
by investigating the nature of things and their various relations, might prevent litigation and give

stability to the jurisprudence of the kingdom. *Hic labor, hoc opus est.**

SECTION II.

Contract of maritime loan for a limited time.

Losses which happen during the existence of the risk, are borne by the lender. *(a)*

§. 1. Losses which happen during the exis-

tence of the risk are borne by the lender. *a* Art. 11. h. t. L. 6. ff. de naut. fœn. Kuricke, tit. 6, pag. 762. Pothier. n. 37.

But as soon as the time limited has elapsed, the risk ceases, as to the lender, and the maritime interest becomes due, though the vessel be afterwards lost: *post diem præstitutam, et conditionem impletam, periculum esse creditoris desinit.* (*b*) part. 4. cap. 4. n. 87. pag. 384. Pothier, n. 36. Valin, art. 11. pag. 13.

The risk ceases with the limited term. *b* L. 4. ff. de naut. fœn. ßtypmannus,

* Notwithstanding the liberal wishes of our authour, whose work the compilers of the Napoleon Commercial Code had before them, and whose hints it would have done them the honour to attend to, they have copied sevility the 13th article of the ordinance, without amending or explaining it as to the important point to which the text refers. *Code du Commerce.* *No.* 328. It was expected by many that this new Commercial Code which was announced with so much pomp, would have settled all the points which were left doubtful by the celebrated Ordinances of Louis XIV. instead of which we find that where it is not a mere copy of their texts, there is very little in it to be commended: Bonaparte's legislators do not seem to have possessed a spark of the spirit of the great Colbert, and have by no means improved his immortal works by their new fangled code ; unless it can be called an improvement to have loaded the mercantile profession with new and ignominious shackles, as, for instance, by punishing imprudence as a crime, and that too, by means of the *correctional police, Nos.* 586. 592. or to have changed the ancient French expression *au marc la livre*, into *au marc la franc No.* 331. without adverting that the *marc* is full as obsolete at this day as the *hire*, and that a grave legislative work is disgraced by this Revolutionary pedantry.

.2.   I have often seen contracts of this sort, *for three*
Clause,
at so   *months and pro rata, not exceeding one year.* The
much per term is then limited to one year, at the expira-
month
not ex-   tion of which the risk ceases, as to the lender, and
ceeding   his principal, and interest, then becomes due.
one year.

a Vid·   The terms of the clearance are of no conse-
Traité
des assur- quence to the lender in estimating his risk.* (*a*)
ances ch. 13. sect. 1. §. 2.

§. 3 Of a   A ship which is not heard of, is presumed to
ship
which is have perished within the time limited, at least, un-
not heard til the borrower proves the contrary. (*b*)
of.   *b* Valin, art. 13. h. t. [Emerig. Traité des assurances, ch. 13. sect. 1.]

§. 4. If   As soon as the peril commences, the lender has
the vessel
return be- an undeniable right to the whole interest, although
fore the   the peril should be abridged or lessened. (*c*)
expira-   tion of the time limited. *c* Suprà ch. 3. sect. 1.

§. 5. Un-   In Italy, they sometimes lend at gross adventure
limited
time.   for an unlimited time, without designating the
           voyage. It depends then on either of the parties
           to terminate the contract, when he thinks fit, pro-
d Targa   vided it be done at a proper time and under pro-
ch. 33.
not. 11.   per circumstances. (*d*) *Our money left by renew-*
12. 14. 15. *al or continuation*† spoken of in the 10*th art. h. t.*
pag. 145. has some relation to this custom.

§. 6. Time   The course of the time limited is not interrup-
of demur- ted by a demurrage or delay in port during the
rage.
           route: because whether the stay be voluntary or
           forced, it is possible that the ship may perish by

---

* In France vessels are sometimes cleared out for one or
two years, without designation of places. Those voyages are
called *en Caravan*, the vessels go from port to port in quest
of freight, or of profits until the time limited for their return.
Those voyages are also frequent in Holland. *Vid.* 2. H. Black,
604. *Giener and Meyer.*

† Vid. ante. ch. 5. Sect. 3.

the perils of the sea. *(a)* In order that a delay may suspend the time, there should be an express agreement to that effect; but such stipulations are not used among us, except in charter-parties of affreightments or articles of associations for privateering. *a* Styp-mannus part. 4. ch. 2. n. 80. pag. 383.

A special agreement is equally necessary to justify a deduction for the time during which a vessel is laid up for refitting or otherwise, from the term limited by the contract, unless, from the circumstances of the case, the laying up of the vessel be considered as a general average. The law would be the same as to demurrage occasioned by a fear of enemies or pirates.

SECTION III.

Of contracts for an entire voyage, with a designation of it, or limitation of time.

The ordinance has not provided for the case of money lent *for a limited time with a designation of the voyage,* but *(b)* says, that there, the voyage designated would be the principal object of the contract and the time merely accessory. It is just, he adds, that the borrower should arrive at the place of his destination, in order that he may be in a situation to pay the principal and interest. We presume that the time has been added, not as a period for the termination of the risk, against the lender, before the voyage is ended, but as a measure for the increase of interest, in proportion to the length of time beyond the period stipulated. Sect. 1. If there be a time limited and designation of the voyage. *b* Targa, ch. 33. not. 13. pag. 146.

The question is so decided in matters of insurance. " If the voyage be designated by the poli-

a art. 35.
lit. des
ass.
cy, the Insurer shall bear the perils of the whole
voyage: on condition, always, that if its duration
exceed the term limited, the premium shall be increased in proportion, but the insurer shall not be
bound to return any part, if it be less." (*a*)

b L. 6. ff.
de naut.
fœn.
On the first view of the subject, it appears that
the same rule should be extended to contracts of
maritime loan.   But 1. the law (*b*) decides, that
the lender does not bear the loss unless the ship perish within the time limited. *Si navis intra præs-
titutos dies periisset.* The ordinance does not militate with this general rule. It ought, then, to
have effect, under the modifications which I shall
here mention. 2. Legal presumptions are *stricti
juris :* the ordinance provides that if the voyage be
designated in the policy, the Insurer shall be pre-
pared to have undertaken the perils of the whole
voyage, for an augmentation of the premium; but
the ordinance has not established the same presumption, in cases of maritime loan, against the lender.
Therefore we cannot supply the omission. The
contract must contain some special clause on the
subject, or a clause indicating that the lender has
undertaken to bear the perils of the whole voyage.

For a
voyage
not excee-
ding six
months,
and pro-
rata if it
be longer
I have seen contracts of maritime loan, on a voyage out and home, at the rate of 12 per cent. (more
or less) *for a voyage not exceeding six months and
pro rata if it continue a longer time.* This signifies, that if the voyage continue for six months,
the 12 per cent. shall then be due to the lender,
and if it require a longer time, the interest shall
be increased in proportion. But if the ship perish, at any time during the voyage designated,
the lender forfeits all claim to the principal and interest even for the six months.

I have often seen contracts of maritime loan, for a voyage out and home, at *two per cent. a month.* In this case the interest is not due until the end of the voyage ; and the amount is regulated by the duration of the voyage. But if the ship perish, the lender has no claim.

For a voyage at 2 per cent. a month.

I lend a sum for the entire voyage. I stipulate for 12 *per cent.* for the first six months; and I add that *the interest for that time shall be due notwithstanding any accident which may occur subsequent to it.* The ship perishes after the period mentioned. (*)— May I demand interest for the first six months ? According to the principles which I have laid down, it would seem that my demand is not legal; for, if it be true that interest is but an accessary inseparable from the principal, it follows that the loss of the latter includes the loss of the former, and that such an agreement is illegal. But the contrary is the practice, and we can only justify it by the particular circumstances of each case.

Agreement, that the first six months shall be due notwithstanding any accident subsequent to that term.

First case. During the first six months, the ship arrives, for instance, in the West Indies, or has made several short voyages *en caravane,* in the Mediterranean. The borrower has made some profit which he might have secured on shore, and remitted a part of it in bills of exchange to pay the interest for the first six months. If he fail to fulfil his agreement, it is just that he should be compelled to do it, notwithstanding any subsequent accident ;— because, in this supposed case we find two sorts of voyages : the first, from the place of departure to that where it was lawful for the borrower to appropriate a part of his profits to the payment of the interest for the six months elapsed: the second, from the time of leaving the last place to the arrival at the place of destination. Here is a sort of *renewal or continuation of*

* See Marshal's observations on this case, 650.

V

the contract. And I think that the borrower could release himself from every obligation, by sending the amount of the principal and interest, on the expiration of the six months; which he could not do, if, instead of the stipulated clause, the contract was in the usual way. Such an agreement, not authorized by the Ordinance and inconsistent with the nature of the contract, is not proper. It ought to be restricted and modified as much as possible.*

Second case. If the ship perish after the expiration of the first term, but before she has arrived at any place where the borrower had intended to touch in his course, I believe he would be released from every obligation. A Farmer is not bound to pay rent for ground which has been carried away by the torrent and has produced nothing. (*a*)

a Targa, ch. 33, not. 14. pag. 147.

Valin, (*b*) says that " usurious lenders have invented a way of indemnifying themselves in a case " where the vessel does not return within the ordinary time, by stipulating, that, *if she do not return* " *by a certain period, they shall receive interest at* " *the rate of one half per cent. a month both on the* " *capital and the maritime interest.*" But since they are allowed to stipulate for any rate of interest that they think proper, I see no reason why they should be prevented from augmenting an interest already due, in a case where the vessel does not return within the time limited. By a contract of maritime loan of which I have spoken, (*c*) Lavabre, Doerner & company, stipulated for a maritime interest of 28 per cent, "*for the space of* 30 *months*, from the 30th Nov. 1776, and 1-2 per cent per month, *as well on the principal as the interest* for any time beyond the aforesaid 30 months." The legality of this, never was contested.

§. 2. Agreement that after a certain time the borrower shall pay 1-2 per cent. per month as well on the interest as on the principal

b art 2, h. t. pag. 5.

c Emerig Traité des assurances, ch. 13, sec. 16.

In fine, these and other cases which might be put, have not been foreseen by the Ordinance. They must be decided on general principles.

* Marshal, 640.

In the years 1777 and 1778 I saw contracts of maritime loan, on goods, to go to and from the French West India Islands. The interest was fixed at so much per month, with a clause, that in case of war the principal and the interest accrued should be sent from the Islands, in bills of Exchange. This clause is valid, because in case of war, we may suppose that the money was only lent on the outward voyage. But here I believe

§. 3. Agreement that in case of war the principal and interest due shall be transmitted in bills of exchange.

1. The bills ought to be at the risk of the lender, for whom the borrower acts only as an agent. His situation is not to be rendered worse, contrary to the natural order of things. It is enough if he pay the principal and interest at the time or place where the risk ceases ; *(a)* it is enough, if, with good faith and in consequence of orders to that effect, he convert this sum into Bills of Exchange, by the fate of which he is not to be affected.

a Infra. ch. 9. sec. 2.

2. In the case mentioned, as the money is presumed to have been lent only for the outward voyage, the interest, stipulated at so much per month, ceases when the vesssl arrives at the Islands.

I have never seen except in time of a war, a stipulation that in case of peace, the interest stipulated at so much a month shall be reduced to the usual course of the place, on the unexpired time. But if such a case were now to happen we should take as the period of peace, the cessation of hostilities and be guided by the ordinance of the 4th Febuary, 1783.(*)
reduced to the usual course of the place.

§. 4. Agreement that in case of peace the interest stipulated at so much per month shall be reduced to the usual course of the place.

* That Ordinance or rather Proclamation is merely for the purpose of fixing the time of the cessation of hostilities between Great Britain and France, graduated according to the different latitudes and parts of the world. It is such as issues in every maritime country at the end of every maritime war, and therefore unnecessary to be inserted in this translation.

SECTION IV.

Places of peril and change of the ship.

§. 1.
change
of the
voyage.
All that I have said in the *Traité des Assurances,* ch. 13. on the subject of the *route*, the *voyage* and the places of the perils will apply here.*

a Art. 11.
h. t. Styp.
part 4.
cap. 2. n.
105. pag.
585.Targ.
cap. 33.
not. 6.
pag. 142.
Kur. tit.
6. pag.
762.
The lender is not responsible for any loss which occurs out of the places designated in the contract, except in cases of deviation occasioned by necessity or the perils of the sea. *(a)* A voluntary deviation, discharges the lender from the consequence of any ulterior peril, although the ship return to her legitimate track.*(b)*

Locc. lib. 2. cap. 6. n. 9. pag. 994. Poth. n. 18. *b* vid. Emerig. Traité des Assurances, ch. 15. Sec. 16.

§. 2.
change of
the ship.
The lender is not answerable for a change of the ship without necessity. Losses occurring in any other ship than that which is designated in the contract, do not affect his rights. On this subject Pothier reports the following decision of our admiralty :

" A. lent to B. a certain sum for a voyage to the
" East Indies, on merchandize shipped on board
" the *Duc de Penthievre.* B. arrived at the Isle of
" France with his vessel, where he put the goods on
" board of another vessel called the *Pondicheri*, by
" virtue of an order from the governor of the Island,
" directing the captain to take it from him. He made
" a protest before a Notary, declaring that being obli-
" ged, by superior orders, to quit his vessel and put
" his goods on board of another, the perils, which
" A. had agreed to bear on the *Duc de Penthievre,*
" should be, hence forward, transferred to the *Pon-*
" *dicheri.* The *Pondicheri* was captured by the En-

* Marshal 392. 655.

" glish and the *Penthievre* arrived at her port. A.
" demanded his principal and interest. B. contend-
" ed in reply, that the risk had been transferred to
" the *Pondicheri* and produced a certificate from
" the East India Company, attesting that the gover-
" nor of the Isle of France had ordered the captain
" of the *Pondicheri* to take him on board. To this
" A. answered, that the certificate proved no more
" than that B. who could not go in the *Pondicheri*
" without an order from the governor, had obtained
" the order : but it did not prove that he had been
" obliged to go in her : that without necessity, B.
" could not, unless with the consent of A. change
" his situation and subject A. to the risk of the *Pon-*
" *dicheri*, when he had undertaken those of the *Duc*
" *de Penthievre.* By a sentence of the Admiralty
" 23d June, 1758, from which there was no appeal,
" B. was adjudged to pay the money."

But if the change of the ship be of necessity,
from the perils of the sea, the lender must bear the
risk of the substituted vessel. For instance, the
first vessel is taken for the service of the king, or is
declared unseaworthy, or is wrecked. The borrower, whose goods have been landed before the accident, may ship them or their returns in another vessel, at the risk of the lender. *(a)*   I ought to re- *a* Infrà.
mark that the additional freight, which may have ch. 11.
been paid to the substituted vessel, is a gross aver- 5. & Sec.
age which is chargeable to the lender ; and that then 3. §. 3.
the party comes within the provisions of the Declaration of 1779, art. 9.*

---

* This Ordinance is published at large at the end of the original of this work, 2d Emer : 625. But we think it sufficient to insert here by way of note the 9th art. referred
to by our author. It relates to the transhipment of merchandize in cases of *unavoidable necessity.*

Art. 9. In case the said merchandize should have been trans-
shipped on board of another vessel, the insurer shall run the
risque of the said merchandize until their landing at the place
of their destination, and shall moreover be obliged to bear (to

CHAPTER IX.

Of the Payment of Maritime monies.

a·Chap. 3.
Sec. 4.

I have already spoken *(a)* of the common legal interest which the borrower must pay after demand made. We shall now inquire in what manner, to whom, and at what time and place the sum lent and the maritime interest ought to be paid.

SECTION I.

Is a bottomry bill * negotiable ?

§. 1. Is a bottomry bill nego- tiable if made payable to order.

b Emerig. desass, ch. 18. sec. 3.

A policy of insurance is a negotiable instrument, when it contains a clause that the loss shall be paid to the bearer *without order or procuration.*(*b*) So it is with respect to bottomry bills if they are payable to *the order of the bearer.* Therefore they may be endorsed and delivered from one to another. Against the bearer of such a bill we cannot plead as a set off,

---

the discharge of the insured) the averages of the said goods, the charges of salvage, loading, storage and reshipment, together with the duties which shall have been paid, and the extra-freight, if there be any.

The ordinance is dated 17th Aug. 1779, and entitled " *Declaration of the King concerning Insurances.*"

The English law is similar. Marshal 656.

* We use the term *bottomry bill,* in this place, by way of example, as the novelty of the French term, *bill* of *gross adventure,* to an English ear, might probably subject us to a charge of innovation if we were to apply it. Yet there appears to be no valid objection to the incorporation of it into our legal language. It is so comprehensive as to include every instrument of writing which contains a contract of bottomry, respondentia, and every other species of maritime loan, and we know of no word of similar import.

a debt due from the original creditor himself, because in such a case, we must consider the endorsed bill, as if it had been drawn in favour of the bearer himself.

But if the bill had not been drawn *payable to order*, then the drawer would be entitled to the same exceptions or set off against the bearer, that he would have had against the original payee; because, in that case the endorsement has no other effect than the assignment of a mere *chose in action.*[*] It would be the same if the bill were not expressed to be *for value received* or *in merchandize*, because, in such a case, the endorsement is a naked authority to receive the amount.

The holder of a bottomry bill who has paid its value, becomes the owner of it. He incurs the maritime risks and the maritime profits belong to him.

§. 2. Nature and effect of this negotiation.

On the return of the ship, if the borrower be insolvent, the bearer of the bill is entitled to an action of guaranty against the endorser, in the same manner as on bills of exchange or negotiable notes. This doctrine is very well maintained by Casaregis, (a).

Guarantee in case of the insolvency of the debtor.

a disc. 55.

This guaranty extends no farther than the principal sums; *habetur regresssus contra girantem* † *ut*

---

* The phraseology of our common law appeared to us better calculated to convey, with perspicuity, the sense of this passage to an American reader, and it is therefore adopted in the text.

† *Girantem.* The meaning of this word had entirely eluded our research until it was proposed to a learned friend who seems to be never so happily engaged, as when he is unlocking the copious stores of his mind to the enquiries of the younger part of his profession. It is Italian *law-latin* and is derived from the

a in loc. cit. n. 2.

*valutam** *per eum receptam restituat. Casaregis.(a)* It also covers the cost of protest and common legal interest from the time of the protest : but not the maritime interest, for the endorsement is not a guaranty of the contract. In short, the guaranty here spoken of, would not take place, if the indorser should take the bill at his own risk and without recourse. This depends on the agreement of the parties.

SECTION II.

In what manner, at what time and in what place ought the money to be paid,

§. 1. The bill ought to be paid in money.

a Pothier, des obligations. n. 242 et 530

b 27th November 1779.

When the risk is ended the borrower must pay the principal and maritime interest in money. He cannot offer merchandize in payment. *(a)* If the contract was made in the West Indies or the Levant, to be paid in France, the money stipulated is valued in livres tournois. The Arrêt of the council of state, (*b*) concerning the fees of the consulate, established for the trade of the Levant and Barbary, enjoins " the deputies † to keep the accounts in French money. Therefore they must value the current money of the sea-port towns in livres tour-

---

Italian word *girare*, to draw, in the same manner as the English verb, to murder, is transformed into *murdrare* in our indictmens. *Girantem* therefore signifies *the drawer*.

* *Valutam*, the value, is also an Italian word latinized. But it may be understood with less difficulty than that which has just been explained.

† The deputies of the French Nation in the ports of the Levant are two respectable merchants, elected annually by the other French merchants residing within the same consulate.— They are assessors to the consul in his judicial functions, which in those countries he is permitted to exercise. They have also a variety of prerogatives and privileges which need not be detailed here.

nois, as well in paying as in receiving. And they shall establish this valuation on the course of ex.. change in their ports respectively and it shall be proved by the certificate of two known merchants *a* Emerig. nominated for that purpose by the Ambassador of Traité des Ass. the King at Constantinople and by the consuls and ch. 9. vice consuls in the other Islands. *(a)* sec. 8.

The borrower has received money on the goods or the vessel. It is but just, then, that a little time should be allowed after the arrival of the vessel, for the collection of the freight or to sell the merchan- dize, so that he may be able to fulfil his obligations. In Sweden, it is customary to allow twenty days and the legal interest does not commence until that time has elapsed. *Postquaim navis salva redict domum, mercatori indulgentur viginti dierum induciæ ad distrahendas merces, et conficiendam pecuniam, quam creditoribus suis solvat, unâ cum usuris. Quod si pecunia credita diutius maneat apud debito- rem, reliqui temporis post illos dies elapsos non am-* *b* Loccen- *plius maritimæ usuræ. Sed communes usitatæque* cenius, *solventur, quia tunc desiit esse periculum creditoris.* lib. cap. 6. n. 11. *(b)* I have seen contracts which allowed a delay of pag. 994. fifteen days and even a month.

If the contract do not provide for any days of grace *c* L. 186. I think a reasonable time should be allowed to the ff. de reg. jur. §. borrower, to enable him to raise funds : *nihil peti* 27. inst. *potest antè id tempus quo per rerum naturam per-* de inut. stip. *solvi possit.* *(c)*

I think that time should be allowed even if it be If it be stipulated, in the contract, that the payment shall stipulated that the be made immediately on the arrival of the vessel. ayment *Quod dicimas debere statim solvere, cum aliquo scili-* shall be made im- *cet temperamento temporis intelligendum est : necer-* mediately on the arrival.

Z

a L. 105 *enim cum sacco adire debet. (a). Quod dixi inconti-*
ff. de solut
et lib. L. *nenti, ita accipiendum cum aliquo spaco.(b)* In
135. § 2. all these cases, the judge has the power, according to
ff. de
verb. ob- equity and the circumstances of the case, to grant a
lig. certain delay, which without injuring the creditor,
b L. 21. ff. will enable the debtor to pay the debt,(*b*) saving the
de judic. common legal interest, which runs from the time
L. 2. ff. when the debt became due, and not merely from the
de re judi-
cata. L. time of action brought.
105. ff. de solut. L.2. ff. de legat. 1.

If the money was lent for the outward voyage or
for a limited time, the principal and maritime interest ought to be paid at the place where the stipulated risk ended, although the voyage be not com-
c supra ch. pleted.   Formerly the payment was made to a slave
1. Sect. 1. factor* as we find from the laws before cited *(c)*
At present it is made to the creditor or his appoint-
d Styp- ed agent. *Si in itum navis: accipiatur solutio eo loco*
mannus
part 4. *quo itur, vel à servo qui simul mititur, vel à factore*
cap. 2. *creditoris; si in reditum: accipiatur in portu, ex*
n. 90.
pag. 384. *quo quis solvit.(d)*

Risque of
money   If, at the place where the stipulated risk ends,
not de- there be no person to whom the principal and
manded
at the interest, can be paid, the borrower may make a
place of judicial deposit of it or carry it with him.   In the
payment.
e Locce- latter case, legal interest shall not be chargeable until
nius, lib 2 his arrival, but the money or effects which he em-
cap 6 n
10 & 11 barks, shall be at his risk *(e)* If, in order to fulfil
f Suprà his engagement, he voluntarily draws bills of ex-
ch. 8.
Sect. 3. change, they are on his own account, unless they
are drawn by the order of the creditor. *(f)*

An agreement that the bills of exchange drawn by
order of the creditor, should be at the risk of the borrower, would be inconsistent with the nature of the
contract and usurious: for it is sufficient if the borrower pay the principal and interest at the place

---

* It was usual then, to send a slave with the merchandize or
money, in order that he might demand the return of the loan at
the time or place stipulated for the expiration of the risk.

where the term expires, without permitting him to place himself in a worse situation.

As the borrower may apply to the judge of the §.4, competent place where the term expires, in order to be permitted judge mitted to make a deposit, so the other party may commence an action before him for what may be *a* Ordidue. The creditor may also sue in the court of admiralty nance of miralty of the place where the contract was made. 1673. tit. 12 art.18. *(a.)*

The *Ordinance de la Marine* does not authorize the Admiralty to condemn the borrower to pay the money, provisionally and notwithstanding an appeal.*

What is said in the Ordinance on the subject of Arbitration. arbitration does not apply to Maritime Loans. If tion. arbitrators be nominated, their sentence cannot be enforced by execution.

—————

SECTION III.

Of Prescription or Limitation of actions.

The statute of Marseilles, *(b)* speaks of adven- *b* lib. 3. tures shipped on a joint concern and of maritime chap. 25, partnerships. It decides that after the expiration pag. 402. of four years from the time of the return of the ship, the acting partner cannot be called

———

* In France, in most commercial cases, the court before which the suit is first brought, may order, by its judgment, that the money shall be paid provisionally, any appeal notwithstanding, the party to whom the money is paid giving security to refund, in case on an appeal the judgment shall be reversed. It seems that such provisional orders cannot be made in cases of Maritime Loans, as they are not among the enumerated cases for which this remedy is provided.

upon to account. But this limitation does not apply to maritime loans. The marine ordinance has
established none. The lender's right of action is
not barred until the expiration of thirty years. The
plea or exception given by the 48*th* art.(*a*) does not
apply to this contract.*

a tit. des
assuran-
ces.

If the bill be drawn payable to the order of the
lender and he negotiate it, the holder is obliged to
use diligence against the borrower, within the time
allowed by the ordinance of 1673, (*b*) counting from
the day the bill becomes due. After the expiration
of this time † the holder forfeits his right of action
against the endorser. In such a case, it is not considered as a contract of maritime loan, but merely as
a negotiable note.

b tit. des
lettres de
change,
art. 13.
and 32.

In respect to security, ‡ it is to be wished that it
were regulated by the rule established concerning
bills of exchange by the *Ordinance du commerce.* (*c*)
They are barred after three years, counting from the
day that they have become liable. But, until it is determined by a new ordinance, we must conform to
the common law, as it is laid down by M. Pothier,
(*d*)unless the money has been left in the hands of the
borrower by renewal, in which case the bail are discharged. (*e*)

c tit. 5.
art. 20.

d Traité
des oblig.
u. 671.

e Infrà
ch. 10.
sect. 1.

---

* There is no limitation of action against the original owner of property found derelict at sea, unless there be proof
of an intention to abandon wholly. *Bee's. Adm. dec.* 82.

† Five years.

‡ In France, when a Bill of Exchange is protested for *an acceptance*, the holder may compel the drawer and endorser to give
security for its payment when due ; but the securities must be
paid within three years after the bill become due, and they consequently become liable to pay the money, otherwise the Ordinance may be pleaded in the same manner as our statute of limitations.

CHAPTER X.

Of Security.

Nothing is more frequent than to see persons become security for others in contracts of maritime loan. If they have no personal interest to serve, they are very imprudent. It is true, they do not bear the perils of the seas, but they are responsible for the good faith of the borrower, who, in general possesses nothing ; and who, through misconduct or ill success, is often unable to fulfil his engagements. He who is wise will not be security for any one. *Non inscitè doctores nostri dixerunt, titulos de donationibus et fidejussoribus esse fatucorum hominum.(a)* [a] Cugas on the rubrick of the code. de precario.

Those who require security, are not free from solicitude, *propter fragilitatem cautionis :* as says the *Law* 66. §. 1. *ff. ad s. c. Trebell.* A poor debtor gives poor security. *Quem enim homo tenuis locupletem pro se fidejusorem inveniat?*

—◦—

SECTION I.

In general the security is bound by the same obligations as the borrower.

In general the security is bound by the same obligations to the lender, as the borrower himself, unless there is a particular clause to the contrary in the contract. (b) The security is bound to pay the principal and interest not only in case of the safe arrival [b] Pothier des oblig. n. 404. pag. 198. Casaregis disc. 63.

of the ship, but if she do not return,* as we find
from the decisions before reported (*a*). He is bound,
ipso jure to pay legal interest, from the time of
delay of payment. His body is liable to execution
in the same manner as that of the principal. He
may be arrested for the whole and directly, without
the benefit of apportionment or discussion : such
advantages are unknown in matters of commerce.

According to the arrêt reported by *Bezieut,* (*b*)
the joint debtor on a bottomry bill, is liable for the
costs adjudged against the other, although process
was issued only against the other. In short, the security comes under the jurisdiction of the Admiralty, even in the case where he alone is sued.(*c*)

But " those who have been security for money
lent at profit are discharged on the completion of
the voyage, if the creditor leave the principal in the
hands of the debtor, for another voyage *without their
consent. (d)* This renewal operates as a new contract, as to the security, according to the principles
laid down by *Soulatges,* (*e*) and *Boutaric*(*f*). The
latter author says, "the security is discharged, although the new contract be imperfect and insufficient to cancel the first obligation of the debtor.
As in the case of a renewal or tacit continuance of a
lease after the expiration of the stipulated term, and
other similar cases, where it is evident that the security is not bound."

By a bill of the 10th Oct. 1764, *Jean Gayole,* an
officer on board *la Vierge de la Garde,* capt. Mar-
cel Isoard, borrowed of *Francois Pascal,* the sum
of 400 liv. at a maritime interest of 10 per cent. on

---

* That is to say provided the *goods* on which the money was
lent are *saved,* or were secured on shore before the loss of the
ship. See the cases cited above by our authour, ch. 3, §. 3

the cargo of the ship, for a voyage from Marseilles to Genoa and return. *M. Jartroux* became security for the payment of the money, with maritime interest. Some months after, the vessel returned to Marseilles. *Gayole* paid *Francois Pascal* 40 liv. being the amount of the maritime interest, and sailed on a new voyage.

Pascal, not being paid his capital and accumulating interest, filed a petition in our admiralty on the 11th March, 1769, against *Gayole* and *Jartroux,* claiming the 400 liv. with maritime interest, and common legal interest since the delay of payment, deducting the 40 liv. which he had received. *Jartroux* plead that the money had been left by renewal and that by this act he was released from his security. *Pascal* denied that it had been left by renewal or continuation.

On the 5th May, 1769, a sentence was rendered, " condemning *Jean Gayole,* the defaulter, to the payment of the 400 liv. and maritime interest at the rate of 10 per cent. with common legal interest since the demand and costs, deducting the 40 liv. which had been paid. Execution against his body, after a stay of eight days. And as to *Jartroux,* he is ordered to adduce proof within eight days that the money was left in the hands of *Gayole* by renewal, for a new voyage, in failure of which" &c.

This proof was deducible from the petition of Pascal. He had received the maritime interest for the voyage from Genoa ; and now he demanded the principal and a maritime interest which could be due only in consequence of a renewal of the contract. The interlocutory judgment was therefore unnecessary and moreover the renewal was presumable from the lapse of more than four years and the subsequent voyages which the borrower had made.

Jartroux appealed from this sentence. It was reversed by an arrêt of the Parliament of Aix 18th June 1770, on the report of M. de Ramatuelle. The petition of *Pascal* against *Jartroux* was rejected and he was condemned to pay the costs.

SECT. II.

Is the security responsible for the fraud of the borrower?

I have lent a thousand crowns to Pierre, at maritime risque, upon your security. He loads his vessel with goods purchased with this money. He afterwards borrows other sums also at maritime risque of which he makes no use. The ship sails and is lost. *Notwithstanding the loss of the vessel*, the ordinance (*a*) authorises me to demand this money from Pierre because he has fraudulently borrowed more at maritime risque than the value of his interest.

a art 3. h.
t.

But Pierre is a fugitive. He is insolvent. I demand the money from you, for which you have become security. You reply, " as a security I am liable to all actions which result directly from the contract of maritime loan. But the vessel is lost, with every thing on board. If Pierrie had acted honestly you would not have been entitled to any action against him or me. You do not accuse me of being an accomplice in the fraud. Content yourself, therefore, with the penal action which the law allows against him: an action which is admitted *stricti juris* and should not be extended to another, and which in *odiam fraudis*, raises for your benefit from the bottom of the sea, a right which had been swallowed up by the waves. No plank remains for you after this shipwreck, but the person of the borrower, whom the law permits you to pursue, but not me, whom the accident has released from every obligation."

These objections are plausible; but they are at variance with the spirit of the contract of security. *a* ch. 19. *The Guidon de la Mer*,*(a)* allows an action against art. 8. *b* disc. the borrower and his pledges jointly, and such is 62, n. 37. the doctrine which *Casaregis* maintains.*(b)*

In the year 1749 *Jean Baptiste Boule* lent 3,000 Jean-Baptiste livres to captain V. upon the cargo of the ship Boule *L'Heureuse Marie*, upon the security of Jean-An- v. V. and toine Fille. *Jean-Antoine Fesquet* also lent 2,000 Jean-Antoine livres to the captain upon the same goods and with toine the same security. The ship perished in the British Fille channel. It was proved that the two sums borrowed 1753. by *captain V.* exceeded the value of his interest which amounted to only 2195 livres. Under the authority of *art. 3. Boule* filed a petition against *V.* and his security claiming the 3,000 livres. On the 4th December, 1751, he obtained a sentence against both V. and his security and on the 11th of June, 1753, this sentence was confirmed by an arrêt.

Encouraged by this decision *Jean Fesquet* de- Jean Fes-manded the amount of his loan. *Fille*, the security, quet v plead that the security is not liable for the fraud of same. his principal. *Fesquet* replied that the security was not only the guarantee of payment in case of safe arrival, but also of the validity of the contract. The ordinance,*(c)* does not affix a penalty properly so *c* art. 3. called; it annuls the contract against the borrower, h. t. who ought to restore the money loaned with common egal interest, and for this the security is answerble.

On the 8th of October, 1754, a sentence was rendered against *V.* and *Fille*, jointly for the sum

A A

borrowed with legal interest of 5 per cent. from the time it was received and costs and execution against the body. This sentence, being conformable to the arrêt already pronounced in favour of Boule, had the force of a definitive judgment (*nota*, maritime interest was not allowed, because the contract was not considered a maritime loan.)

Antoine
Bouvet
v
A and
Canelle,
1777.

There is a decision at variance with this. Upon the security of *M. Canelle, Antoine Bouvet* lent 1200 livres to captain *A*. on the cargo of the *Elizabeth* for a voyage *en caravane*.* The vessel was lost. It was proved that the captain had borrowed, from *Bouvet and others*, more than the value of his interest. *Bouvet*, relying upon the 3d art. claimed the money from *A*. and *Canelle*. On the 26th of August, 1754, a sentence passed by default, against them jointly for the sum demanded with interest and costs. *Canelle* appealed. On the 28th, February, 1777, an arrêt was pronounced, which "reversed the sentence, and by a new judgment, disregarding the petition of *Antoine Bouvet* of the 12th July, 1774, concerning *Antoine Canelle*, released the said *Canelle* from the court and its process, and condemned the said *Antoine Bouvet* to pay the costs, except on the default."

If the ship perish, he who has borrowed beyond his interest, is presumed to have had nothing at risk. This presumption, established by the ordinance, is *juris et de jure*. The contract is then declared null. It is therefore just that the security should be answerable and that he should pay the sum lent with legal interest: and the more so, because, in general, the security is the partner of the borrower. The important part of commerce which is carried on by means of the contract of maritime

---

* This term is explained *ante* ch. 8. Sect. 2 *in not*.

loan, would languish extremely, in consequence of the little confidence that is placed in seafaring persons, if the bond of the security were to be weakened by exceptions which are contrary to the spirit and nature of the contract. I am therefore of opinion that we should conform to the decision in the first of the two arrêts which I have reported.

SECTION III.

Of the joint obligation of the securities.

A captain borrowed, at bottomry, upon goods, the sum of 2,000 livres and one of his friends became his security. The goods were squandered. The borrower and his security became bankrupts and obtained a release by paying ten shillings in the pound. The lender having received 1,000 livres from the captain, applied to his security for the balance and was offered 500 livres. He refused to accept this sum and a controversy took place, in consequence of which merchants were chosen as arbitrators between them. This was in 1774. They decided that the offer of the security was legal. It was accordingly accepted, because it was conformable to the general opinion of the law, at that time in Marseilles.

In the numerous failures which took place in that year, the bearers of indorsed bills submitted to this practice, without difficulty. A single exception occurred.

Laurent D. drew a bill for 2421 livres payable to the order of Zacharie B. who endorsed it to the order of Antoine-Joseph and George A. They endorsed it to Pierre V. who passed it to Antoine

Bellon. The drawer and the three endorsers became bankrupts. D. by his composition* engaged
to pay 40; Zacharie B. 60; mess. A. 55; and V.
32 per cent. on their several debts. On the 28th
June, 1775, Bellon filed his petition in the consular
tribunal of Marseilles against the drawer and the
three endorsers, praying that they might be condemned *in solidum* to pay the sum due, relatively to
the whole amount of the bill and so as to effect the
full payment thereof.

On the 16th of March following, a sentence was
passed by which the drawer and endorsers were
condemned to pay "the aforesaid sum of 2421
livres in the proportions of their respective divi-
dends, with interest, deducting, nevertheless, successively, the sums which Bellon may have received from the said D. B. A. and V."

By this sentence, it was decided that by virtue of
the action *in solidum*, Bellon was entitled to claim
from the assignees of each of the four bankrupts,
but that he could not pretend to a dividend from
each on the whole of his original demand, and until
it were fully satisfied, but only the balance which remained due to him, after deducting successively
the payments which he had previously received.

Bellon appealed from this sentence to the Parliament of Aix. He contended that the borrower and
the several endorsers were indebted to him *in solidum ;* that each and all were bound to pay the whole

* The French bankrupt law turns upon a very simple principle. Whatever composition is agreed upon by a certain majority of the creditors in number and value with the debtor, is
made binding upon the rest of the creditors by a rule of court,
provided there is no fraud.—The law in its details consists only
of provisions to direct the mode of enforcing those agreements,
to prevent fraud therein and punish it when discovered.

sum: that the bill must exist in its integral state until the whole was paid: that the sums which each of them should pay, should be simply *on account*, without prejudice to his rights: in a word, that he was entitled to demand of each set of the assignees a dividend on the whole sum originally due, and that the original claim should exist against each until the debt were entirely satisfied. He added that the question was new, that it had never been discussed by any authour and that it ought to be decided upon principles of justice.

I appeared as counsel for the defendants. I contended that the usage of Marseilles had always been to allow the bearer of paper to sue each person for no more than the balance actually due: from which it followed that if the creditor had received 50 per cent. from one debtor, his debt being reduced to a moiety, he could claim no more than the remaining half from the next debtor; and so on as to the others. For example; I hold a bill of 2,000 livres and I will suppose, for the sake of facility in the calculation, that the drawer and each of the three endorsers have declared a dividend of 50 *per cent.* I apply, first, to the drawer, who pays me - - *L* 1,000

Next, to the first endorser, who
pays me 50 *per cent.* on the balance due me - - - - 500
The second in the same manner - 250
And the third - - - 125

_____
L 1,875
I am then a loser of - - - 125
_____
L 2,000

Instead of applying, first, to the drawer, and then to the first, second and third endorsers, I may select either of them, by virtue of the action *in soli-*

dum. The operation, though complicated as to them, remains simple and unique as to me, without being altered with respect to them, who, in conse-, quence of their respective guarantees, will not be really bound for more than the proportion which they would have paid if things had remained in their original state.*

a Savary, Parere 4. 48. 90.
b art. des lettres de change, ch. 16.
c vid. Su-prà.
d on the 12th art. tit. des lettres de change.
e on the 33d art. of the same title.
Traité du con-trat de change, ch. 5. n. 159. tom. 2. pag. 159.

After having thus stated the question I observed that, formerly, the bearer was obliged to make his election among the different sets of assignees(*a*) that this error was refuted by *Dupuy,(b)* and corrected by an arrêt of the Parliament of Paris, of the 18th May, 1706, reported in the Journal des Audiences. I admitted that, before that arrêt, the actual question never had been agitated; but I said that it had not escaped *Dupuy(c)* nor *Boutaric(d)* nor *Jousse, (e)* nor *Pothier,(f)* all of these writers agree that after suing one, the others cannot be sued but successively for the balance remaining due. Yet I would admit that the question had not been discussed by these authours and I would endeavour to supply the omission by these remarks;

1. The *concordats*† of a bankrupt, subscribed by three fourths of his creditors, has the effect of a law, to which the others are obliged to submit. The ordinance has given this effect to it, for the publick good. The smaller number must submit to the fate which the majority has agreed upon and each creditor not otherwise secured by judgment or mortgage must support the loss agreed upon by the general consent. The bearer of a bill is legally presumed to

---

* That is to say ; if they had not become bankrupts they would have owed no more than the balance ; having become such, their assignees owe no more than a dividend on that balance.

† Deed of compromise or settlement with creditors.

renounce a part of his claim to each joint debtor. This renunciation is implied. It results from the nature of a concordat to which he must submit.

2. I am a creditor only for what is really due to me and not for that which has been paid. Having many endorsers, the action *in solidum* enables me to call upon each of them; but in so doing I must be guided by two laws: the one resulting from the nature of the subject, the other prescribed by royal authority. According to these laws I act, and in claiming from each debtor, I can exact only the sum really due. My bill is for 2,000 livres. I apply to the first creditor, whose *concordat* is fixed at 50 *per cent.* and I receive 1,000 livres because he owes me 2,000 livres Upon receiving this sum my bill is reduced to 1,000 livres. I can claim no more than this sum from the second, by the action *in solidum*. His *concordat* is also 50 *per cent.* and I receive from him 500 livres being the moiety. There remains but 500 livres and by the same reasoning, I receive from the third debtor 250 livres. By this means, my action *in solidum* produces all that it is capable of effecting according to the nature of things and the law. I sued each person because I was the creditor *in solidum* of each bankrupt. But each creditor is only bound to pay what remains due in proportion to his *concordat*.

This argument was refuted with equal spirit and energy by a *consultation* of M. M. Simeon the father, and Pascalis, advocates of Bellon, and by the *consultations* of M. M. Aubrey, Frouchet and le Gouve advocates of the Parliament of Paris.

The opinion of M. de Castillon, attorney-general, was in favour of Bellon and a reversal of the sentence. But by an arrêt of the 18th June, 1776, on the report of M. de Bellon, in the great Hall of the Parliament, it was confirmed with costs.

The same question was then under debate in the Parliament of Paris, in consequence of certain bills of exchange drawn by M. and endorsed by L. They had become bankrupts and obtained a release from their respective creditors.

By a singular coincidence of circumstances the Parliament of Paris decided directly contrary to that of Aix on the same day. It was there decided that the bearer of a bill had a right to demand the whole sum from each creditor, until it was paid.

Bellon appealed to the council of state* and obtained from the king the following arrêt.

" Having heard the report of M. Moreau de Beaumont, member of the royal board of trade, the king in council, having regard to the aforesaid petition, has reversed and doth reverse the aforesaid arrêt of the Parliament of Aix of 18th June, 1776, and all its consequences. And in so doing, has examined the demands and contestations, upon which the said arrêt was passed, with all their circumstances. Has ordered and does order that the parties shall proceed in his council upon their demands and contestations in the manner indicated in the ordinance to be determined according to right. Done in the king's council of state, held at Versailles, the 24th February, 1778.
　　　　　　　Signed,
　　　　　　　　　Huguet de Montaran."

Another arrêt was passed on the 23d October, 1783, which rejected the petition in opposition, that had been filed by Zacharie B. and the others.

------

* Before the French revolution, the king's council of state was a court of revision, in important cases, as the House of Lords is in England.—Its jurisdiction in civil cases is now supplied by the *Cour de Cassation.*

Thus the question was decided in favour of the holders of paper. Each of the joint debtors owes the whole sum. The claim is indivisible against any one. *Promittentes singuli in solidum tenentur. In utrâque enim obligatione una res vertitur.*(a) The bankruptcy of the joint debtors cannot affect the individuality of the debt, which does not cease to be the same against each person and which preserves its entire existence until it is fully discharged.*

a §. 1. inst. de duobus reis.

---

* The same rule appears to be settled in England, in equity as well as at law, that a creditor who has several securities for the same debt, may prove the whole of it against each of his debtors who are bankrupts, and receive a dividend from each on the whole sum, so, however, that he receives but one satisfaction. See Cooper's Bankrupt Law 267—and the cases there cited.

B B

CHAPTER XI.

Of the extinction and nullity of the contract of maritime loan.

In maritime loans we recognize two kinds of nullity: the first, when the contract contains some internal defect, which makes it illegal in its very commencement; and the other, when it becomes void by the loss of the things upon which the loan was made.

The latter does affect the existence of the contract considered in itself. It releases the borrower from his personal obligation, by reducing the contract to the value of the portion which may have been saved. This is a condition which operates as a release of the borrower who is only obliged to pay in case of the safety of his property. We may say, that, as to certain effects, the *nullity* here spoken of, is similar to abandonment in cases of insurance.

SECTION I.

Comparison of art. 11. 16. 17. *h. t.*

According to the 11th art. "all contracts of maritime loan shall become void upon the loss of the thing upon which the loan was made, provided it happened by accident, within the time and place of the risk."

The 16th art. directs that lenders shall contribute to general and not to simple average or particular damages, if there be not an agreement to the contrary.

The 17th adds, that "in case of wreck, the contract shall always be reduced to the value of the goods saved."

There is no doubt that the contract becomes void by the loss of the ship on the voyage. "Such is the nature of the contract of maritime loan, that if the thing upon which the loan is made, perish, by accident, the contract is of no effect and the lender can claim nothing. This is what is meant in the 11th art. where it is declared that the contract shall be void in this case. It is also the common law of the nations of Europe."(a)

§. 1. If there be an entire loss? a Valin ibid. pag. 12. Cleirac, sur le Guidon, ch. 18. art. 2, pag. 331.

If there be a general average, and the thing upon which the loan was made be not wholly lost, the lender contributes to it instead of the borrower. This preserves the contract in its full force, and the borrower is obliged to fulfil his engagement, without being allowed to complain, because the gross average does not affect him. This will hold, however, where the original value of the borrower's property does not exceed the sum borrowed. But, for example, if my goods were worth 3,000 livres and I had borrowed 1,500 livres, the average would be borne equally by the borrower and myself, and if my part which was not lent was insured, my proportion of the average would be paid by the insurers.(b)

§. 2. If there be a general average? b Supra. ch. 7. sect. 1. §. 2.

Simple average does not affect the contract; and not being any obstacle to the safe navigation of the vessel, it is borne by the borrower if there be no particular stipulation to the contrary.(c) "The

If there be a particular average. c Supra, ch. 7.

sect. 1. §. 1.

condition of the contract of maritime loan, and the
obligation of the borrower which it contains, exist,
when the thing on which the loan is made, remains
on board during the whole term, without being captured or lost, *whatever damage they may suffer
from mere accidents of vis major.* And the borrower
is obliged, in this case, to pay the whole sum lent,
with maritime interest, without claiming any deduction on account of the deterioration which his goods
may have suffered."(*a*)

But in case of wreck or any other accident of *vis
major,* the contract is void and is reduced to the
value of the things saved. *M. Pothier,(b)* very
well observes, that the case of wreck is only mentioned in the 17th art. by way of an example. Therefore when a capture, ship-wreck, foundering,
stranding, arrest of princes, &c. takes place, it is
a legal total loss: there remains nothing but the
salvage. The personal obligation of the borrower is
extinct; the lender has nothing but an action *in rem*
on the salvage and *the contract is reduced to the value
of the effects saved.*

Opinions
of Valin
and Po-
thier.
c on art.
11. h. t.

M. Valin observes(*c*) that "from this article it
does not follow that if the loss be not total the contract exists integrally. The reason is that he who
is bound to support the loss, when it is entire,
bears a proportion when it is less. Thus" he adds
" if it be a moiety or a third, the contract is redu-
cible to that proportion. This is so just, that a stipulation to the contrary would be usurious and
therefore void." (But according to the ordinance,
if the partial loss do not proceed from gross average
or *vis major,* it must be borne by the borrower if
there be no stipulation to the contrary.)

M. Pothier explains himself in a manner less equivocal. "We have seen," says he, "that the arri-

val of the thing upon which the loan was made, whatever damage it may have suffered, by what accident soever of *vis major*, preserves the obligation of the borrower who must pay the sum lent and the maritime interest. What if only a part of the thing return and the remainder has been lost or captured ? as, for example, if the vessel has been pillaged by pirates who take away only a part of the cargo ? In such cases the condition applies only to what is saved and the contract is void as to the remainder." The authour here alludes to cases of *vis major*, the effect of which is to convert into salvage all that escapes the accident.

But if the goods of the borrower had been entirely landed before the accident, the contract would not be affected provided the goods or their proceeds could be laden on board of another vessel. The change of the ship would then be at the risk of the lender.*(a)*

§. 4. If the thing had been landed before the accident.

a Vid. sect. 3. §. 3. of this chapter, and also Suprà. ch. 8. sect. 4. § 2.

If the borrower cannot find another vessel in which to ship the goods or their returns, he becomes released from responsibility, by rendering an account of the articles saved in the place where the goods are landed. Vid. infra. sect. 3. §. 3. where I shall again speak of the arrêt in the case of Armelin.

In cases of insurance on goods out and home if they are landed before the wreck, the insurers are answerable for the returns laden on board another vessel. But if the insured could not find any other vessel to lade his goods, I think he could not require a reduction of more than one third of the premium ; for we cannot abandon to the insurers any other goods than those which were on board at the time of the accident. The decision pronounced by the arrêt in the case of the Armelin is no argument

a Vid. Emerig. Traité des ass.

against the insured, whose privileges are much less extensive than those of the borrower.*(a)* ch. 12. sect. 16. ch. 13. sect. 8. §. 3. and ch. 17. sect. 8. §. 2.

If the effects on board at the time of the accident, were worth less than the sum borrowed, *b* ch. 13. sect. 8. §.

If the effects which were on board at the time of the accident were worth less than the sum borrowed, the contract would still exist as to the surplus.* It was so decided by a sentence of our admiralty, 17th May, 1776, in favour of Simon Gilly, which I have reported in my Traité des assurances.*(b)* This sentence was confirmed by an arrêt of the 16th July, 1779, on the report of M. de Perier.*(c)*

3. tom. 2. pag. 42. *c* Journal du Palais de Provence pour l'année, 1779, by Me. Janety, pag. 394. Vid. infrà, ch. 12. sect. 2. §. 3.

§. 5 Unseaworthiness or stranding. *d* Vid. Suprà. ch. 3.

If the effects of the borrower are landed in consequence of the innavigability of the ship, and he cannot provide another ship for them, they are to be considered as *goods saved* to the value of which the contract must be reduced.*(d)*

sect. 3. pag. ch. 8. sect. 4. §. 2. and infrà sect. 3. §. 3.

If they are shipped in another vessel, the risk of the lender is transferred with them; but in such a case, if, after the accident, the goods decay or deteriorate in consequence of the delay, either on shore, in the new vessel or otherwise, so as to be less in value than the amount of the loan and interest, I believe the lender would be obliged to bear the loss: because the contract is broken by *vis major*.

It is the same of a vessel which is thrown on rocks and set a-drift. If the average paid be so great as to

* It must be understood that there was originally on board goods to the value of the sum borrowed, and that a portion of them was landed at some time previous to the accident. The case cited does not support the position without this limitation. If the borrower had not shipped to the amount of the loan, the lender could demand only legal interest for that part which was not employed in the voyage and exposed to its perils.

put it out of the power of the lender to fulfil his engagement, the deficiency must be borne by the lender, according to the spirit of the declaration of 1,779.

SECTION II.

Right of the lender to the effects saved.

It follows from what has been observed in the preceding section, that the personal action against the borrower is barred by accidents arising from a *vis major.* * Nothing remains for the lender but an action *in rem* against the things saved and the action *negotiorum gestorum* against him who has managed or taken care of it, and in whose possession it may be. The lender may pay himself, from the effects saved, both his principal and interest, if they be sufficient. But if they are not, he has no recourse against the person. §. 1. Nature of the action which the lender has against the effects saved.

M. Pothier,(a) asks "whether under the 17th art. the borrower must pay maritime interest on the sum to which the goods saved amount; and he replies in the negative." For when the ordinance says " *the contract shall be reduced to the value of the goods saved,* the term *contract* comprehends all the obligations which it contains, the stipulation to pay the sum lent and also that of maritime interest. All these obligations are reduced to the value of the effects. For all that may be due to him, the lender can demand only the value of the effects saved and nothing more." Is the interest due in proportion to the thing saved. *a* n. 48.

---

* The case of *Jones,* vs. *the schooner Massachussetts,* was a suit on a bill of lading of goods at the *Havanna* to be delivered in Charleston. They were delivered, but they had sustained damage in the latter port. This was held not a subject of admiralty jurisdiction. *Bee's Adm. dec.* 116.

And I ought to add that he can demand this value only from the person in whose hands the goods may be, who has preserved them for account of the concerned.

The effects saved are pledged to the lender.

From the moment of the accident, the lender is seized, of right, of the effects saved. He has a special lien upon them for the payment of his debt, saving the freight and salvage.

Lien on the freight.

a Pothier n. 52. Traité des assurances ch. 17. sect. 9. quest. 1.

If the money was lent upon the hull, the lien of the lender embraces not merely the wreck of the ship, but also the freight on the merchandize saved. *(a)* Nota. The subject of liens which is very extensive, shall be discussed in the following chapter.

Abandonment is not necessary.

b Valin art. 13. h. t.

In order to relieve himself from his engagement, it is not necessary that the borrower should abandon. The loss by *vis major, ipso jure* releases him from the personal action which flows from the contract.(*b*) All that takes place after the accident, principally concerns the lender, whose right of action against the borrower ceases, unless he himself has recovered the goods or has been in fault.

Apportionment between the insurer and lender.

c ch. 17. sect. 12.

In my treatise on insurance (*c*) I have spoken of the division of the effects saved between the insurer and the lender.*

---

* There our authour lays it down as a rule that there can be no apportionment between the lender and the insurer, but that the former must be preferred. He adds that neither this doctrine nor the opposite one are founded on the principles of justice, but that it is a point on which the law may arbitrarily decide. 2. Emer. 236. But we think differently. For the insurer has an evident interest in the preservation of the thing insured, and money lent for its preservation, as for instance, money lent on bottomry for the repairs of a ship insured, operates for the be-

The borrower can claim nothing from the effects Appor-tionment between the bor-rower and lender.
saved until the lender be wholly satisfied. The or-
dinance establishes nothing on this point. The
spirit of the ordinance is opposed to it, for the creditor never comes into apportionment with his
debtor on the thing which is the pledge for the pay- *a* Salgado Laby-
ment of the debt. *Contentio super prælatione non* rinth. cre-
agitur inter creditorem et debitorem; sed inter dit. part. 1. cap.
creditores ipsos.(a) 16. n. 23.
pag. 143. and part 3. cap. 3. n. 59. pag. 379.

For instance, the goods which I
shipped, were valued at *L* 6,000.
I had borrowed at risque - - *L* 3,000
On a maritime interest of 15
per cent. - - - - - - 450
—————
L 3,450
—————

The ship is lost. The nett produce of the goods
saved amounts to 3,450 livres. The whole of this
sum belongs to the lender and I can claim no part of
it: because the effects saved are pledged to the
creditor and all beyond the amount borrowed is lost.
This is the true sense of the 17th art. h. t. and the
opinion of Pothier, who very properly refutes that
of Valin. *Nota.* The debtor cannot divide with
the creditor to his prejudice; but in some cases the *b* Suprà sect. 1.
creditor may demand an apportionment with the §. 2.
debtor.*(b)*

nefit of the underwriters, and the lenders of such money ought
to be preferred. Indeed the same reason will not apply in
cases where the money lent at maritime r sque, was borrowed
for the purpose of purchasing goods which are afterwards insured. Still it may be said that without that money, the subject matter of the contract of insurance would not have existed.
But ought not the insurers to be told previous to making the
insurance, that the goods have been bought with money taken
up at risque?

C c

M. Pothier,(*a*) observes that if the loan "be made only on a part of the cargo, as on two thirds or three fourths, the lien extends only to that proportion of the effects which are preserved from wreck. The contract is reduced, not to the whole, but to that proportion, and the remaining third or fourth belongs to the borrower, free from any claim, or if the surplus is insured, it should be abandoned to the underwriters." This distinction did not escape M. *b* art. 11. Valin.(*b*) It flows from true principles.

SECTION III.

Does the contract become void by the ill success of the voyage?

§. 1. General observations. In the contract of insurance, an abandonment cannot be made but in cases of a loss by *vis major*. Every other damage is considered as an average, which is regulated between the parties. By this means, the law provides for the real interest of the insured, and gives every one his due.

The borrower does not appear to have been treated in so favourable a manner, since he is obliged to bear simple average or particular damages. But is he exonerated from the payment of the principal and maritime interest, only where there is an entire loss of the thing upon which the loan was founded? Shall there be no indulgence, if the voyage be lost by any other accident than the *vis major* provided *c* tit. des against in the 46th art?(*c*) I borrowed a sum with assurances. which I purchased a small adventure and shipped it for a certain port. The fear of enemies or something else obliges the vessel to return: am I bound to pay the whole principal and maritime interest, although the voyage is frustrated and the goods disembarked are not worth half the first cost ?

This case is not provided for in the ordinance. The omission must be supplied by calling to our aid the application of general principles. The object of the contract is, that the vessel shall reach some specified place, where the borrower may sell his merchandize, purchase returns, and make such a voyage, as will enable him to comply with his engagements. It is only on his *successful return* that he has promised to pay the principal and interest. The accident renders this successful return impossible : therefore the *object* has not been accomplished, the condition is not fulfilled, the contract cannot exist in its original state and ought, necessarily, to be rescinded.

If, by accident, the voyage be broken up before it is commenced, I believe that the sum borrowed ought to be returned, without entering into any modifications, which are of no use but to occasion law-suits. The maritime interest is not due and common legal interest is due only from the time of demand and refusal. The doctrine of M. Pothier,(*a*) may be applied to this case.

§. 2. Relinquishment of the voyage before its commencement.

a n. 39.

If, by accident of *vis major*, the voyage be broken up, after the commencement of the risk, without a possibility of preventing it, by a change of the ship or otherwise, I think the contract would be void, except as to the amount saved ; upon which the lender would have a lien for his principal, maritime interest and damages. I have already reported,(*b*) the arrêt of the 28th June, 1765. *Jean Joseph Marseilles*, gave, by way of maritime loan, the use of

Relinquishment after the voyage is commenced.

b Suprà ch. 5. sect. 4. §. 2. pag, 489.

divers kitchen and table utensils, valued at 1043
livres, to *M. Pinel*, who promised him 110 *per
cent.* maritime interest. The ship, being intimi-
dated by enemies, returned to Toulon. Our admiralty decreed that the whole maritime interest
amounting to 1,247 livres should be paid to the
lender. The arrêt reversed this sentence. But, as
Jean-Joseph Marseille was obliged to receive the
utensils in the same condition as they were when returned and to pay the premium of insurance which
had been effected for his account, the Parliament,
by way of indemnity directed the amount of the
premium to be paid by the borrower and that the
lender should pay the costs. The contract was considered as void by the non-performance of the legal
condition; and the sum adjudged to *Jean-Joseph
Marseilles* was given more as a compensation for the
use of his utensils, than as a portion of the stipulated
maritime profit.

If the vessel, in consequence of an accident, never returns.   If money be lent upon the cargo, to go and return,
and, in consequence of being rendered unfit to navi-
gate or other *vis major*, the ship do not return, and
no other can be provided for the goods which have
been landed, or their returns, the contract is void.
The borrower then becomes the mandatary of the
lender and has full power to dispose of the effects
saved for the account of the lender, in order that he
may be re-imbursed. The question was decided in
this manner by an arrêt of the 30th June, 1761.(*a*)
La Vierge de la Garde arrived at Cayenne. *Margarel* landed his goods. The vessel was then declared
unseaworthy. *Armelin* demanded payment of his
bottomry bill. *Margarel*, for whom I was counsel,
replied that he was not obliged to pay the loan, but
upon his safe return: that he had promised an interest of 100 *per cent.* under the expectation of being
able to ship the returns at Cayenne : but, in consequence of the ship being declared unseaworthy, he

a Vid. ch. 3. sect. 3.

had been obliged to convert the returns into royal paper, which had depreciated in value. The Parliament of Aix condemned *Margarel* to pay the principal and interest, not in money, but in the same bills which his sales had produced. By this, it was decided that as the vessel did not return, in consequence of an accident, the contract was broken; and that *Margarel* became the factor and legal mandatary of *Armelin*, as to the goods landed. But if the borrower, having it in his power to ship them in another vessel, preferred disposing of them, he voluntarily broke the voyage, and ought to pay the whole loan with maritime interest. Thus it was decided by the arrêts and judgments reported *d. loco.* See also what I have said suprà. ch. 7. sect. 1. §. 4. ch. 9. sect. 2. §. 1.*

The contract ought not to be affected by the ill success of the speculation, occasioned by the particular juncture of affairs or the badness of the merchandize. The lender is not answerable for such events because they are perils of the land; this subject I have already treated upon.(*a*) If the contract of maritime loan, was in the nature of a partnership we should regard the good or bad success of the speculation; but the action *pro socio* has no relation with that which flows from *pecunia trajectitia.* As I have more than once observed, they are contracts, which are different in their nature and each is governed by laws peculiar to itself. Traité ass. ch. 12. sect. 47.

§. 4. If, owing to particular occurrences the speculation of the borrower is not successful.

a Suprà ch. 7. sect. 2. §. 4. ch. 9. sect. 2. §. 1, and Emerig.

* Money was lent on a bottomry bond, conditioned that if the vessel should perform the voyage, the money should be paid in twenty days after her arrival; if she should be lost through the perils of the seas, or by fire, or by the enemies of the United States, the bond to be void. The vessel was captured by a British cruizer, and condemned as lawful prize: upon appeal, the condemnation was reversed, and full compensation received by the owner, for vessel, cargo and freight, by virtue of an award of the commissioners under the treaty of November, 1794. It was held that the obligee could not recover in an action of debt brought on the bond. 3. Tyng's Mass. Rep. 443.

CHAPTER XII.

Lien of the lender upon the effects at risk.

Whether it be owing to the difference between our usage and the Roman law or to the *ordinance de la Marine* having omitted to develop several essential points, there is a considerable difficulty here, which can be removed only by the application of the common law. " For it is a certain maxim, that a lien, never takes place without an express law to authorize it; and another rule, not less general, is, that liens, of every sort, are regarded with a jealous eye, because they are prejudicial to third persons. It is for this reason that they are never implied. It is always necessary that there should be a formal obligation executed which produces a conventional lien, or an express law which creates a legal lien, *a* Dup- otherwise there is no lien, nor can there be by any lessis, construction or implication; *neque enim tacitas hy-* tom. 1. pag. 687. *pothecas sine lege fingimus.*"*(a)*

" If we attend to principles we shall find that there is no hypothecation or lien without a contract in writing *b* M. le expressly granting the same. Other contracts cre- Camus, ate actions: but *actions*, in themselves, do not on the create liens, until judgment, and then, only from the art. 183. de la day it is rendered : excepting in cases where the Coutume de Paris law gives a tacit lien, as in actions against guardians, n. 23. &c.*(b)*

Liens are *stricti juris.* They cannot be extended from one case to another. Respecting them we cannot argue by deduction or analogy. The lien must be created by the law itself. *Privilegia, cum sint stricti juris, nec extendi possunt de re ad rem,* ^{a Leprestre, cent.} *nec de personâ ad personam.(a)*

^{1. ch. 31.}

de pignor. lib. 4. quœst. 21. n. 44. pag. 372   Ansaldus, disc. 26. n. 35. ^{pag. 3.}
Dernusson, de la subrogation, ch. 3. n. 17. and 52. ^{Merlinus,}

If the thing which is the subject of the lien be ^{b L. 8. ff. quib.} extinct, the lien is lost : *re corporali extinctâ, pig-* ^{mod.} *nus hypothecave perit.(b)* ^{pign. Salgado, de}

part. I. cap. 43. n 14 pag. 324. Negusantius. part. 6. memb. 3. n. 9. pag. ^{labyr.}
574. Merlinus, de pign. lib. 5. tit. 5. quœst. 34. pag. 602. ^{cred.}

SECTION I.

View of the Roman laws concerning liens on the ship and cargo.

Among the Romans, he who lent money to purchase, build, repair, or rig a ship, had a lien on the ship, as a security for his debt. *Qui in navem extruendam vel instruendam credidit, vel etiam emendam, privilegiam habet.(c)* But this was ex- ^{c L. L.} clusively personal. It was only good by way of ^{26. and 34. ff. de} preference against simple contract creditors and had ^{reb. auth.} no effect against those who were secured by express ^{judic.} hypothecations. *Eos qui acceperunt pignora, cum* ^{d L. 9. c.} *in rem actionem habeant, privilegiis omnibus, quæ* ^{qui potior inpign.} *personalibus actionibus competunt, præferri cons-* ^{ibiq. Cujas and} *tat.(d)* ^{Godefroy.}

^{Stypmannus, part.}
n. 18. pag. 411. Loccenius, lib. 3. cap. 2. n. 2. pag. 1012. Vinnius, pag. ^{nus, part.}
100. and 233. Scotanus, pag. 393. ^{4. cap. 5.}

Kuricke, in his celebrated questions,(e) contends ^{e quœst.} that the Roman laws, gave an absolute hypotheca- ^{13. pag. 866.} tion to him who lent money to purchase, build, repair or rig a vessel. But this authour, perhaps, had no other design than to adapt the texts which he cites to modern customs.

I ought to remark that according to the Roman law, if one among those who held hypothecations on the ship, furnished money for her repairs, or to purchase provisions during the voyage, he was preferred to the others, because he preserved the common pledge. *Hujus enim pecunia salvam fecit totius pignoris causam.(a)*

a L L. interdum 5 and 6. ff. qui potior in pign. habeat.

The same law prevailed in favour of one who held an hypothecation on the cargo or furnished money to pay average or freight. He was preferred to the others who had similar liens because the common pledge would have been lost without his assistance. *Si quis in merces sibi obligatas crediderit, vel ut salvæ fiant, vel ut naulum exsolvatur, potentior erit; licet posterior sit: nam et ipsum naulum potentius est.(b)*

b L. 6. § 1. ff. eod.

If the aid was furnished by a third person, who had no previous lien on the ship, he would have only a personal privilege and be excluded by the actual holders of hypothecations. This is the true sense of the famous law *interdum ;* * as any one may be convinced by comparing the different texts of the law which have a reference to it. This is also the opinion of the authours already cited, to whom may be added *Ansaldus,(c) Vinnius(d)* and *Donnellus.(e)* The last writer has left nothing to be said upon the subject.

c disc. 90. n. 14.
d quest. lib. 2. cap. 4.
e de pignor. pag. 580.

---

* Interdum posteriori potior est priori: utputa, si in rem istam conservandam impens sem est, quod seguens credidit; veluti si navis fuit obligata, et ad armandam eam vel refriciendam ego credidero. Dig. Lib. XX. Tit. 4. Qui potiores in pign. l. 5.

SECTION II.

French laws concerning liens on the ship and cargo.

In many instances we have adopted the texts which have just been cited, as shall presently be seen. The *personal privilege*, mentioned in the Roman law, is unknown in our jurisprudence. Every privilege includes a tacit and exclusive lien, at least as to the thing which is the subject of it. *Livoniere,(a)* says that "a common hypothecation is governed by the date of the contract and that a privilege is regulated by the degree of favour due to each particular claim, and is preferred to common hypothecation, though prior in time.*

§. 1. The law *interdum* adopted among us.

a Regle du droit, ch. 4. sect. 1. pag. 439.

It is not doubted that ships are personal proper-ty.(*b*)† From which it follows, that on the gene-

Can the ship be charged with hy-

b Cleirac pag 399. n. 11. Furgole, on the ordinance of 1731. art. 23. pag. 100. Valin art. 1. tit des Navires, &c.

pothecation.‡

* To explain this : suppose that A. builds a ship and gives an actual moitgage to B. thereby to secure a debt due to him : afterwards the ship sails on a voyage, is damaged by storms and puts into port to repa r : C. furnishes money for the repairs, which gives him a lien at the French law, on the vessel even without an express hypothecation.—On the vessel arriving home, his lien will be preferred by *privilege* to the prior actual mortgage, by reason of the *favour* due to his claim ; on the same principle, and for the same reason, mariners for their wages will be preferred to the same mortgage, though they have only a tacit and posterior lien.

‡ By the French law real or immoveable property only is susceptible of being hypothecated ; moveable or personal pro-perty cannot be hypothecated withou an actual delivery of posses-sion, in which case it cannot be said to be properly hypotheca-ted, but pledged ; this follows necessarily from its moveable and trans tory nature. But ships, which may be more easily traced & followed, and with less danger of fraud, are so far assimilated to real property by the law of every commercial country, that they may be mortgaged or hypothecated in the same manner as land. This is the subject of which our authour treats in this paragraph.

† An arret rendered 7th December, 1674, by the court of accounts, aids and finances of Provence (reported in Boniface

D D

ral principles of law, they cannot be charged in
mortgage or hypothecation.(*a*) In fact, by an edict
of December, 1666, which may be found in Boniface tom. 4. pag. 691. and which was passed at the
instance of our chamber of commerce, it was ordered that all vessels should be considered as move-
ables, and not be taken, nor considered as real property in sales which may take place nor be charged
with any mortgage.

a Bro-
deau,
cout. de
Paris, art.
90. n. 4.
Catelan,
tom. 2.
pag. 285.
Graverol,
pag. 159.
Daix.
pag. 683.

This rule has been modified by the ordinance of
1681.(*b*)   After having decided, in the first article,
that all ships and other vessels shall be considered
as personal property, it adds, in art. 2. nevertheless
all vessels shall be bound for the debts of the vendor,
until they shall have made a voyage in the name and
and at the risk of the purchaser: unless they have
been sold under a judicial decree."   Art. 3. of the
same title decides that " the sale of a ship, while on
a voyage or by private signature,* shall not operate
to the prejudice of the creditors of the vendor."

b tit. des
Navires.

tom. 5. pag. 666. confirmed a deliberation of the magistrates of
St. Tropez by which ships and fishermen's nets were charged
with the personal tax.

M. Jullien, on the statute ; tom. 2. pag. 293. reports contrary arrets rendered by the same court. The question again
arose in the following case. Captain Hermieu, commander of the *Diamant*, sailed from St. Tropez, in 1774, on a
voyage to the Levant. His ship was taken by the English in
1780. Upon his return to St. Tropez, the captain was sued for
the tax called *tallage* imposed in 1779. He refused to pay it,
1. Because his ship had been taken by the English. 2. Because
ships of the sea are personal property, not subject to *tallage*
which in Provence is a tax that is laid only on real estates.
An arret of the 20th February, 1782, was rendered by the
court of accounts, aids and finances of Provence, in favour of
captain Hermieu with costs. M. Gassier for the town of St.
Tropez and M. Guerin for captain Hermieu. *Note, by the Author.*

* An instrument under the private signature of the parties,
is considered in France as a *simple contract* as with us, and as not
binding upon any third party, without express notice ; whereas
notarial instruments have not only the effect which deeds executed with the solemnities of sealing and delivery have with us

M. Valin writes, at great length on these two last articles. But, 1st. The ship sold is liable for the debts of the vendor, until she has set sail under the name and at the risk of the purchaser.

2d. As the formality of a decretal sale is un-known in *Provence*,* the liens of creditors con-tinue, although the ship may be sold at auction by the lieutenant of the admiralty : for among us, ju-dicial auctions not preceded by a general instance of *discussion,* do not remove the lien.

------

but in many respects are considered as matters of record, es-pecially when the original instrument remains deposited in the Notary's Office. Hence the distinctions taken in the French law between *actes sous singe privé* (acts or instruments under private signature) and *acts notaries,* or *actes publics, actes passes pardevant notaries* [acts or instruments executed before a nota-ry] the former of which are considered as *simple* and the latter as *solemn* contracts. Hence also the distinction between *debtor chirographaires* (simple contract debts, or debts evidenced by private writing only) and *debts privilegiés* [privileged debts, debts evidenced by notarial acts or by judgments or other mat-ters of record] which have in France privileges analogous to those which our law confers on specialties and judgments of record.

* It must be recollected that M. Emerigon wrote this work at Marseilles, in that part of France which was formerly called *Provence,* where it seems that a *Decretal Sale,* that is to say a sale by Judicial Decree was not made in the same form or with the same effects as in the other parts of the kingdom, where it was considered as notice to all the world and bar-red all prior liens, whereas in Provence, as our authour calls it, such liens were not removed without a special proceed-ing called *discussion.* These details are altogether uninter-esting to us, but it was necessary that our authour's meaning should be elucidated, lest false conclusions might be drawn from his promises.

3d. If the ship be sold at a judicial auction* or by publick contract,† the purchase will be exclusive of creditors by simple contract.

4th. As soon as the vessel has sailed under the name and at the risk of the purchaser, all the debts of the vendor lose their lien on her.

5th. A sale made during the voyage or by private signature before the departure, shall not prejudice the creditors of the vendor, even by simple contract who come in concurrence with a purchaser who has paid the full price.

§. 2. Lenders on the hull have a lien on the ship.

a art. 7. h. t.

The ship, her tackle, apparel, furniture, provisions and even her freight are liable for the principal and interest of money lent on the body and keel for the necessities of the voyage.(*a*)   This lien is allowed to the lender, although the money was furnished to the owners themselves or the captain, if within the case mentioned in art. 8. h. t. and before explained in ch. 4.

What if the vessel do not put to sea ?

b Suprà, ch. 1. sec.. 4.

In order that the lender may be entitled to this lien, it is sufficient if the money have been furnished, bonâ fidê, *on the hull, for the necessities of the voyage;* although the voyage should be broken up, and the vessel seized before she has put to sea.   It is true, that in this case, there would be no maritime interest, because there was no risk.(*b*)   But the

---

* In France judicial sales are made at the bar of the court in presence of the judge and of the clerk, who records the proceedings, the cryer calling the bids as auctioneer. They are not made, as with us, by a ministerial officer out of doors.

† That is to say by an instrument before a notary.—It will bar all creditors who are not possessed of a lien created by an instrument of record or by act of loan.

lien would still continue on the vessel, according to art. 7. and 8. the meaning of which is general.

In the following section, I shall examine, to what rank this lien must be assigned. In my treatise on insurance *(a)* I have discussed the question, whether the lien of the lender extends to the freight already received in the course of the voyage. *a* ch. 17. sect. 9.

The lender on the hull has a lien on the freight.

The clause in a policy which enables the assured to abandon the freight, was authorized by the declaration of 1779.(*b*) I do not believe that it was authorized between the lender and borrower. The contract of insurance is susceptible of any conditions which the parties may think proper to make. The insurer may take upon himself only a part of the risks, and the declaration of 1779, allows the insured to agree that he will make only a partial abandonment. But from the nature of the contract of maritime loan, the lender must bear every risk and pay general averages. From which it follows, by analogy of reasoning that the lender has a lien on what is saved from a wreck and the freight due to the ship. It is his money which caused the thing to exist. Without that aid the voyage would not have taken place. Hence it would be contrary to justice to exempt the freight; it would, in certain cases, make a shipwreck profitable to the borrower. In a word, it is sufficient that the borrower has not been authorized to make such a stipulation and he must be bound by the common law.(*c*)

What, if the borrower on the hull has relinquished the freight?

b Emerig. Traité des ass. ch. 17. sect. 9.

c The law allows no average or salvage in bottomry bonds Marsh. 659, 663.

If money be lent to the captain, during the voyage, for the necessities of the ship, the lien extends to the whole ship and freight.(*d*)
ship and freight ? *d* art. 7. h. t.

Does the lien extend to the whole of the

But if the money be lent to the captain, in the place where the owners reside, without their consent, the

a art. 8. h. t. lien extends no further than to the interest which the captain may have in the vessel and freight.*(a)*

b Infrà sect. 3.

If it be furnished to a captain who was authorized to provide tackle, apparel and furniture, the lender has a lien on the whole vessel.*(b)*

Money furnished to one joint owner gives a lien only on his own interest in the vessel and freight.

§. 3. lien of the lender on the cargo.

c art. 7. h. t.

d Pothier,

The cargo shall be bound for the payment of money which was lent for the purpose of providing it.(c) When the money is lent for the voyage out and home, all returns voluntarily shipped on board the same vessel, are subject to the same lien.*(d)*

n. 34. Stypmannus, part. 4. cap. 2. n. 20. pag. 378. Suprà ch. 5. sect. 1. §. 2.

Effects disembarked before the accident.

The borrower is not obliged to put effects at risk further than to the amount of the sum that has been lent to him. If he puts more on board, he encreases the pledge of the lender, but this addition, voluntary on his side, is not irrevocable. During the voyage, he may unlade the surplus; and the lender has no right to complain. The 14th art. h. t. says, that "he who has borrowed money by way of maritime loan, shall not be exonerated by the loss of the vessel and cargo, *unless he can prove that he had effects on board to the value of the sum borrowed.*" From which it follows, that if the borrower prove that he had effects on board, at the time of the accident, equal in value to the amount of the sum lent, he is released from every obligation, and the contract must be reduced to the value of the effects saved from the wreck.

The lender does not bear the perils of the sea, except as to those effects which are on board of the vessel at the time of the accident. *Suscipiens periculum pro iis solùm tenetur, quæ tempore periculi aut naufragii, in navi fuerunt.(a)* This, then *a* Loccenius, lib. should be the single object of inquiry.*(b)* 2. cap. 5, 982. *b* bid. Traité des assurances, ch. 17. sect. 8. §. 2. p. 217. n. 7. pag.

The lender upon the ship and cargo, has a lien, Lien of *in solidum* upon both. The ship and cargo form the lender on but one fund, as to him. The borrower, by a the vessel conjunction, *re ét verbis*, has made his interest, in and cargo. the two, but one capital. This capital is subject, without division, to the lien of the lender, who may pay himself from either or both.

The lien of the lender comprehends his principal, §. 5. The interest and other charges.*(c)* In fact, the obliga- lien extends to tion to pay the principal and interest, arising from the capi- the same source, the same lien extends to both. tal and interest. *Non tantùm sortis, sed etiam usurarum potior est,* *c* art. 7. says the law 18, ff. *qui potior in pign.(d)* h. t. ibiq. der the title, de la saisie, art. 16. tom. 1. pag. 347. Pothier, n. 48. and Valin, 57. *d* Ibiq. Cujas, lib. 1. resp. Scvolæ. Charondas, resp. 202, f. 266. pag. 9. Brodeau Sur Louet, v. Dépens. n. 2. tom. 1. pag. 538. and un-

The lien is not the less valid, because the bill is §. 6. The lien ex- private.*(e)* tends private. *e* Basnage, des hypotheques pag. 318, Valin, on art. 16, tit. though de la saisie, tom. 1. pag. 344, Suprà, ch. 2, sect. 1, and ch. 4, sect. 5. the bill be

In order to have the advantage of his lien against And al- a third person, it is not necessary that the lender though the hol- should prove the useful employment of the money. der does It is sufficient if his title be clear.*(f)* not prove the useful the money. *f* Valin, art. 7, h. t. Pothier, n. 52, (Suprà, ch. 4, sect. employ- 7. §. 4, ch. 6, sect. 3, §. 2. ment of

SECTION III.

Priority of liens on a ship which has not com-
menced her voyage.

I have built a vessel, or have purchased one on credit and have ordered repairs and rigging. I have taken up money at bottomry on the hull. I have only paid a part of what is due to the workmen and furnishers. She is seized by these creditors. In what order are they to be paid?

Texts of the ordinances.

The *Consolato del Mare,*(a) says that "if a vessel just built be sold at the instance of creditors, before she is launched, or before she has made her

a ch. 32.

first voyage, the carpenters, caulkers and other workmen, as well as those who furnished the timber, pitch, nails and other articles which are necessary in the construction of a ship, are preferred to all other creditors, of what sort soever they may be: even those who have lent money, under a written declaration, that it is to be employed in the building of the ship."

b art, 17.

Ordonnance de la Marine.(b) "If the vessel sold have not made a voyage, the vendor, carpenter, ship builders, caulkers and other workmen employed in her, together with the creditors for the timber, cordage and other articles furnished to her, shall be preferred to other creditors and by a concurrence among themselves."

1st. rank the vendor.

By the 17th art. the vendor of the vessel is placed in the first rank of privileged creditors of a ship, which has not performed her first voyage. This is according to the common law of the kingdom, by which he who sells, upon credit, has a lien upon the article sold, for the price of it.

The workmen.

The carpenters, caulkers and other workmen are included in the same rank with the vendor.

Material men.

In the same rank also, the ordinance has placed the creditors for timber, cordage and other articles furnished to the vessel.

Concurrence of the above persons.

All the above creditors are paid in equal proportions, without any preference. *Nota.* If the ordidinance did not preclude it. I would say that we discriminate between the body of the vessel in the state she was before the sale from the repairs that she has undergone, so that the vendor might have the original and leave the surplus to the material men and workmen. But the ordinance directs that the whole shall be divided among them in proportion to their respective claims.

If the person who undertakes to build the vessel have received the price agreed upon and do not pay the workmen and material men, are they entitled to a personal action against the owner and a lien on the ship? *If the building was undertaken at a stipulated sum?*

The law 1. ff. *in quib. caus. pign.* says, that if a third person lend money to an architect or undertaker, which is employed in the erection of an edifice, and if this loan had been effected by the order of the owner, the lender shall have the same lien as if the loan had been made to the owner. *Pignus insulæ, creditori datum, qui pecuniam ob restitutionem edificii extruendi mutuam dedit, ad eum quoque pertinebit qui redemptori, domino mandante, nummos ministravit.*

The law 24. §. 1. ff. de reb. auctor. jud. gives a lien also on a house erected or repaired, to the person who lends money for the purpose, by order of the owner, to the undertaker. *Quod privilegium ad cum quoque pertinet, qui redemptori, domino mandante, pecuniam subministravit.*

" But if the money was borrowed without the knowledge or order of the owner, and he pay the undertaker, the lender would have no action but against the borrower. But if the owner has not paid the undertaker, the third person would have a lien, whether the loan had been made with or with-

E E

out the order of the owner, provided he had taken proper precautions."(*a*)

M. le Camus,(*b*) proposes this question. "Whe-ther a dealer in timber, who has sold timber to a house carpenter, who has undertaken the building of a house, may, after the timber has been employ-ed in the building of a house, proceed against the owner thereof, for the materials furnished or the price of them. It is necessary," says he "to make this distinction: whether the work is done by the day or by *the job*, and we must also distinguish the time. For if the timber be not yet used, I think the vendor might recover it: but if it be used, *est pars ædium*, and the vender has no remedy but by attaching, in the hands of the owner, whatever may be due to the undertaker. The owner is in no man-ner bound to the vendor, because he has purchased nothing from him and moveable property is not subject to liens, not coupled with possession."

Such then is the provision of the common law: those who have furnished the undertaker, without the order of the owner, *domino non mandante*, have no lien on the house. Does the same law prevail respecting advances to an undertaker of a vessel?
The *consolato del Mare*,(*c*) says,

"The carpenter, or caulker who undertakes a piece of work for a stipulated sum, ought to pay the men who work under him: but the owner should give them notice, that they may not be de-ceived. If he do not notify them, they may attach the thing for their wages, and it shall be liable for the payment of their wages, costs and interest. But if they had received warning, they shall have no lien."

M. Valin,*(a)* quotes this chapter of the Consulato. [a art. 17. tit. de la saisie, pag. 349.] But he does not admit the application of the princi- ples of the common law to vessels. "It is an important observation" he remarks, " on the subject of liens of carpenters and other workmen employed in the building of a ship, that they should *work by the order of the owner*, in order to be entitled to this privilege. If they were employed by an under-taker, who has received the stipulated price of the work from the owner, they have no lien upon the ship and have no remedy but a personal action against the undertaker, upon whose good faith they acted. This, however," he adds " is to be understood in cases where the workmen and material men knew that it was *a job* and that they had no busi-ness with any one but the undertaker." This qua-lification brings the doctrine of the authour very nearly within the law of the Consolato.

By the declaration of May* 16, 1747, his majesty declares " that when merchants build vessels, by contracting with master-builders for a particular sum for the whole work, inasmuch as the material men and workmen have no remedy but by personal action against the contractor, under whose orders they laboured, they shall be at liberty to attach, in the hands of the owner, the debts due from him to the contractor ; and they shall be preferred to all other creditors of the contractor."

But this declaration of the king has not been registered in the Parliament d'Aix. It was register-ed in that of Bourdeaux, with this modification ; inserted at the suggestion of the attorney general, " that contracts by *the job* for the building of a ves-

* *A declaration of the king* is an ordinance, by which the king explains, modifies or annuls, in whole or in part any edict or ordinance, &c. Ferr. *in hoc verb.*

sel, should not be executory, unless they were pre-viously registered in the registry of the courts of admiralty."

There is nothing which is regarded with so much favour as debts for work and labour furnished to a vessel. Commerce and the country at large are in-terested in them. It is right that the workmen and material men should enjoy the *real lien* which is given them by the ordonnance de la Marine. *(a)* They cannot be deprived of it, unless it is proved that they contracted on the faith of the person and not of the thing.

a tit. de la saisie arr. 16 and 17.

Claude Frichet furnished a quantity of iron to a vessel built by captain *Cresp*, in which *Thomas Bouis* owned thirteen shares. The vessel was seiz-ed by the creditors of *Cresp*, before she put to sea. *Bouis*, who had furnished the whole of his propor-tion, endeavoured to confine the lien to the captain's interest. But our admiralty gave *Frichet* a lien on the whole vessel; and the sentence was confirmed by an arrêt of the 13th March, 1747, on the report of *M. d'Étienne*. *Cresp* was the contractor for the building of the vessel; but *Frichet* acted on the faith of the vessel, not of the person : *navi magis, quam ipsi crediderat*.

According to the *arrêts* of *M. de Lamoignon*,*(b)* he who has delivered seed grain to a farmer to sow, is preferred to the owner in the crop which it produ-ces." It is true that this opinion is very much con-troverted. We find in *Decormis*,*(c)* and in the new edition of *Duperier*,*(d)* two arrêts of the Parlia-ment of Aix, which, *for the prevention of frauds*, give the preference to an owner without whose knowledge the seed had been furnished. This, at once, revives the *domino mandante*, of the laws be-fore cited.

b tit, des actions personel-les et d' hypothe-que, art. 113.

c tom. 2. col. 1221.

d tom. 3. liv 1. quæst. 16. pag. 74.

But these laws, which can be adduced here only by way of argument, cannot controvert the express provision of the *Consolato de la Mare*, nor that of the maritime ordinance. The carpenters, caulkers and other workmen employed in building, together with the creditors for the timber, cordage and other articles furnished to the vessel, ought to enjoy the privilege allowed to them, unless they have been warned in due time that if they do not secure the payment of their claims against the contractor, they shall have no lien on the ship. And I do not believe that a simple registry of the contract, would be considered as a notification within the meaning of the *Consolato*, it requires that the notice should be given to the workmen and other material men, in order that they may not be deceived.

We have before seen that the *Consolato del Mare*, (a) declares that the workmen and material men shall be preferred to all other creditors; even to those who have lent money with a written declaration that it is to be employed in the construction of a vessel. This chapter does not say that lenders shall have a lien on a ship seized before she has put to sea. Art. 17. tit. de la Saisie does not speak of them. From which it follows that they have no lien. In fact, the contract does not really become a maritime loan until the moment of departure; and if the vessel does not sail, *pecunia non erit trajectitia.*(b)

2d Rank. Lender on bottomry. *a* ch. 23.

b L. 1. ff. de naut. fœn.

Nevertheless, as the lien which is given to lenders on the hull,(c) is indefinite, I believe that in order to reconcile the ordinance with itself, we should place, after the persons spoken of in the 17th art.(d) those who have lent on the hull.

c art. 7. h. t. *d* tit. de la saisie.

Suppose you have a ship on the stocks. You sell
her to me, on credit, for   -   -   *L* 4,000
I have borrowed at bottomry
(which I have paid to the work-
men and material men.)   -   -   -   4,000
There remains due to them,   -   -   4,000

                                                              L 12,000

The ship is seized and sold for,
nett   -   -   -   -   *L* 9,000

The vender shall be fully paid   -   *L* 4,000
The material men and work-
men will receive   -   -   -   4,000
The lenders divide among
themselves by privilege   -   -   -   1,000

                                                              L 9,000

If the nett produce should be only 7,000 livres
the moiety of this sum would belong to the vender
and the remainder to the material men and workmen. The lenders would be entitled to no part,
but they would have a personal action against the
debtor. *(a)*

a L. 10. C. de oblig. et act.

The same privilege, it seems, may be allowed to a
person who furnishes money, not on bottomry, for
the building of a ship and who has neglected to
substitute himself in the place of the workmen and
material men. The laws 26 and 34, *(b)* may be
applied here. But as on the one hand these laws
give no more than a personal privilege, unknown
among us, and on the other, art. 17. *(c)* does not
speak of money furnished by a third person, I do
not see upon what ground this lien is allowed.

Money furnished by a third person.

b ff. de rebus auct. judic.

c tit. de la saisie.

The Mess. M. bought the ship *la Perle.* They Joint owner
sold a moiety to Joseph Solary, for 26,021 livres. who fur-
The ship required repairs and Solary undertook to nishes the
superintend them. He expended 12,498 livres of his part-
his own money. He then sold his interest back to ners.
M. for 38,519 livres, for which they gave him their
promissory notes.

Mess. M. failed and Solary demanded his money,
by privilege* on the vessel, which had not yet left
the port. On the 30th May, 1750, a sentence was
given by the consulate tribunal, which allowed
Solary a privilege on a moiety only of the net proceeds of the vessel, of which a sale was ordered.
On the 3d June, 1751, an arrêt was passed by the
Parliament of Aix, on the report of M. de Galliffet,
confirming this sentence, because the right of Solary was limited to the moiety which he had re-trans-
ferred and he was neither a workman nor had he
furnished any materials.†

---

* *Privilege* by the French law is a right to be paid out of the
proceeds of a ship or other thing by virtue of a tacit lien created
by operation of law. It differs from *hypotheca*, in as much as
that is created by deed. For instance mariners have a *privilege*
on the ship for their wages, the holder of a bottomry bond has
an *hypotheca*, or as we should call it a right by hypothecation or
mortgage.

† An owner may borrow money, on bottomry, for fitting out
his ship for a voyage, and hypothecate his ship therefor. Cro.
Jac. 209, *Sharpley* v. *Hurrel*, 2. Bl. Com. 458. A master, if
part owner, may take up money on bottomry to the value of his
own share, in places where the owners reside, 2. Molloy, b. 2.
c. 2. s. 14. 15. Hence it may be inferred that any other owner
may do the like. But, *quere*, whether a bottomry bond executed by the owner *at home*, creates a lien on the ship which
can be enforced in a court of admiralty ? 4. Cranch, 332. *Blaine*
v. *ship Charles Carter.* The owner of a ship, covered by a bottomry bond, to an amount beyond her value, has not an insu-
rable interest. 2. N. Y. Cas. in error, 110. *Smith* v. *Williams*:

SECTION IV.

Priority of liens on a vessel which returns from a voyage.

1. mariners.   "The wages of mariners employed in the last voyage shall be paid in preference to all other creditors," art. 16. tit. de la saisie.(a)

a Consolato del Mare, ch. 33, 105, 135, 136.   Cleirac, sur les judgmens d'Oleron, art. 8 n. 31. pag. 46 and under the title de la jurisdiction, art. 18 n. 4. pag. 419. Basnage, des hypotheques, pag. 70. Pothier, n. 54 Kuricke quest. 12.*

* In Minors et al. vs. the ship Mary, wages were decreed upon the captains certificate that they were due though the vessel was in port, not earning freight. Such certificate is the best evidence, where the shipping articles are not produced. Bee's Adm. dec. 119 If a voyage be interrupted without the fault of the crew they shall receive wages during the time they work on board the vessel in port. The act of congress for the regulation of seamen, [V. 1. p. 134.] must be strictly followed, it being penal. Bee, 48. Peters, xcv. in not. If the mariners suffer imprisonment under the 7th clause of that act, they shall not also forfeit wages under the 5th. Bee, id. By the act of congress [ut sup. cit. sect. 9.] every vessel must carry certain proportions of provisions, under penalty of paying double wages. In one case, there was an unavoidable deficiency of bread, but a larger proportion of beef and water than the act requires, one third wages decreed. Bee, 80. Where the esculents designated in the act cannot be procured or become damaged or wasted, others may be substituted and the master is the sole judge of the expenditure. Peters 220. *Quere*, whether he is the *sole* judge? Must he not afterwards be able to show that the putting of the crew on allowance was ex necessitate? The act applies only to seamen of vessels bound *from* the United States and not to those shipped in foreign ports, ib. 223. They do not forfeit their wages by absence without any fault of their own. Bee, 134. Pet. 115, nor prize money. Hopkinson 60. Bee 395. Nor by the capture of the vessel if they were on board ib. 190. The right to wages is founded on the *service* not on the articles, ib. 395, and the owner is bound if the vessel is insufficient, ib. 254. If the seamen die before the voyage is performed, his representatives shall have his wages up to the time of his death, but not beyond it, ib. 255 And see a deci-

I have before cited the laws 5 and 6, ff. *qui potior* 2d. loans during *in pign. hab.* which say that the last creditor is the voyage. sometimes preferred to the first : *interdum posterior, potior est priori.* He, for instance, is thus preferred, who furnishes money during the voyage to purchase provisions, without which the vessel could not return: *si in cibaria nautarum fuerit creditum, sine quibus navis salva pervenire non poterat..*

According to this principle, writers generally *a* Stypm. agree that among lenders at bottomry, the common part. 4. ch. 6. n. order of liens should be reversed, and the last should 150, pag. be preferred to the first.*(a)* 420.
Locc. cap. 6. n. 8. pag. 993. Vinn. pag. 95. Casa. disc. 18. n. 14. Marq. lib. lib. 2. 2. cap. 8. n. 78.

Kuricke, in his celebrated questions,*(b)* opposes *b* quest. this opinion. He contends that all the lenders 25. pag. 880. should come in by concurrence, because, by means of their money, they enabled the voyage to be performed.

The former doctrine is recognized by the Ordi- *c* tit. de la saisie, nance.*(c)* It provides that after the sailors, those art. 16. who have furnished money during the voyage, for the necessities of the ship, shall be preferred.*(d)* *d* Valin, ibiq. pag. Pothier, n. 53. 343.

---

sion to the same effect by Judge Davis of the Massachussetts District where the question is very elaborately discussed. 2. Hall's Law Journal, 359. Bee, 441. Contra, judge Peters whose decision is confirmed by judge Washington. Peters 155. In a late case in this district, judge Houston adopted the opinion of the latter judges. An appeal was prayed and we may therefore expect to see this question finally settled by the supreme court of the United States.

Where the voyage is commenced in time of war the wages are not to be diminished in consequence of a peace. Bee 423. Secus, where the voyage is not commenced before that event, ib. 429.

F f

Before his departure from Marseilles, a certain captain, borrows money at bottomry. He arrives at Martinique where he borrows a further sum for the necessities of the ship. He reaches Cape Francois where he again borrows for the same purpose. The third lenders shall be preferred to the second and those to the first. *Sic erunt novissimi, primi; et primi, novissimi.* But the creditors in each of these classes shall take by concurrence among themselves, without regard to the dates of their respective contracts.*

Those whose merchandize has been sold during the voyage for the necessities of the ship.

a ch. 105.

In the same manner we must place in the second rank, those whose merchandize the captain has sold, in the course of the voyage for the necessities of the ship. The *Consolato del Mare*,(*a*) says, " if the captain stand in need of money to enable him to prosecute the voyage and he can find no person who will lend it to him, and the consignees have none, he may sell merchandize to the amount required. And those whose merchandize is thus sold, shall be preferred to all others, excepting the sailors in their claims for wages."†

b art. 45.

The ordinance of Wisbuy,(*b*) says, "the merchant to whom the merchandize" (sold for the ne-

---

* But if the obligee of a bottomry bond suffer the ship to make several voyages without asserting his lien, and executions are levied on the ship by other creditors, the obligee losses his lien. 4. Cranch, 328. Blaine vs. the ship Charles Carter. In this case the same order of liens as we find in the text is laid down by the court.

† But note, ante, ch. iv, sect. 13. Pet. Adm. dec. 67. 79. In such case, there is an implied hypothecation upon which suit may be maintained in the admiralty. Bee's Adm. dec. 116. A captain pawned his own person to procure the ransom of the vessel. He afterwards redeemed the pledge by borrowing money on bond in another port. On his return to England he recovered this money in the admiralty. A prohibition was prayed in the case but denied. Vin. 529.

cessities of the ship) "belonged, or the creditor who shall have lent money shall have a special lien and right of attachment against the vessel."

It was not through negligence that the ordinance, (*a*) has omitted to provide for merchandize sold to supply the necessities of the voyage, because in the 19th art.(*b*) the master is permitted, in case of necessity, during the voyage, to borrow money at bottomry, or to pledge his rigging or to sell a part of his cargo, on condition of paying for it at the rate at which the rest may be sold. The money arising from the sale is considered as money lent for the necessities of the voyage. He has then the same lien as a lender at bottomry.* They should be paid in concurrence.(*c*)

a art. 16. tit. de la saisie.

b tit. du capitaine.

c Valin, tom. 1. pag. 343.

The ordinance(*d*) places in the same rank those who have lent money for the repairs, victuals and equipment before the departure.
art. 16. tit. de la saisie.

3rd. Lenders before the departure.

In 1775, I was consulted, whether those who have furnished timber and cordage ought to be placed in the same rank. I answered in the affirmative. For it is of little importance whether money or materials be furnished. Material men, indeed, should be more favourably regarded, because there is no doubt about the employment of the articles which they furnish; but it is not so certain that the money lent has been appropriated to the vessel.† This explanation *non est extensiva, sed intellectiva.* Such is our law.

Material men.

---

* Pet. Adm. dec. 277. Gardner et al. vs. the ship New-Jersey.

† But if material men take other security, the ship is released from the lien. In the Maryland district court, Gordon filed a libel against the ship Alexander, for cordage furnished. Brown, who had purchased the vessel from Wilson, who was the owner at the time when the cordage was furnished, appeared as clai-

Workmen. *a* pag. 318. V. infrà, sect. 7 § 2.

Workmen employed in the building or repairing should be placed in the same rank if they are not paid. It was so decided by an arrêt reported in *Basnage.(a)*

4th. Shippers of small adventures. *b* ch. 56.

The *Consolato del Mare,(b)* says that "if any merchandize shipped in a vessel, and mentioned in the bill of lading, be lost, the ship must pay the value, but without prejudice to the seamen's wages."

Chapter 61, adds, that "the captain ought not to stow the merchandize in damp places, nor nigh to the mast, helm, sink or in other situations where it may be damaged. If it be injured by water from the deck, sides, masts, sink, helm or other open places, in consequence of the hold not being properly covered, the captain is answerable for the damage. If the captain be insolvent, the ship is liable; and those who are thus injured are preferred to all other creditors except the seamen."

The vessel is bound to the cargo and the cargo to the vessel. *Reglement pour la navigation of rivieres, art.* 18. *in Cleirac, pag.* 597.

It seems that the lien of those whose merchandize has been lost or diminished by average resulting from any other cause than the peril of the sea, ought to be placed first ; even before the seamen, because such losses or damage generally proceed from their fault. It would be much more just to give shippers the preference to those who have lent money before

---

mant, and contended that the lien was destroyed in consequence of Gordon's having taken a note at six months in payment of his bill when it was presented, and so the court decided. An appeal from this decision was prayed and granted, 10th May, 1810. On the doctrine of liens created by the law maritime, the reader is referred to a decision by judge Winchester of the Maryland district, in the case of Stevens vs. the Sandwich. Pet. Adm. dec. 233, *in nota.*

the departure; because the former are ignorant of the provisions and loans that have been furnished in the place of equipment. But the Ordinance,(*a*) places them only in the fourth rank, although the second is allotted to them by the Consolato. *a* art. 16. tit. de la saisie.

The Ordinance, in the place cited, divides the creditors into but four ranks; and "as to simple contract creditors and others not privileged" it says, " they shall be paid according to the laws and customs of the place where the decision may be made."

It is to be remarked that the Ordinance does not say that there shall be no more than four ranks of privileged creditors. Its provisions are not so exclusive. We are then permitted to add other creditors to the above, if there be others who are entitled to a lien on the ship. In this class are the insurers to whom the premium has not been paid. I think they should be placed in the fifth rank.(*b*) Vaisseaux, tom. 1. pag. 343. V. Traité des ass. ch. 3. sect. 8. *5th. Creditors for the premium of insurance. b Valin, on the 16th art. tit. de la saisie des*

Le Guidon de la Mer,(*c*) speaks of renewal, that is, the renewing, from one voyage to another, of *securities for money lent by maritime loan.* "These renewals," it provides, "have no special lien on the profits of the voyage but are to be considered as among the youngest privileged creditors. If the merchant reserve the profits of each voyage and leave the principal in the hands of the master to be again employed, his right shall not be good against the tradesmen and victuallers, nor those who have lent their money by bottomry for the particular voyage." *6th. Money left in the hands of the borrower by renewal of the contract. c ch. 19. art. 2,*

In the 10th art. h. t. it is also said that " money left by renewal or continuation of the contract, shall not come into concurrence with that which is actually furnished for the same voyage."

From the terms of the 10th art. and its coinci-, dence with the *Guidon de la Mer*, I suppose that the creditor for money left by renewal, ought to have a lien ; but it should be declared to be posterior to all others and not be prejudicial to the owners of the ship, unless they had authorized the renewal contracted for by their captain.

Raoul vs.
Durand,
1765, The *St. Jacques*, equipped at *Arles*, by the own-ers residing at that place, sailed on a coasting voyage, under the command of captain Durand. On the 21st February, 1764, she was at Marseilles. The captain borrowed of André Raoul, commissary of the navy, the sum of 150 livres on the hull, *for a year*, at the rate of 24 *per cent.* On the 24th of March ensuing, he borrowed from the same person, the further sum of 150 livres on the hull, for a voyage from Marseilles to Arles and back again, at the rate of 5 *per cent.* On the 25th December ensuing, he borrowed from the same person for a similar voyage, the like sum and at the same interest.

Neither of these sums were paid when they became due. But the interest was regularly paid up to the 21st September, 1765. The captain became embarrassed in his affairs and he was discharged from the command of the vessel. Raoul filed a petition against Durand claiming 450 livres with interest and costs and also against the owners, praying a joint execution.

On the 23d December, 1765, a sentence was rendered by the Parliament of Arles, by which the captain was condemned to pay the whole sum with interest and costs. The sentence was declared to be common and executory against the owners, *only as to the last loan of* 150 livres, &c.

From this sentence, the owners appealed. Raoul came to consult me. I told him that his claim for the two first loans had been rejected very properly and that there was nothing due to him, upon which a common execution could be issued, but the last loan; for the ship had made several voyages after the 15th December, 1765. Consequently the owners were no longer responsible for the contracts of the captain. Raoul followed my advice. He acquiesced in the decision and departed with as much as he could obtain.

On the 10th art. h. t. M. Valin observes that "it is only those who do not foresee the consequences of this article, that can come within its provisions. All that is necessary, is to conceal the existing contract and make another instead of renewing the old one. This authour has carefully guarded against authorizing a practice which is but too common. Those who are guilty of it, commit a *crimen falsi,* and deserve to be severely punished.

The 17th art. *(a)* places the vendor among the privileged creditors on a ship which has not yet put to sea. But the 16th art. of the same title, in prescribing the order of liens upon a vessel which returns from sea, takes no notice of vendors.

7th. The vendor. a tit. de la saisie

Nevertheless, by the common law of the kingdom, by the statute of Marseilles,(*b*) and by the deliberation of our Chamber of Commerce, in 1730, approved by the Parliament of Aix, the vendor on credit may reclaim the thing sold, which he finds existing in the same state, in the hands of the purchaser, to the exclusion of other creditors, in order to pay himself.

b pag. 380.

The vendor of a ship which is not yet paid for, may then reclaim it by action, to pay himself, provided he yields the preference to those creditors.

who are privileged by the 16th art. just cited.* It would be repugnant to the most common rules, if the vendor of a ship on credit, should be obliged to yield to simple mortgage creditors, or if he were compelled to come into concurrence with simple contract creditors, whose claims have no connection with commerce.

This case often occurs among us. The privilege of the vendor has always been recognized by other creditors, that is, by those whose debts have no direct relation to the ship. But seamen, those who have lent money for the necessities of the ship during the voyage, those who have made advances for the repairs, victuals and equipment before the departure, and shippers, are preferred to the vendor. The ship, by putting to sea under the name and at the risk of the new owner, ceases to be liable to the creditors of the vendor; and with more reason the vendor ceases to have any lien, excepting that which results from the general rules of law.

----

* By the French Law the seller of merchandize and indeed of any thing else, may pursue the property in the hands of the purchaser for the payment of the consideration money as long as it can be identified. As to houses, lands and ships, he may pursue the objects sold even in the hands of a third person. This may appear rigorous to an American lawyer, who will immediately suppose the case of a bonâ fidê purchaser without notice. But the hardship will disappear when it is considered that in France a deed or bill of sale is not accompanied as it is among us, with a receipt in full endorsed or at the foot for the whole consideration money, but the credit given and the terms of payment are always expressed on the face of the instrument of sale. Therefore the case of a bonâ fidê purchaser without notice can never occur. If the vendor should endorse a receipt in full on the bill of sale, he would undoubtedly lose his lien, and be driven to the new security which he had thought proper to take from the purchaser.

SECTION V.

Priority of liens on the Cargo.

The charges for unlading, porterage and storage are placed in the first rank by the L. 6. §. 2. ff. *qui potior in pign. Si merces horreorum, vel areæ, vel vecturæ jumentorum debetur ; hic potentior erit.* 1st. Charges of unlading.

In the second rank, the captain should have a lien on the produce of the cargo, for the freight and general average.*(a) Ipsum naulum potentius est.(b)*
21. h. t. tit. du jet.   Kuricke, quest. 11.   *b* L. 6. §. 1. ff. qui potior in pign. 2d. Freight and general average. *a* art. 24. tit. du fret. art.

If, in the course of a voyage, the shipper require money to save his goods or repair injuries which may have happened to them, the lender shall have a lien subsequent to the freight and general average. *Si quis in merces sibi obligatas crediderit, ut salvæ fiant.(c)*
of the cargo. *c* d. L. 6. §. 1. 3d. Particular articles furnished during the voy. age for the safety

All those who lend money on the cargo or on small adventures, before the departure, come into concurrence. The 7th art. h. t. gives them an equal privilege, without regard to the dates of their respective contracts.*(d)*   ch. 5. sect. 1. §. 2. 4th. Lenders before the departure. *d* Vid. Suprà,

If the merchant borrow by way of maritime loan in an intermediate port, in order to increase his adventure the second lenders are not preferred to the first. They come into concurrence, because money borrowed in the course of the voyage, has not had for its object the preservation of the common stock. *Si diversi creditores mercatori, sub obligatione mercium navi illatarum, pecuniam nauticam dederint, nullum inter eos esse prælationis jus, ra-* Lenders in an intermediate port.

G g

a Kn-
ricke,
quest. 25.
pag 880.
Locee
nius, lib.
2, cap 6.
n. 8. pag.
993. Vin- *tione temporis, sed omnes pares haberi, ac simul concurrere, communis est jurisconsultorum opinio ; quam etiam in foro mercatorio itâ in usu esse, ex relatione fide dignâ quorundam celebrium mercato-rum compertum habeo, quorum fidem sequar (a)*

nius ad L. L. Rhodias, pag. 95. Marquardus, lib. 2. cap. 8. n. 79

Does the
vendor of
merchan-
dize come
in co. cur-
rence
with the
lender on The privilege of the lender by maritime loan is of publick importance *ad summam rem publicam, navium exercitia pertinet. (b)* This privilege, there-fore must be preferred to that of a vendor, who has not been paid for his merchandize.
the cargo? *b* L. 1. §. 20. de exercit. act.

c L. 5. §.
15. ff. de
tribut.
act.

d liv.
3. ch. 5.
de pig-
nore dato
in navi
bus pro
aliquâ pe-
cuniâ. A person purchases merchandize on credit and also borrows money by maritime loan on the same effects. From the moment of the loan, the effects become pledged to the lender, who furnished mo-ney only on the faith of the goods : *merci magis, quàm tibi credidit. (c)* The statute of Marseilles, favourable as it is to a vendor, nevertheless places him after the lender.(*d*)
pag. 375.

e ch. 4.
sect. 6. We have before seen, *(e)* that the dishonesty of the borrower cannot operate to the prejudice of the rights of the *bonâ fide* lender. The 7th. art h. t. in giving a privilege to him who furnishes money to complete the cargo, does not impose upon him the burthen of proof as to the employment of it. It suffices that the goods are put on board in order to render them liable to the claims of the lender.

f tit. de
la saisie. The 17th *(f)* art. in speaking of a vessel which has not yet put to sea, places the vendor among the privileged creditors and gives him a preference to the lenders on the hull, because the risk does not commence until the ship has weighed anchor. But the risk of the lading commences the moment it is put on board. The right of the shippers to a lien

is consummated by lading the goods and that of the lenders by the departure of the ship. Now since the vendor of a ship which has put to sea, is excluded by the lenders on the hull, the vendor of merchandize on board should be excluded by the lenders on the cargo.

Thus, I cannot but disapprove of a sentence which our Seneschalsea tribunal* rendered on the 20th August, 1777, in the case of the heirs of captain Orange, by which an absolute and exclusive privilege, notwithstanding there were lenders at maritime risque, was given to Mess. Ferreol and Bignan; for the amount of certain linens which they had sold to the captain and which were found yet in existence at Cape Francois at the time of his decease. Mess. Ferrol and Bignan held a note payable to order, *for the value received in merchandize.* They had not furnished the goods *as a part of the cargo;* the bill had none of the features of a maritime contract about it, and ought therefore, to have yielded the preference to the respondentia creditors. The vendor, who is not paid, may reclaim his good, if he find them on board or elsewhere, still in the same state in which they were sold: but his lien cannot operate to the prejudice of the lender, whose right is established by publick law.

With much greater reason, every sort of privilege should be refused to a vendor, whose goods are no longer in being. In 1767, Etienne B. bor-

---

* Tribunal de Senechanssèe. Before the late revolution, France was divided into Bailiwicks, for the administration of justice. In every one of those districts there was a judge called Seneschal *(steward)* and his tribunal was called Seneschalsea (in French Senechanssèe.) In some Bailiwicks, that judge was called Baillif, and his tribunal, bailliage (Bailiwick or county court.) This tribunal had cognizance in the first instance, of civil suits to any amount and also of criminal causes; subject to an appeal to a superior court,

rowed divers sums at maritime risque on his cargo.
He purchased oil from M. Ferry, to the amount of
14,000 livres payable on the safe return of the vessel. The vessel returned to Marseilles. A dispute
arose between the vendor on credit and the lender.
The sentence of the judge and consuls,* gave the
preference to the latter, and it was confirmed by an
arrêt of the Parliament of Aix, on the report of M.
de Beauval. He who buys merchandize on credit
may dispose of it according to his own pleasure.
If he ship it, it is because he supposes he will find
a better market. If he borrow money by maritime loan *on the goods*, the lenders have a lien and
special privilege on the effects embarked and their
returns, in preference to a vendor, who cannot reclaim the thing sold, much less its returns, to the
prejudice of the lendor.

---

* In France, before the revolution, all causes relating to the
Land Commerce, such as the sale and delivery of goods, partnerships, factorage, bills of exchange, promissory notes,
bankruptcies, settlement of accounts between merchants, &c.
were decided by a court established in every trading town, under the denomination of Judges and Consuls. They were ex-
perienced merchants, annually elected by the body of merchants and traders established in the respective towns. All
causes of maritime contracts, such as insurance, maritime
loans, fitting out and repairing of ships, mariner's wages,
freight, &c. came within the jurisdiction of the court of admiralty. Those two jurisdictions have been merged since the revolution into the tribunals of commerce, which are established
much on the same principle as the Judge and Consuls, formerly
were. There are no longer any courts of admiralty. Causes
of prize and spoilation are determined as formerly by a council
of prizes sitting at Paris, from whose decision there is an appeal to the Council of State.

SECTION VI.

*Claim of Property.—Severance of Property.**

He who has furnished the timber with which the *a* §. 1. ff.
vessel is built cannot reclaim it, because it has be- rer. do-
come a part of the ship. *Navi tabula cedit,* says min.
the L. 26.(*a*) The materials of which the ship is §. 3. ff.
composed and the ship itself, are considered as de pign.
different things. *Aliud est materia ; aliud navis.*(*b*) Cujas.

But if the materials can be detached from the
ship without ruining it, as, for instance, the masts,
cordage, sails and anchors, the furnisher may reclaim them by the action *ad exhibendum,* according

---

* The title in the original is *revendication, distraction,* which
I have endeavoured to render more familiar to the English
reader.

By the civil law, he who has sold goods for cash or on credit may demand them back from the purchaser, if the purchase
money is not paid according to the contract. The French a-
dopted this law into their system under the title *revendication,*
which signifies re-claiming or re-demanding. See the 85th
Parere, [answer or opinion] of Savary, where this subject is
well treated.

If the creditor seize more than his own goods, the owner of
that part may demand a separation, [*distraction*] of the property.

We have no technical terms in our legal grammar wh'ch answer precisely to these, and it is to be regretted that we have not
adopted the principle. However prejudice or part'ality may
deride the manners or abhor the morals of this nation, we
should not be ashamed to imitate the'r wisdom. It is not unu-
sual for merchants on the eve of bankruptcy to purchase goods
on credit, in order to enable them to bubble on the stream of speculation a little longer or to pay, what is called, their accommoda-
tion notes. The latter case is a fraud which deserves the seve-
rest punishment. See an attempt to introduce the principle of
the action of *revendication* into our law, in the form of an action
of replevin, in the case of *Haskins* vs. *Latour,* 2 Hall's Law
Journal, 181.

a L L. 6
and 7, ff
ad exhi-
bendum.
L. 23. §.
5. ff. de   rei vindicat.

to the general rule established by law.(*a*) *A fortiori*, we may reclaim such articles if they be found not on board the ship.

Of the vendor's lien. In the preceding sections, I have spoken of the lien which the vendor of a ship or merchandize may claim in certain cases.

Severance of property. If the property of the borrower be ordered to be sold judicially, the lenders may require a severance or separation of the effects upon which their lien operates.

Captain André Orange, commander of the *Heureuse Therese*, had borrowed from different persons the sum of 29,942 livres on his hull and cargo. He arrived at Guadaloupe, where he died and the vessel returned to Marseilles.

The mother of Orange's children empowered Francis Guichard, one of the lenders, to demand the freight, and to dispose of the vessel and cargo. A short time afterwards, she took possession of her husband's property with *benefit of inventory.**

The lenders sued in a body and required a severance of the effects which were subject to their lien and attached, in the hands of Guichard, the sums which he had received.

Me. Seytre, the attorney, in a suit brought by the creditors at large for the distribution of the effects of the deceased, having obtained a provisional order for 600 livres to defray the costs thereof, sued Guichard

* Justinian established in favour of the heir, a liberty of accepting the inheritance, with what is called *the benefit of an inventory*, that is, a condition that he should not be liable beyond the value of the property of the deceased. Harg. and Bull. Co. Lit. 191. a. V. [3.]

for this sum. Guichard pleaded the attachment laid in his hands by the lenders at maritime risque.

He contended that they had a privilege and lien on the property in his hands, which was bound to them, to the exclusion of all other creditors : and that therefore the costs must be demanded else-where.

On the 17th of August, 1775, a sentence was rendered against Me. Seytre. An appeal was pray-ed. The case was reduced to the point whether the lenders' application for the severance of the property bound to them was well or ill founded. On the 17th of July, 1776, an arrêt was passed, on the report of M. de la Boulie, which confirmed the sentence, whereby the question was fully settled. A definitive sentence was rendered on the 20th August, 1777, by which the severance was ordered, as prayed by the lenders for whom I contended. This sentence is now the law on this point. The following is an abridg-ment of the argument that I wrote on the subject.

The action of severance takes place when, in a suit for the distribution of effects, I claim certain specific goods which belong to me or on which I have a lien or qualified right of ownership. It would not be just if I were obliged to follow the windings of a general suit involving various rights and demads and to see the thing which is mine or which ought to be mine in consequence of a special privilege, absorbed by the costs of court. Thus, the owner of a thing, of which a deceased person was simply the possessor, may reclaim it and have it severed from the general mass of the property in controversy. So likewise we may reclaim *a deposit which is still in existence.* The debtor may also claim or cause to be *severed* from the general estate of the deceased a pledge which he had given, by paying or tendering to the heir the sum for which it had been given.

The vendor on credit, according to the rigour of the law, is not entitled to a right of claim or of severance. For when one trusted to the credit of a purchaser, as soon as the article is delivered to him, the property is changed, although the price be not paid. *(a)* Nevertheless, according to our usages, the vendor on credit, who has not been paid, may, by virtue of a tacit lien and *quasi* right of property, if there be a suit for the distribution of the general property of his debtor, require the severance of the chattel which he sold and for which he has not yet been paid; for the purpose of having it sold at auction, and being paid out of the sale in preference to every other creditor, or to take as much of it on valuation as will pay his debt. *(b)* In this case, the severence is not a revocation of the first sale. It operates as a new sale; because the price having been trusted in the origin of the transaction, on the credit of the purchaser the primitive alienation had been complete. *(c)*

a §. 41. inst. de rer. devis. L L. 19, 53. ff. de contrah.
emp. L. 38. §. 2, ff. de liber. caus.
b Meynard, liv. 2. ch. 45. Dollive, liv. 4. ch. 10. actes de notoriété de Provence, pag. 176.
c L.. 5. §. 18. H. de tribut. art.

The estate of an insolvent or deceased debtor when in a course of distribution undergoes a kind of division. All that is subject to personal actions or general actions of lien or privilege, forms one mass, and all that is subject to real actions of property or *quasi* property forms a particular which is distinct from the general mass.

What has been said applies to what is called, in cases of bankrupts, the right of *pursuit*. The vendor of merchandize, who has not been paid, may seize it. And he may have it severed from the rest in order that it may be sold for the payment of his privileged debt. By this means, the property of a bankrupt becomes divided into two classes: the first is the property of the general creditors, and the other is subject to the respective liens of particular creditors or to the *quasi* right of property to a thing yet in existence.

This distinction or division takes place every day in commercial partnerships. The partnership is as one person.*(a)* The property of the partnership, considered in one point of view is not the property of the individuals in their particular capacity.*(b)* The creditors of the partnership are preferred in the joint property to the creditor of one of its members, although prior in date, and even to the dowry of the wife of one of them.*(c)*

a L. 22. ff. de fidejuss.
b Dupuy, des lettres de change. ch. 16. pag. 76. Journal du Palais, tom. 1. pag. 779.
c Journal du Palais

tom. 1. pag. 776. Journal des Audiences, tom. 3. pag. 178. Toubeau, tom. 2. pag 101, &c.

The creditors of two different firms, although they are composed of the same persons, have their respective privileges against each partnership.*(d)* D. and Mess. D. and A. had made a joint composition with their respective creditors in which the property of D. personally and the joint property of D. and A. were confounded and the creditors were mingled together. But an arrêt was passed 30th June, 1767, by the Parliament of Aix, by which the property was divided into two parts.

d L. 5. §. 15. ff. de tribut. act.

If the same person keep two shops, *duas tabernas*, the creditors of one have a preference on its contents to the creditors of the other and so *vicé versâ.(e)* The creditors of two different partnerships have their respective liens on their several effects. They are divided into two orders of distribution, because the respective creditors have contracted rather with the firm than with the person. *Unusquisque enim eorum, merci magis, quàm ipsi credidit.*

e L. 5. §. 16. ff. de tribut. act. Straccha, de decoc. tor. part. ult. n. 20. Ansaldus, disc. 4. Brodeau sur la coutume de Paris, tom. 2.

pag. 447. n. 6. Toubeau tom. 2, pag. 381.

The contract of maritime loan is more of a real than personal nature.* The lender lends to the ship or the cargo. He acts on the credit of the *thing* itself, which becomes his debtor. This is the reason why the ordinance (*a*) subjects the ship and freight to the payment of the principal and interest of money lent on bottomry: and makes the cargo liable to the payment of the money which enabled it to be put on board. This privilege is *in rem;* it is a particular privilege or lien on the thing which it affects. It produces a *quasi proprietorship* in the lender, who, by claiming payment from the vessel or cargo, merely reclaims what already belonged to him, in a qualified manner, from the nature of his contract. His loan was to the vessel or cargo: *merci credidit.* He may, then, apply to the thing itself for payment; but it is not in a situation to fulfil its contract if it be involved in a general mass of effects to be distributed.

a art. 7. h. t.

The ship of a bankrupt arrives. His effects are seized, and a suit for distribution takes place. It follows then, from the doctrine against which I am contending, that the seamen, for their wages, the Farmers—general, for the duties, and all others similarly circumstanced should become parties to that complex suit. This cannot reasonably be proposed, for the wages are due by the ship, the duties by the cargo, &c.

---

* This must not be understood in the sense of the common law, in which the word *real* applies exclusively to lands.— In the civil law, every thing is called *real* which relates to property in kind, thus a suit in nature of an action of *replevin* or detinue, would be called a real action. In the same manner a contract made on the credit of property exclusively, is called a *real contract*, in opposition to a contract merely personal. Perhaps, as we say an action, we might also say a contract *in rem.*

Now if, in all these cases, there must be a severance, or rather, if the ship and cargo have never
been included in the general suit of distribution, the
same rule should be observed towards those who
have a privilege of a similar nature as the seamen ; *a* tit. de la
for the 16th art.(*a*) confines itself to establishing the saisie des
order of priorities without altering the nature of the seaux.
privileges.

Another arrêt. In the year 1771, captain Jean-
Baptiste Mourardou equipped the snow *la Vierge de
Grace.* He borrowed at maritime risque on the
vessel 500 livres of André Raoul. 1,000 livres of
Jean-Pierre Plasse and 1,000 livres of Jean-Baptiste
Fabre.

To the two last he sold an interest in an adventure which he had on board, and he borrowed at
maritime risque on the *cargo*, several sums of Jacques Ventre, Jean-Pierre France, Fodrin and Bour-
lier and Francis Gilles. He sailed from Marseilles
and arrived at *Satalia*, in the province of Carama-
nia.* All the merchandize composing his cargo,
the joint and the separate adventures were together.
He sold a great part thereof, which he converted
into the produce of the country, without noting in
his book the price of each separate article. He
continued sailing and trading from port to port to
Damietta, whence he returned to *Satalia*, where
he died 30th March, 1772, of the plague.

The mate brought the vessel back to Marseilles
with part of the returns. The rest was left in the
hands of Roubin, Provencal and Co. who sent the
proceeds by capt. Dauphin. Claire Bourelly, widow
of the defunct, was appointed guardian of his children, and administratrix to the estate.†

* On the coast of Natolia in Asiatic Turkey, the ancient
Anatolia in the province of Asia Minor.

† In the original it is : she took the succession with *benefit of
inventory.* We have already explained what that is, still, as

The lenders required that the snow and the goods on which their money had been secured, should be severed from the mass of the estate and delivered to them, to discharge their respective claims.

A sentence was rendered by the tribunal of Marseilles, on the 17th July, 1776, which ordered, " that the snow should be severed from the general estate of Jean-Baptiste Mourardou, in order that the proceeds thereof should be appropriated to the payment of the claims of Ravel, Plasse and Fabre for the monies lent by them on bottomry with maritime and legal interest and costs."

This sentence rejected the petition of the lenders on the cargo, as well as that of Plasse and Faber, who claimed as partners of the captain in the small adventure; because the returns which had arrived at Marseilles were mixed and confused together. This reason was not a legal one because the whole being the property of the captain, it was subject to the liens of the *respondentia* creditors. They appealed from the sentence. Plasse and Fabre, also appealed, as partners of the captain.

An arrêt was given on the 6th June, 1778, on the report of M. de Beauval, which reversing the sentence, *as to this part*, ordered "that the proceeds of the returns should be separated from the mass of the estate of Mourardou, in order to be distributed among the *respondentia* creditors, to the amount of the sums lent with maritime and common interest and costs; and the remainder of the proceeds" it adds "shall be distributed between the aforesaid Fabre and Plasse, to the amount due to them for their share in the small adventure, with com-

---

more familiar to our readers, we have thought it right, in this as in other instances, to make use of an analogous expression of our own law.

mon legal interest and costs ; saving to the aforesaid Fabre and Plasse, their right to recover a-
gainst the heirs, all further demands, to which they
may be entitled," &c.

———◆———

SECTION VII.

*Concurrence between the lenders at bottomry and
the insurers of those who have privileged or concurrent claims, on the property saved and the
policies of insurance.*

The expenses of salvage are preferred to all §. 1. Ex-
others and ought to be a preferable lien on the pences of
whole.*(a)* salvage.

naufrages. art. 45. tit. des assurances. Vid. Traité des assurances ch. *a* art. 24, and 26.
17. sect, 7. §. 4. tit. des

After the expences of salvage the wreck is affect- Mariners
ed to the seamen for their wages.*(b)* wages.

ch. 17. sect. 11. *b* Traité des ass.

After the salvage and wages, what remains of the Other
wreck is to be distributed among the other credi- creditors.
tors in the order specified in the 16th art. tit. de la
saisie.

In my treatise on insurance,*(c)* I have spoken of Privilege
the privilege which the mariners for their wages and on the freight.
lenders by bottomry have on the freight.

sect. 9. and 11. *c* ch. 17.

M. Valin.*(d)* makes these remaks. " When §. 2. Lien
the solvency of the owner of a vessel which has on the policies.
put to sea becomes doubtful, the material men and *d* art. 3.
workmen may demand, whether he has insured his tit. des
vessel and to what amount and that he may be or- prescrip- tions,
pag. 296. tom. 1.

dered to deposit the policy in the registory of the admiralty, in order that they may have the benefit of their privilege if the policy be effected or cause it to be done. And it is the custom of our admiralty to grant them such security; it not being just that they should run the risk of losing all that is due to them, or at least, a great part of it, in consequence of no insurance being effected. In order to transfer the privilege on the amount of the policy, it does not appear to me necessary that this precaution should be taken by the material men and workmen, excepting in cases were the owner neglects or refuses to do it, when the creditors have a right to cause it to be done in his name. From which it follows, that if the owner has effected an insurance without being constrained to it, I have no doubt that in case of the loss of the vessel, the material men and workmen would be entitled to their privilege in the same manner as if they themselves had effected the policy. But, by an arrêt of the Parliament of Bourdeaux, passed on the report of M. de Marboulin, the father, on the 7th September, 1758, between Mess. Courtés and Foussat, bankrupts and their several creditors, the privilege or lien on the policy which I contend for, on behalf of the material-men and workmen, was rejected, on the principle that there is no law, which authorizes the transferring of a privilege and that every privilege ought to be established by some law."

This decision does not appear to M. Valin to be just, "especially at Bordeaux," he says "where they hold as a maxim, that the price of a thing so far represents the thing itself, that the vendor of moveable property retains his privilege for the price, if he finds it in the hands of a second purchaser. The application of this rule to the case of a privilege on the policy in favour of the material-men and workmen, is so natural, that we cannot conceive how a difference could be made. The produce of the insurance as completely represents the ship, as the price does the thing. It is true that this maxim of the Parliament of Bourdeaux is not adopted in the provinces where the civil law does not prevail: but equity no less requires that the privilege of the material-men and workmen should be extended to the policy, since it is really their property which is insured, at least as far as the ship with her apparel and furniture."

To this I answer that with respect to a separate and specific article the price does not take the place of the thing sold. *In particularibus, pretium non succedit loco rei ; (a)* These authours rely upon different texts of law. *(b)* It follows from this principle, that if a purchaser on credit, has sold the thing on credit, and it ceases to be in existence in its original condition, the first vendor has no privilege for the price against the second purchaser, although the price grows out of the thing which belonged to him and for which he has not been paid. This is the rule which is constantly observed by the Parliament of Aix. With more reason the material-men and workmen, have no privilege on a policy which never belonged to them. For as Cujas says, *(c)* there is nothing necessarily common between the right of pledge and that of property : *nihil commune habet pignus, cum dominio.*

c on the law 6 §. 8. ff. commun divid.

a de Luca, de credito. disc. 35. n. 55 Faber def. 26. C. qui pot. in pign. Duperier, tom. 1. liv. 3. quest. 1. Julian Code, v. discutio, 8. B.

b L. 70. §. 3. ff. de legat. 2d. 1. 3. C. in quib. caus. pign.

In a word, the ordinance gives no privilege to the material-men and workmen but *on the ship.* Consequently, they have none on the policy, according to the rule established in the preamble of this chapter. If the ship were represented by the policy, it would be necessary that a privilege on the policy should be given to the seamen and to every other creditor, mentioned in art. 16. *(d)* By this means, the purpose of insurance would be destroyed. *(e)*

d tit. de la saisie.

e vid. Supra ch. 4. sect. 11. §. 3.

If the effects lost were represented by the sum insured, the insurance would be represented by a re-assurance ; but we have seen,(a) that the first insured has no direct action nor privilege on the re-insurance. Thus, the transfer or subrogation of which M. Valin speaks, is not admissible.

a traité des ass. ch. 8. sect. xiv.

Question on this subject.

This point being thus explained we may resolve some difficulties that have been started on the sub-ject.

Have the material-men and workmen a right to demand of the owner of a ship that has put to sea, whether he has insured the vessel and to what a-mount? I think not. They might have seized the vessel before she set sail, but having suffered her to go, they have nothing but a personal action against the owner and a privilege on the ship. The right of effecting a policy belongs to the insurer and if he become bankrupt, it is the property of his creditors generally.

If, before his bankruptcy, he had caused policies to be effected, they would belong to the general mass of creditors and the material-men and work-men would not be entitled to lay claim to them.

If, while he is in business, the owner assigns to a third person, policies effected before his failure, they would belong to the assignee, exclusive of the material men, workmen and the general mass of creditors. It is true, that during the risk, the po-licy is an *accessory* of the thing insured, as I have observed before.(b)   1st. After the loss of the ship, the policy becomes a substantive right independent of any thing else and gives a right of personal action in favour of the assured, or of his creditors or as-signs.   2d. During the risk, the policy, notwith-standing its dependence on the thing insured, is an

b Traité des ass. ch. 16. §. 3.

eventual debt, capable of being assigned, and does
not belong to the material-men or workmen.

There is an easy method by which they might
secure their interest. They might procure sureties,
who, for a certain reward in the nature of a premium,
would become security for their debt, in case of
the loss of the vessel. For we may become security on a condition and it is not essential to suretyship
that it should be gratuitous : *fidejubendi causâ pecuniam accipere possumus.*(a) Suretyship is different
from insurance and what I have here said does not
militate with the observations in my treatise on in-
surance. a Gode-froy, ad L. 19. §. 1. ff. de donat. et ad L. 6. §. 7. ff. mandati. Heringi-us, de fidej. part. 1. cap. 27. n 119. pag. 352. Corvinus, C. de fi-dejus.

pag. 661. Roccus de assur. not. 76. Duperier, tom. 2. liv. 2. n. 86.
pag. 94.

The material-men and workmen are not co-pro-
prietors of the ship. If they were to make insurance
on account of their privilege, it would be improper
as an insurance, though it might be regarded as a
security and authorized by that name. At least
such is my opinion, for it would be well, in such a
case, to mitigate the rigour of the law and give
them some means of securing their interest.

However, it would be wrong to conclude from
this that seamen may secure their wages: the lender
his maritime profit; the merchant, the profit that
he calculates to make and the captain his freight.
Reasons of publick convenience do not permit them
to secure these objects nor to make insurance upon
them. Ship-wrecks would become too frequent, if
personal interest were not concerned in the preservation of the ship. Moreover, the wages, profits,
&c. depend upon an uncertain event and are conditional debts which have no certain existence, and
are also less susceptible of suretyship than insurance:
instead of which the privilege of the material-men

I ɪ

and the workmen is an acquired and detirminate right, to which these considerations do not apply.

All these questions were discussed in an arbitration which took place under the following circumstances: Jean Chauvin was the creditor of Mess. L. bankrupts, to the amount of 2020 livres for materials furnished to the *Aimable Louise*, captain Bauzau. Etienne Jourdan, ship builder, was also a creditor for a balance of 4138 livres for the building of the ship *Deux Freres*, captain Guerin.

Chauvin proceeded against the bankrupts and their creditors generally, in the Consulate Court of Marseilles for his debt and he demanded a privilege on the policies effected on the *Aimable Louise*, which had been captured by the English. Jourdan also proceeded in the same manner for his debt and claimed the policy on the *Deux Freres* which had likewise been taken by the English.

An award was made on the 31st May, 1783, by M. M. Brés, Gignoux and myself, the arbitrators, by which it was declared that they were entitled to no privilege, as the right of pledge ceased with the loss of the vessels which were bound to them.

It follows from this principle, that the right of pledge which belongs to the lender on the whole effects which the borrower has put at risk, is never transferred to the policies, which the latter has effected on his property. It is true, that for his capital, the lender is preferred to the insurer, as to effects saved from the wreck.(*a*) But that is all. The benefit of the insurance still remains the property of the borrower. It would, however, cease to be so, if Valin's doctrine were adopted. See my Traité des Assur.(*b*)

a art. 18. h. t.

b ch. 17. sect. 12. pag. 234.

In my treatise on insurance,(*a*) I have spoken of § 3. Concurrence between the insurers and mariners, currence insurers and lenders, and also among insurers them- different selves. In this treatise,(*b*) I have spoken of the con- creditors. currence between the lender and borrower and in sect. 11, the present chapter,(*c*) have treated of that between 12. 13 lenders themselves, &c. *b* ch. 11.
c sect. 4 and 5. sect. 2,

In my treatise on insurance,(a) I have spoken of the concurrence between the insurers and mariners, insurers and lenders, and also among insurers themselves. In this treatise,(*b*) I have spoken of the concurrence between the lender and borrower and in the present chapter,(*c*) have treated of that between lenders themselves, &c.

§ 3. Concurrence between different creditors. *a* ch. 17. sect. 11. 12. 13 and 14, *b* ch. 11. sect. 2,

———

SECTION VIII.

Of priority in cases where there are secret part owners by assignment from the original owners.

The cession of a part of a person's interest in the § Gene- ship and cargo or in a particular shipment is common vations. among us. It is a sort of secret partnership. The speculation is made in the name of the assignor, who has the management of it and who binds himself to the assignee to divide the net profits with him, ac- cording to the proportion assigned. I say the *net proceeds ;* by which I mean what remains after de- ducting all costs and charges. If the assignor fur- nished the whole capital, he, of course, must take it back, before dividing any profits, and would be preferred, in this respect, to the particular creditors of his partner.

It is prudent to register the assignment in the of- fice of the admiralty before the departure of the ship : otherwise, the ceded interest in the vessel would *d* tit. des continue to be affected to the debts of the vendor, Navires. conformably to the 3rd art.(*d*)

As the assignor is the manager of the common ad- § 2. Are venture and the chief in the partnership, those who those who lend mo- risque to the assignor preferred to the assignee ? ney at

lend money to him at maritime risque are preferred
to the assignor, although he has furnished his own
proportion. M. commanding the ship l'Aigle and
interested in the vessel and cargo, assigned 6,000
livres of it to Bodington and 4,000 livres to Stamma.
At the same time he borrowed money at maritime
risque from Mess. Orgeas, Soria and Pauquet. The
ship sailed for the Indies and returned. A suit took
place between the assignees and the lenders. The
admiralty gave the preference to the latter: and thus
the question was again decided by the arrêt of the 6th
June, 1778, reported in the 6th sect of this chapter.

§. 3 Are those who lend at risque to the assigner preferred to the assignor? — If the assignor borrow money at maritime risque
on his part and do not ship his proportion, the as-
signor may do it, to the exclusion of the lenders.
The common property does not cease to be in the
custody of the assignor; it is to him a sort of special pledge, *venditor, pignoris loco, quod vendidit
retinet, quoad emptor satisfaciat.(a)*

a L. 31. §. 8. ff. de ædil. edict. L. 13. §. 8 ff. de act. empt. L. 22. ff. de hæred. vendit. L. 14. §. 1. ff. de furtis.

§. 4. What, if the assigned interest be modified by a contract of maritime loan? — I assign an interest in my ship and cargo to the captain or supercargo thereof, who, to guard against
becoming my debtor in consequence of shipwreck,
declares that he takes it only as a loan at maritime
risque. The chief object of the parties has been
to establish a sort of partnership, which shall sti-
mulate the zeal of the agent without being prejudicial to the interest of the owner. This partnership
does not destroy its nature, by the clause of maritime risque, which is only an incident and an accessory to it; for to judge of a contract we must regard its principal feature: *à præponderante naturâ,
contractus judicatur.(b)*

b Daplessis, tom. 1. pag. 370. See the arrêt in Floret's case, reported in ch. 5. sect. 4. §. 2. See also ch. 1. sect. 4. §. 2.

If a captain or supercargo were permitted to a-buse the confidence which is reposed in him and increase the proportion assigned to him by contract-ing maritime loans, such partnerships would soon cease. The industrious mariner would be deprived of this resource, and owners would not risk their goods, if they were liable to cessions which might be fatal to them.

He who lends money to a captain or supercargo, in the place where the owners reside and without their consent, ought to know that the borrower can-not pledge more than his own property in the ship, and if this be an undivided portion of interest which has not been paid for, it is but just that the whole vessel and cargo should remain affected to an owner who has never ceased to have it in his hands and in his power as his specific pledge. He ought to be paid from the whole of the partnership effects, be-cause they have not ceased to be such by a subor-dinate contract of maritime risque, which is nearly incidental to that of partnership. *Illud adnotandum est quòd quando unus contractus incidit in alium per modum pacti, talis contractus dicitur accessorius, et* [a] *pars ipsius contractus principalis ; et ideò illa actio, quæ proficiscitur ex contractu principali, oritur etiam ex incidenti. Et ità ille contractus semper inspici-tur, qui est principalis, non accessorius,(a)*

[a] Manti-ca, de ta-citis, lib. 1. tit. 14. u. 12. pag. 35.

What I have said does not apply, where the as-signee makes bottomry or respondentia bills in favour of the assignor, by way of payment for the property assigned. It is true that the vendor on credit does not extinguish the debt, by receiving promissory or negotiable notes. Such notes are no more than a recognition of the debt and are only given by way of security on the first obligation, which always continues the same : *cedula bancaria datur pro cautelâ et cautione.(b)* But the assignor, who

What, if the as-signee had given bills of gross ad-venture in favour of the as-signer as the consi-deration of the in-terest as-signed ?

[b] Merlinus, de pignor. lib. 5. quest. 30. n. 33. pag. 601.

a Manti-
ca, de
tacitis,
lib. 17.
tit 3. n.
13. pag.
292. Cas-
saregis.
disc. 21.
n. 4. et
seq.
converts the interest ceded into a loan at maritime
risque, becomes a lender; he acquires a new claim
and of a different nature. It is a *novation** of the
debt. *Sine dubio locum habet novatio, quandò ulti-
mus contractus, cum primo non compatitur. Tunc
enim posteriora derogant prioribus.(a)*

M. Louis Aycard was the owner of the ship called the *Actif* and her cargo. He ceded a moiety,
amounting to 70,078 livres, 5s. 4den. to Honnoré B.

B. borrowed at maritime risque from several
persons, 29,871 livres. There remained due to
Aycard 34,007 livres, to pay which he executed
three bills of maritime loan for 12,000, 9,007 and
13,000 livres respectively, in the following form.
" The undersigned Honnoré B. being concerned
in the one half of the *Actif,* her tackle and cargo,
commanded by Pierre Guichard and now at anchor
in the port of Marseilles, acknowledges to have received of Mr. Louis Aycard, the sum of —— at
respondentia, which sum has been employed in the
equipment of the vessel and procuring a cargo for
the said vessel for a voyage to the West India
Islands and back to this place, at the risk and peril
of the said Aycard, to whom, or to whose order, I
promise to pay the aforesaid sum with maritime interest of seven *per cent.*

On the same day, the account current between
Aycard and B. was stated between them in these
terms. " I acknowledge the present account cur-

---

* Novat on, a term derived from the civil law, is the change
which the creditor and debtor make, who substitute one debt in
the place of another; so that the first obl gation subsists no
longer, and the debtor remains bound only by the second. *Novatio est prioris, &c.* l. 1. ff. *de novat. et deleg.* Dom. lib. 1.
tit. 3. sect. 1. It is analogus to what we call in our law *extin-
guishment.*

rent to be just and true, for the balance of which, I admit that I owe M. Louis Aycard the sum of 34007 livres for which sum I have given to him my three bills of maritime loan. Marseilles 23d October, 1773."

B. sailed in the vessel, as supercargo. The ship arrived safely at her port and returned to Marseilles. The moiety of the cargo was not sufficient to pay the debts which B. had contracted, in the West Indies. Aycard as manager of the ship and cargo, claimed the right of paying himself first to the exclusion of the lenders. They contended that they should come in concurrence with him. He has no evidence of his title, they said, but the bills of maritime loan which he took in payment of the moiety, and his title is therefore of the same nature with ours, &c.

On the 23d August, 1779, a sentence was rendered by our court of admiralty, which " rejected the claim of the lenders to come into concurrence, but reserved to them the right of proceeding against Aycard, in the proper manner, for the sums or merchandize to be received and which should remain in his hands on account of B's proportion, after his own debt should be paid.

This sentence was reversed; and the concurrence prayed for by the lenders, was granted by an arrêt of the Parliament of Aix, rendered on the 20th June, 1782, on the report of M. le Blanc de Castillon, a magistrate who nobly follows the footsteps of his father. *Fortes creantur fortibus.*

FINIS.

AN APPENDIX

CONTAINING THE TITLES

DE EXERCITORIA ACTIONE, DE LEGE RHODIA DE JACTU,

AND DE NAUTICO FŒNORE,

Translated from the Digests and Code of Justinian,

AND THE TITLE

DES CÓNTRACTS A LA GROSSE AVENTURE *OU* A

RETOUR DE VOYAGE,

FROM THE

MARINE ORDINANCE OF LOUIS XIV.

A

Translation of the First Title of the Fourteenth Book of the Digest, entitled :.....

De exercitoriâ actione

DIGEST, Book XIV. Tit. I.

Of the responsibility of Ship Owners, for the acts of the Master, and of the action which results therefrom, called actio exercitoriâ.

LAW I.

Ulpianus, lib. 28. Ad Edict.

Utilitatem.... The usefulness of this edict is so evident, that every one must be sensible of it. For, as we are sometimes obliged to contract with masters of vessels, with whose persons or condition we are entirely unacquainted, it is equitable, that he who has appointed such master to the command of the vessel should be bound by his acts, in the same manner as he is bound who appoints an agent, factor or deputy to his tavern or traffick, the necessity being greater to contract with the master of a vessel, than with such agents. For we may enquire into the condition of the agent with whom we contract, but not so with a master of a vessel, for, sometimes, neither the time nor the place will allow of deliberation.

Magistrum Navis. § 1. We call him the *master of a ship* who has the care of the whole vessel.

Sed si. § 2. (But) if we *contract* with any of the mariners, we have no action against the owner, although an action lies against him for the *tort* of any of those who are on board the vessel for the sake of navigating her. For there is a difference between torts and contracts: he who appoints a master, tacitly authorizes you to contract with him; he who appoints mariners, does not so authorize you, but is nevertheless answerable for the frauds and tortious acts which they may commit.

Magistri autem. § 3. Masters are appointed for the sake of letting vessels to hire either to transport merchandize or passengers or to purchase things necessary for the furniture of the vessel: but if he is also appointed to buy or sell merchandize, he binds the owner *hoc nomine.*

Cujus autem. § 4. It matters not what is the condition of the master, whether a freeman or a slave, and whether the servant of the owner of the vessel or of another; nor matters it of what age he is, he who appoints him being to impute all to himself.

Magistrum autem. § 5. We not only call him *master* whom the owner has appointed, but him also whom the master has put in his place, and so the learned Julianus answered to an ignorant owner. Besides, if he knows and suffers him to act as master in the vessel, he is supposed to have appointed him. This opinion appears to me indisputable. For, he who has appointed a master, must answer for all his acts, otherwise those who contract may be deceived, and this is more easily admitted against masters of vessels than against other agents, for the sake of utility. What then if he who appointed the master, forbid him to substitute another in his stead? We must see now whether we can admit the opinion of Julian in this case. Suppose the owner has positively forbid the master to appoint Titius, by name, as his substitute. It must be said, however, that even in that case, the interests of those who navigate must be attended to.

Navem accipere. § 6. *Navis* is a generic name for all vessels, whether they navigate on the seas or in lakes, or in rivers, and it also applies to boats. *(Schedus.)*

Non autem. § 7. The prœtor, however, does not, in all cases, give an action against the owner, but only for such things to which the master *has been appointed,* that is to say: If he has been appointed to that particular thing, as for instance, if he has been hired to carry a burthen, or has purchased something useful for the passengers, or if he has contracted for any thing for the ship's repairs, or with the mariners for their labour and hire.

Quid si mutuam. § 8. What if he has borrowed money, will it be considered as done in the regular course of his business? Pegasus is of opinion, that if he has borrowed it for the use of the object to which he is appointed, an action will lie, which opinion I conceive to be correct. What then if he has borrowed for the sake of fitting out the vessel and hiring mariners?

Unde quærit Osilius. § 9. Hence Osilius makes a query, whether if he has borrowed money for the repairs of the vessel and afterwards converts it to his own use, an action will lie against the owner? And he says; if he borrowed it *hac lege,* for the purpose of employing it on the vessel and afterwards altered his mind, the owner is liable, and must impute it to himself that he appointed such a man; otherwise, if his intention was from the beginning to to defraud the lender, and if he did not specially express, that he borrowed it for the use of the vessel: which distinction Pœdius approves.

Sed et si in pretio. § 10. But if the master deceived him with respect to the price of the things purchased, it will be to the damage of the owner not the lender.

Sed si ab alio. § 11. And if having borrowed
money of another, he should pay with it the one who
had lent money for the repairs of the vessel, I think
that this second lender is entitled to his action in the
same manner as if he had advanced the money to the
use of the vessel.

Igitur præpositio. § 12. The appointment therefore points out a certain rule to those who contract.
For, if one has been appointed to the command of a
vessel, to receive freight money; but not to let out
the vessel, the owner shall not be bound, if the master lets her out, and *vice versa*, if to let to freight and
not to receive or demand it, or if he appointed him
to take passengers and not to take goods on freight,
or *vice versa*, if to exceed his power, he shall not bind
the owner. If he is appointed to let out the vessel for
the freight of certain goods, as for instance hemp or
vegetables, and instead of that he takes in marble or
other articles, it is said the owner shall not be bound.
For there are ships expressly made for carrying
bulky articles, others for the carrying of passengers,
and I know that several owners command their captains not to receive passengers, and also to traffick in
certain regions and in certain seas. There are for instance some vessels which carry passengers from *Cas-
siopa* or *Dyrrachium* to *Brudusium*, and which are
unable to carry burthens; some of them are able to
sail on rivers but not on the sea.

Si plures. § 13. If there are several masters
whose offices are not distinct, what is done by any one
of them shall bind the owner: if their offices are distinct, as the one to take freight, the other to receive

the freight money, each shall bind the owner for what he does in the execution of his particular office.

Sed & si. § 14. But if they have been so appointed, as is done in several instances, so that none of them shall do any thing without the concurrence of of the other, whoever contracts with one of them singly, must impute it to himself.

Exercitorum autem. § 15. We call *exercitor (a)* the person who receives the freights and profits of a vessel. Whether he be himself the owner of the ship, or whether he has hired her from the owner for a time or forever.

Parvi autem. § 16. It matters little, however, whether this *exercitor*, this general or special owner, is a man or a woman, a father or a minor or a slave; but if a minor owns a vessel, the authority of his guardian is requested to legalize his contracts.

[*(a)* The Latin word *exercitor* cannot be rendered by an exactly corresponding word in our language ; it answers to the French word *armateur*, and means not only the actual owner of a vessel ; but he who is in possession of her, whether for himself or for another, who has the care of fitting her out, and who acts as owner, though it may not be in his own right. Thus a special owner, one who holds a ship in pledge to pay himself out of her freights, or one who has hired her for a voyage, or for a limited time, and also he who has the vessel in charge as the agent or factor of the owner or owners, all come within the meaning of the word *exercitor*. The master himself may be *exercitor* in many cases and under a variety of circumstances. The English term " *ship's husband*" comes nearest to the idea which the word *exercitor* conveys to the mind, but it is a word but lately brought into use, and not yet sufficiently defined. It has been generally employed for the *acting owner*, the one of the part owners who has the actual charge of fitting out the vessel, but we do not know that it has yet been applied to a *mere agent*, though perhaps it might be so applied without impropriety. It must be left to time and usage to fix the precise meaning and application of the word.]

Est autem. § 17. It is at the party's election to sue either the owner or the master.

Sed ex contrario. § 18, But on the contrary, this action (the *actio excercitoria)* does not lie, for the owner against those who contract with the master, because he does not want this extraordinary remedy; but he may sue the master *ex locato,* if he employed him for a reward, or *ex mandato,* if gratuitouly. When employed however, in the transportation of provisions, the prefects of the capital and the presidents of the provinces for the publick benefit, will give to owners an extraordinary action, founded on the contract of the master.

Si is, qui navem. § 19. If the *exercitor* of a vessel is in another man's power, and acted as such with his consent, judgment shall be given against him in whose power he is, on contracts made with the master.

Licet autem. § 20. But although an action lies against him in whose power he was, who acted as *exercitor* of the vessel, it must appear that he thus acted with his consent. They therefore are bound *in solidum* (jointly and severally) who have the *exercitor* of a vessel in their power, because the employment of vessels is a matter of the highest importance to the commonwealth. But the usage is not the same with respect to factors not employed in and about the fitting out of vessels. Those who contract with such a person who traffics on his own account, with the consent of his master, parent or guardian, shall only be entitled to relief to the amount of the factor's *peculium,* or hereditary portion. But if a contract has been made with the master of a vessel with the knowledge, though without the consent, of him in whose power he is, shall we give an action *in solidum* against the master, father or guardian as if he had consented, or only an *actio tributoria*, that is to say, extending only to the *peculium* or hereditary portion of his dependent? It is best in a doubtful case to follow the words of the edict, and not to raise an obligation *in solidum* from the mere knowledge of a father or master in the case of vessels, nor from his consent in the case of mere land traffick, and such seems to be the opinion of Pomponius; if, says he, the master of a vessel is in another man's power, and act with his *consent*, then the person in whose power he is will be bound with him *in solidum*, otherwise only *in peculium*.

In potestate. § 21. By those that are in the power of the other person we mean, sons and daughters and servants of either sex.

Si tamen. § 22. If, however, a *servus peculiaris* that is to say, a slave belonging to a minor or to another slave, as a part of his *peculium*, shall act as *exercitor* of a vessel with the consent of the minor or slave to whose *peculium* he belongs, the father or master who has not given his consent shall be held only *de peculis*, but the son himself shall be held *in solidum*. Clearly if they act as *exercitors* with the consent of the father or master, they shall be bound *in solidum*, and also the son, if he gave his consent, shall likewise be bound *in solidum*.

Quamquam. § 23. Although the prœtor allow the action only in case of a contract with the master yet (as Julian has also written) even if the contract is made with the *exercitor* himself, the father or master shall be bound *in solidum*.

Hæc actio. § 24. This action is given against the exercitor *ex persona magistri;* and therefore if you elect to sue one of them, you cannot afterwards sue the other; but if the master pays any thing, the obligation shall be so far diminished: and so if the

M m

exercitor pays any thing either on account of his *honorary* obligation, or in the name of the master, the obligation shall be lessened, because he that pays for me discharges me.

Si plures. § 25. If several act as exercitors of a vessel you may sue all or any of them jointly and severally.

LAW II.

Gaius, Lib. 9. edictum provinciale.

*Non implures....*No man shall be driven to several adversaries who contracted only with one.

LAW III.

Paulus, Lib. 29, ad edict.

*Nec quicquam....*It makes no kind of difference what share he who contracted had in the vessel : it is his business to make the other part owners contribute by *action of partnership.*

LAW IV.

Ulpian, Lib. 29, ad edic.

*Si tamen....*If several act as *exercitors* of a vessel in their own persons they shall be bound according to their respective shares, nor shall they be considered as masters of the vessel for each other.

Sed si plures. § 1. But if several owners of the same vessel appoint one of their number to be the master, they may be sued on his contracts *in solidum.*

Sed si servus, § 2. If a servant to several owners act as *exercitor* of the vessel with their consent, it will be the same as in the case of several *exercitors;* it is clear that if he acts with the consent of one of them, that one is bound jointly and severally with him, and therefore I think that if he acts with the consent of all, they are all so bound.

Si servus sit. § 3. If he who acted as *exercitor* of the vessel with the consent of his master was a servant, and the master aliens him, he who aliened him is still bound, and likewise if the servant dies, he shall be bound, for he is bound for the master of the vessel though he is dead.

Hæ actiones. § 4. These actions will lie for ever for or against the heirs : so if a servant dies who acted as *exercitor* of a vessel with the consent of his master, this action shall be given after the year, although actions *de peculio* are to be brought within the year.

LAW V.

Paulus, Lib. 29. ad Edict.

*Si eum....*If you have for master of your vessel a person who is in my power, I have an action against you if you contract with him. The same if he is our common servant. You will however have an action against me *ex locato* for having hired the labour of my servant, &c. (*The remainder of this § is uninteresting, and relates only to the hiring of slaves, &c.)*

Item si servus. § 1. Also if my servant acts as *exercitor* of a vessel, and I contract with the master or captain appointed by him, this will not prevent me from having my action against the captain, either *jure honorario* or *jure civili,* for this edict does not prevent any other person from having his action against the master; and the remedy given against

An Essay on

the owner by this edict is cumulative, and the right of action against the master is not taken away by it.

LAW VI.

Paulus, Lib. 6. Brevis Edicti.

Si servus non....If a servant or slave acts as *exer-citor* of a vessel without the consent of his master, an action is given against him with this difference, that if it is with his master's knowledge, the action is *quasi tributoria*, if without his knowledge, the action *de peculio* lies.

Si communis. § 1. If a slave belonging to several persons act as exercitor of a vessel, with the consent of his masters, then an action lies *in solidum* against every one of them.

LAW VII.

Africanus, Lib. 8. Quæstionum.

Lucius Titius....Lucius Titius appointed *Stichus* master of his vessel: he having borrowed money, acknowledged that he had received it for the repairs of the vessel. It is asked whether *Titius* is answerable in an *actio exercitoria* in like manner as if the lender should prove that the money had been actually employed in repairing of the vessel? It is answered that the lender has an action, if when he lends money the vessel was actually in want of repairs : that it is not, however, necessary that the lender should take upon himself the charge of repairing the vessel, and thus do the business of the owner (which must, undoubtedly, be the case if he is obliged to prove that the money has been laid out in repairs:) it is enough that he knows that he lends it for a purpose which falls within the master's power and authority. This cannot be done other-wise but by his knowing also that the money he lends is necessary for repairs. Therefore, although the vessel be in actual want of repairs, yet if *much* more money should be lent than was necessary for those repairs, no action *in solidum* is given against the owner of the vessel.

Interdum. § 1. We must also enquire whether the money was lent in such a place where the thing for which it was borrowed could be purchased. What if one has lent money to purchase a sail on an island where no sail at all can be had? In short, the lender must use *some diligence* about this matter.

Eadem. § 2. The same thing, nearly, may be said respecting the *actio institoria*, that is to say, the ac-tion founded on the acts of *factors in the land trade.* For here the lender must also know that the money was necessary to purchase the merchandize which the agent was entrusted to buy, and it is sufficient if he lent it for that special purpose, the lender is not obliged to take upon himself to see that the money is actually so employed.

THE

Second Title of the Fourteenth Book of the Digests, entitled....

De lege Rhodia de Jactu.

DIGEST, Lib. XIV. Tit. II.

Of the Rhodian Law concerning Jettison.

LAW I.

Paulus, lib. 2. Sententiarum.

Lege Rhodiâ. The Rhodian law ordains, that if goods are thrown overboard for the purpose of lightening the vessel, as it is done for the good of all, all must come into a contribution for the same.

LAW II.

Same, Lib. 34. ad Edictum.

Si laborante: While the vessel labours, if a jettison be made of goods which were laden on freight, the owners of them have an action *ex locato* against the master of the vessel, who has an action *ex conducto* against the owners of the goods saved, that they may make good the damage by contribution. But Servius answers, that you must sue the master *ex locato,* that he may retain the merchandize of the other passengers, until they shall have contributed their share of the damage. Nay, although the master retains the goods, he has, moreover, an action *ex locato* against the freighters; but what if they are only passengers who have no goods on board? It is certainly more convenient, if there be any goods, to retain them. But if there are none, and if he hired the whole vessel, he must bring his action *ex conducto* as against passengers who have hired places in the vessel; for it is extremely just that those who have saved their goods by the loss of those of others, should contribute to the damage.

Si conservatis. §. 1. If the goods be preserved, and the ship is hurt or disabled, no contribution is to take place, because there is a difference between the things that belong to the vessel and those for which a reward is received. For if a smith breaks his hammer or his anvil, it must not be imputed to him who has given him work to do. But if that damage has happened by the act of the passengers, or from fear of danger, they must make good the damage by a contribution.

Cum in eadem, §. 2. Several merchants had loaded various quantities of goods on board the same ship, in which there were several passengers both freemen and slaves. In consequence of a violent tempest a jettison became indispensable. It was asked whether all must contribute to the jettison: and whether those must contribute who had goods on board which did not load the vessel, such as pearls, jewels, &c. and in what proportion they must contribute? and whether there must also be a contribution for the heads of freemen, and by what action it could be enforced? It was determined that all must contribute who had derived an advantage from the jettison, because it was a tribute due by those things which had been preserved, and therefore, that the owner of the vessel was bound to contribute for his share: the amount of the jettison must be apportioned according to the value of the goods.

No estimation can be made of the body of a free-man. The owners of things lost have an action *ex conducto* against the master of the vessel. It has also been agitated whether an estimation is to be made of the cloths and jewels of every person ? and it was unanimously agreed that they should contribute, but not such things as are on board for purposes of consumption, as provisions. And this is so much the more reasonable, because if they should become scarce in the course of the voyage, what every one has is to be used in common.

Si navis : §. 3. If the vessel is ransomed from pirates, Servius, Ofilius and Labeo, say, that all ought to contribute to the ransom. But whatever is carried off by pirates is to be considered as the loss of him to whom it belonged; nor is he obliged to contribute who ransomed his own goods.

Portio autem : §. 4. There must be a difference, however, in the valuation of the things that are saved and of those that are lost; nor is it any matter whether those which have been lost would have been sold for a higher price, because the loss and not the profit is here to be estimated—but as to the things which are to contribute they must be valued, not at the price for which they were bought, but, at that for which they may sell.

Servorum : §. 5. Nor can an estimation be made of servants that perish at sea, any more than of sick men who die abroad or throw themselves into the sea.

Si quis : §. 6. If any of the passengers cannot pay, it will be no detriment to the master, for he is not to enquire into the circumstances of every one.

Si res: §. 7.   If the things that have been thrown overboard appear again, the contribution is discharged; but if it has already been made, then those who have paid, have an action *ex locato* against the master, that he may recover it *ex conducto* and pay what he shall have recovered.

Res autem: §. 8.   But the thing thrown overboard remains the property of the owner, nor does it belong to the finder, for it is not considered as derelict.

LAW III.

Papianus, Lib. 19. *Responsorum.*

Cum arbor: If a mast or any other thing belonging to the vessel be thrown out in order to avert a common danger, a contribution is due.

LAW IV.

Callistratus, Lib. 2. *Quæstionum.*

Navis onustæ: If, in order to lighten a vessel, which has been so much loaded, that she cannot enter a river or port, some goods are put into the boat, that the vessel may not be in danger either at sea or in the river or port, and if the said boat perishes, those whose goods have been saved in the ship, must come into contribution, with those who lost theirs in the boat, in the same manner, as if a jettison had been made.   This Sabinus proves, lib. 2. *Responsorum.* Otherwise, if the boat has been saved with part of the merchandize, and the vessel has been lost, there is to be no contribution for the loss of those who lost their effects aboard the ship, because there is no contribution except in case a vessel is saved by a jettison.

Sed si navis: §. 1. But if the vessel, having been lightened during a storm by a jettison of the goods of one shipper, is lost in another place, and the goods of some shippers are saved by the *divers* for a reward, those who saved their goods by means of the divers, must contribute to him whose goods have been thrown overboard for the sake of lightening the vessel, as Sabinus justly answered. But on the contrary, those who so preserved their goods are not to have a contribution from him whose effects were cast into the sea to relieve the vessel if they should afterwards be found by the divers, because it cannot be said that *their* goods were cast into the sea for the preservation of the ship.

Cum autem: §. 2. But if a jettison is made from the vessel and the goods of some person which remained on board have been spoiled or damaged, is he obliged to contribute? for he must not be loaded with a double loss; viz. the damage which his goods suffered and that of contribution. But it may be answered that he is to contribute, estimating his goods at their present value: as for instance, goods of two persons are respectively worth twenty pieces, and some of them are so damaged by the sea water as to be reduced to ten: he whose goods remained unhurt shall contribute for twenty and the other only as for ten pieces. We must consider, however, while we adopt this opinion, what has been the cause of the damage of the goods, that is to say, whether they have been damaged in consequence of the jettison or by some other cause, as for instance, from their being stowed in some corner where the water penetrated, for in this case they must contribute. But if from the first mentioned cause the owner must not bear the burthen of contribution, because he suffered from the jettison itself. Again, what if the goods have been spoiled by being wet with the sea water occasioned by the jetsison? But a much more subtle distinction is made, to wit, whether the damage or the contribution is greater, as for instance, these things were worth twenty pieces, the contribution is ten and the damage is two pieces—after deducting the damage the remainder is to contribute. What then if the damage amount to more than the contribution? As for instance, if the things have been damaged to the value of ten pieces and ought to contribute two? Undoubtedly they ought not to bear this double burthen. But let us enquire whether they ought to contribute any thing. For what is the difference whether I lose my goods by throwing them overboard or have them damaged by sea water? In like manner, as you relieve him who lost his goods, so ought you to assist him who had them damaged by the jettison; and thus answers *Papirius Fronto.*

LAW V.

Hermogenianus, Lib. 2. *Juris Epitomarum.*

Amissæ navis. The loss of a vessel is not to be made up by the contribution of those who have saved their goods from the shipwreck. For the equity of contribution only obtains when the ship is saved by a jettison agreed upon at a time of common danger.

Arbora cæsa. §, 1. If the mast be cut away, in order to save the ship and goods, the *equity of contribution* takes place.

LAW VI.

Julianus, Lib. 86. *Digestorum.*

Navis adversâ : A ship disabled by a storm, her rigging mast and yard destroyed by the lightning is carried into *Hippona :* and there having hastily purchased new furniture and apparel, sails to *Ostia,* where she lands her cargo in safety. It is asked whether the owners of the cargo are bound to make good the damage of the owner of the ship ? I answer, they are not: for this expense was incurred more for the sake of refitting the ship than to save the cargo.

LAW VII.

Paulus, Lib. 3. *Epitomarum Alfeni Digestorum.*

Cum depressa: If a ship is lost or cast away, whatever any body saves of his own, he saves for himself, in like manner as what is saved from a fire.

LAW VIII.

Julianus, Lib. 2. *Ex Minicio.*

Qui levandæ. Those who throw any goods out of a vessel in order to lighten her, are not desirous to abandon them as derelict. But they mean to reserve to themselves the right to take them away, if they should find them, or to look for them, if they should suspect where they are: in like manner as a person who throws down a burthen on his way, intending soon to come back with others to retake it.

LAW IX.

[Αξιωσις] The petition of *Eudæmon* of *Nico-media* to the emperor *Autoninus;* " May it please the emperor. *Having been shipwrecked on the coast of Italy, the Revenue Officers from the Cyclades Islands seized our property and plundered us of every thing.*"

To which the Emperor answered:

" *I am indeed the Sovereign of the world, but the law is the Sovereign of the sea. Let this matter be determined by the maritime law of Rhodes so far as it is not in opposition to our law.*"

A similar answer was made by the Emperor Augustus.

LAW X.

Labeo, Lib. 1. *Pithanon à Paulo Epitomatorum.*

Si vehenda. If you have undertaken to carry slaves on board of your vessel, and if one die during the voyage, no freight is due for him. *Paulus* says that in this case we must inquire into the nature of the contract, whether freight was to be paid for those who were shipped on board, or for those who were carried to their place of destination; but if the latter is not proved, it will be sufficient for the master of the vessel to prove that the slave was shipped on board.

Si ea conditione, § 1. If you have hired a vessel on condition that she should carry your goods, and the master without being compelled to it by any necessity, and knowing it to be against your will, has trans-shipped them into a worse vessel, and your goods perish with the vessel into which they have been lately transferred, you have an action *ex conducto locato* against the master of the first vessel. *Paulus* says, it is different if both vessels have perished in that voyage, without any fraud on the part of the master. The same law will obtain if the master was detained by authority and prohibited to sail with your goods. Likewise if the master has taken your goods on condition that he should pay a penalty to you if he did not land them by such a day at the place of their destination and has incurred the penalty without any fault of his. Of consequence the same law must obtain if it is proved that the master being detained by sickness could not navigate. And we must pay the same if his vessel was disabled without any fault or fraud on his part.

Si conduxisti. §. 2. If you have hired a vessel of two thousand *jars (amphoræ)* and have shipped jars on board, you ought to pay freight for two thousand jars. *Paulus* says, if you have hired the whole vessel, you must pay freight for two thousand jars. It is the contrary if you have stipulated to pay freight for so many jars as you shall ship on board, for then you are only bound to pay for so many jars as you have actually shipped.

A

Translation of the Second Title of the Twenty-second Book of the Digests, Entitled....

De Nautico Fænore.

DIGEST, Lib. XXII. Tit. 2.

Of Maritime Loan.

LAW I.

Modestinus, Lib. 10. *Pandectarum.*

Trajectitia. What is called *maritime money (pecunia trajectitia)* is money which is carried beyond the sea; if it should be consumed in the same place it will not be *maritime.* But it is to be considered whether the merchandize purchased with that money has been purchased with that view. And it is material that it should be carried at the peril of the creditor. Then the money becomes *maritime.*

LAW II.

Pomponius, Lib. 3. *ex Plautio.*

Labes ait. *Labeo* says: if there is nobody on the part of the borrower on whom process can be served to compel him to pay the maritime money, the fact must be proved by testimony, and it will be equivalent to a legal demand.

O o

LAW III.

Modestinus, Lib. 4. Regularum.

In nauticâ. In a maritime loan, the lender undertakes the risque from the day that the vessel is
appointed to sail.

LAW IV.

Papianus, Lib. 3. Responsorum.

Nihil interest. It matters not whether the maritime money has been taken without being at the
risque of the lender, or whether it ceased to be at
the risque of the creditor after the expiration of the
term or performance of the condition: in either of
these cases no more than the common legal interest
shall be due ; and never in the first case, nor in the
second, from the time that the risque ceases, shall
goods pledged or hypothecated be retained for a
higher interest.

§. 1.   The daily reward of a servant sent for the
purpose of recovering the maritime money shall not
exceed *double* the lawful interest of one *per cent.*
a month.   If the stipulation of interest to be paid
after the risque expires does not amount to the whole
legal interest, it may be supplied by another stipulation for the servant's labour.

LAW V.

Scævola, Lib. 6. Responsorum.

Periculo pretium. The price or compensation
of risque, is whatever is given over and above the
money received on a penal condition not actually
existing, provided the contract is not of a gaming

or wagering species, from which the condition is to arise; as *if you manumit, you do not do such a thing, if I shall not recover from sickness, &c.* But there is no doubt where money is lent to a fisherman to purchase fishing tackle, to be repaid *in case he shall catch fish,* or to a prize fighter to fit himself for the combat, to be repaid *in case he shall come off conqueror.*

§. 1. But in all these cases a simple contract without a stipulation is sufficient to sanction the obligation.

LAW VI.

Paulus, Lib. 25. Quæstionum.

Fœnerator. A person having lent money at maritime risque has taken in pledge some goods shipped on board of the vessel; and further, in case these should not be sufficient to satisfy the whole debt, other goods, shipped on board of other vessels already pignorated to other lenders, are pledged to him in case there should be any residue. It is now asked, whether if the ship out of which he was to have been paid, the whole be lost, it is to the damage of the lender or whether he has yet a recourse on the residue of what was shipped on other vessels? I answer; in general, the diminution of the pledge is to the damage of the debtor and not of the creditor, but when maritime money is thus given, *the lender has no right to demand his money* unless the vessel arrives in safety at the stipulated time; the obligation of the debt is extinguished by the non-existence of the condition, and therefore the lien on the pledge is also gone, even on those that are not lost. If the vessel is lost within the time fixed for the end of the risque, the condition

of the stipulation is extinguished: therefore there is
no ground for prosecuting a lien on the pledges that
were shipped on board of other vessels. At what
time then is the creditor to be admitted to prosecute such liens? Only when the condition of the
obligation is actually in existence, and in case the
pledge should be lost by another accident or should
sell for less than the amount of the money due, or
if the vessel should be lost after the time when she
ceases to be at the risque of the lender.

LAW VII.

Idem, Lib. 3. *ad Edictum.*

In quibusdam: Maritime interest is due on certain contracts agreeably to the stipulation. For if
I lend ten pieces on the condition that *if the ship
arrives safely I shall receive the principal with a
certain interest,* then I may receive the principal
with the interest stipulated.

LAW VII.

Ulpianus, Lib. 77. *ad Edictum.*

Servius ait: Servius says, that the penalty of a
maritime loan cannot be demanded, if the creditor
had it in his power to receive his money within the
limited time.

LAW IX.

Labeo, Lib. 5. *Pithanon à Paulo Epitomatorum.*

Si trajectitiæ. If the penalty of a maritime loan
has been stipulated for in the usual manner, although
on the day of payment no body should be alive that
might be said to owe the money, yet the penalty is
forfeited in the same manner as if the debtor had
left an heir.

Translation of the Twenty-third Title of the Fourth Book of the Code Entitled ....

De Nautico Fœnore.

CODE, Lib. IV. Tit. XXXIII.

LAW I.

Impp. Dioclet. and Maxim. A A. Honorato.

Trajectitiam : It is clear that maritime money lent at the risque of the creditor, bears an interest different from that of the legal rate, only until the arrival of the vessel at the port of his destination.

LAW II.

Iidem, A A. Chosimaniæ.

Cum dicas : If you say that you have lent money on condition *that it should be returned to you in the Holy City,* and if you do not declare that you undertook the uncertain dangers of the seas, there is no doubt that you cannot recover any more than common legal interest for money so lent.

LAW III.

Iidem, A A. Juniæ.

Cum proponas. If you declare to have lent money at maritime interest on this condition, *that you should be paid after the arrival at* Salo *of a vessel which the debtor represented to be bound to* Africa, so that you only undertook the risque of the voyage to Africa; and by the fault of the debtor the ship was seized for contraband goods on board of her, the reason of the law will not permit that the damage of the loss of the goods, which happened, not by the stress of weather, but, by the greedy avarice and insolent behaviour of the debtor, should fall upon you.

LAW IV.

Iidem, A A. Sucharisito.

Trajectitia. But the loss of maritime money lent at the peril of the creditor, before the vessel reaches the place of her destination must not fall upon the debtor, otherwise, without an agreement of this kind the debtor should not be freed from his engagement even by the misfortune of shipwreck.

EXTRACT. EX JULIO PAULO.

Lib. 2. Sentent. Tit. 14.

Trajectitia. Maritime money in consideration of the risque which the lender runs, may, while the vessel is at sea, bear an indefinite interest.

*Translation of the Fifth Title of the Third Book
of the French Ordinance concerning the Marine,
entitled :.....*

Des Contrats à la grosse Aventure *ou* à retour
de voyage.

TITLE V.

*Of contracts of Maritime Loan, otherwise called, of
gross adventure, or return voyage.*

Article I. All contracts of *maritime loan*, otherwise called of *gross* adventure. or, of *return voyage*
may be made either by a publick notary, or under a
private signature.

II. Money may be given upon the body and
keel of the ship and upon her rigging, tackle, provisions and outfits jointly or separately, and upon all,
and any part of her lading, for one whole voyage, or
for a time limited.

III. We forbid all persons to take up, at maritime
risque upon their ships or goods on board thereof,
more than their real value, under pain of being
obliged, in case of fraud, to pay the whole sums
notwithstanding the vessel should be lost or taken.

IV. We also forbid them, under the like penalty,
to take up any money upon the freight for the voyage to be made, or upon the profit expected on the
lading, or even upon the seamen's wages, except it
be in the presence and with the consent of the master, and under one half of the aforesaid wages.

V. We moreover forbid all persons to advance any money to seamen at maritime risque upon their wages and voyages, except it be in the presence and with the consent of the master, under pain of confiscation of the sums lent, and a fine of fifty livres.

VI. The masters shall be answerable in their own names, for the whole amount of the sums taken up by the seamen with their consent, if they shall exceed one half of their wages, and that notwithstanding the loss or capture of the ship.

VII. The ship, her rigging, tackle, apparel and provisions, and even the freight, shall be by privilege, affected for the payment of the principal and interest of money given upon the body and keel of the ship, for the necessities of the voyage and the lading shall be bound for the money borrowed to procure the same.

VIII. Such as give money upon bottomry to a master without the consent of the owners, if they live in the place, shall have no security nor privilege upon the ship, any further than the part that the master may have in the ship and freight, though the money was borrowed for fitting out the ship or for buying provisions.

IX. However, the parts of such of the owners as refuse to furnish their proportions for fitting out the vessel, shall be affected for the money lent to the master for the equipment and provisions of the ship.

X. Creditors for money formerly due on such things and left outstanding by renewal or continuation of the contract, shall not come in competition with those that have actually lent for the last voyage.

XI. All contracts of maritime loan shall be void after the entire loss of the effects upon which the money was lent, if that happened by accident, and within the times and places therein expressed.

XII. Nothing shall be reputed *accident* that is occasioned by the internal defect of the things themselves or by the fault of the owners, master or merchants, except it be otherwise provided by the contract.

XIII. If the time of the risque be not specified by the contract, it shall last as to the ship, her rigging, tackle and provisions, from the day she sets sail, until she arrives at her intended port and is moored at the wharf; and as to the goods, it shall last from the moment they are laden on board the ship, or lighter to be carried thither, until they be unladen and carried on shore.

XIV. A person lading goods, and taking up money upon them at maritime risque, shall not be acquitted by the loss of the ship and lading, unless he makes it appear that he had there, upon his own account, effects to the value of the sum borrowed.

XV. However, if the person that has taken money at maritime risque, make it appear that he could not ship goods to the value of the sum borrowed, the contract, in case of loss, shall be diminished in proportion to the value of the effects laden, and shall only subsist on the overplus; upon which the owner shall pay the interest, according to the current rate of the place where the contract is made, until the actual payment of the principal. And if the ship arrive in safety, there shall be due only the legal interest, and not the maritime profit of the overplus of the effects put on board.

P p

XVI. Those that give money at maritime risque shall contribute, in discharge of the borrower, to general average, such as ransoms, compositions, jettisons, masts and ropes cut away for the common safety of ship and goods; but not for simple average or particular damages that may happen, except there be some agreement to the contrary.

XVII. However, in case of shipwreck the contract of maritime loan shall be reduced to the value of the effects that are saved.

XVIII. If there be a contract of maritime loan and an insurance upon the same cargo, the lender shall be preferred to the insurers upon the effects preserved from shipwreck, for his capital and no further.

INDEX.

ABANDONMENT, by the borrower, is not necessary, in order to release himself from the
contract. - - - - 40, 208
If the owner abandon his interest in the
vessel and freight, he is no longer liable
for the acts of the master. - - 102
In such a case, whether engagements con-
tracted by the master, in the course of
the voyage, still exist against him? - 104
A stipulation by the lender *to abandon in
case of innavigability* is illegal. - 163
ACCIDENT, what shall be so termed. 166, 295
ACTIO INSTITORIA, the, explained. - 103
ACTIONS, of the several kinds, principal, ac-
cessory and contrary. - - - - 96
ACCOMMENDA explained. - - - 42
ACT OF MAN, of loss by the - - 167, 295
ADMIRALTY, jurisdiction of - - 30. 231
French courts of - - - 43
ADVENTURES may be sold by the master du-
ring the voyage to purchase necessaries, 94
Such a sale is among the per: of the seas
for which ensurers are liable, and, in case
the ship do not perish, it gives the owner
of them a lien upon the ship and freight. 95
And an action against the owners of the
ship. - - - - - 118
But freight is due upon them and they
must contribute to gross average, - 94

The goods thus sold are to be paid for at
  the price for which similar goods on
  board were sold for.   -   -   -   95
AGENT, does not, generally, contract in his own
  name.   -   -   -   -   -   114
  But he who does is bound, even though he
  designate his character, and such character, in certain cases may be inferred. 115
ANTWERP, ordinance of, quoted and commented upon, *passim*.
APPORTIONMENT of effects saved.   -   208
ARBITRATION, on the subject of Maritime
  Loans is not provided for by the ordinance.   -   -   -   -   -   187
  The award of an, cannot be enforced by
  execution.   -   -   -   -   -   *ib*
AVERAGE, the lender does not contribute to a
  simple, unless there is an express stipulation to that effect.   -   -   -   160
  A stipulation that the lender shall be free
  from gross average is illegal. 40, 162, 221
  Reason of the different provisions respecting simple and gross average.   -   161
  In England, no average on bottomry
  bonds.   -   -   -   -   160, 221
  Where a ship is obliged to put into port
  for the benefit of the whole concern,
  the charges of loading and unloading
  the cargo and taking care of it and the
  wages and provisions of the workmen
  hired for the repairs, become general
  average, *in not*.   -   -   -   162
BANKRUPT law of France, principle of the 196
  And of England.   -   -   -   201
BOTTOMRY, see *Maritime Loans*.   -   -
BILL OF EXCHANGE, the master has no power
  to draw upon his owners, for necessaries.   -   -   -   -   106, 117
  Law of France respecting the protest of a, 188

Borrower, may retract and rescind the contract by his own act. - - - 147
Must prove property on board in case of a loss. - - - - - 31
If he is not able to procure a vessel for the return cargo, he must account for the proceeds of the outward cargo. - 59
Caravane voyage *en*, explained. - 174
Cargo, liens on the, see *Liens*. - -
Captain, see *Master*. - - - -
Chancelier nature of the office of a - 45
Claim of Property, see *Material-men*. -
By the civil law, he who has sold goods may reclaim them if he is not paid according to the terms of the contract. 245
But not if he endorse a receipt upon the bill of sale. - - - - - 240
Colbert cited. - - - - - 173
Companies, the *Royal Exchange* and *London Assurance*, have the privilege of ensuring and lending at bottomry exclusive of all other corporate bodies, except the *South Sea* and the East India companies, which may lend money on ships or goods on board ships or to persons in their service. - - - - - 26
Commissary of the Navy, his duty. - 133
Commissions, cannot be ensured or hypothecated in France. - - - - 39
Comptrolling, in France. - - - 45
Concordat, what it is and its effects. - 198
Condition, of a bottomry bond, when it is fulfilled. - - - - - - 26
Consignee, hypothecation cannot be made to a - - - - - - 30
Contraband, loss by, is not one of the perils of the sea. - - - - - - 167
Council of Prizes, its jurisdiction. - 43
Of State, its jurisdiction. - - 244

COLONNA DI, the contract explained.   42
COUR DE CASSATION, its jurisdiction.   - 200
CUJAS, quoted, *passim.*
DEMAND, how made in Rome.   -   -   20
    If not made at the place stipulated as the
        termination of the risk, the borrower
        may make a judicial deposit of the mo-
        ney, or carry it with him.   -   - 186
DECRETAL SALE, how made.   -   - 219
DECLARATION OF THE KING, explained.   227
DERELICT, at sea, will be restored after any
        length of time, unless there be proof of
        an institution to abandon wholly.   105, 188
    Quantum of salvage on a   -   -   - *ib*
    A vessel with *slaves* on board but no white
        person considered as a derelict.   -   *ib*
DEMURRAGE, is not allowed without an express
    stipulation.   -   -   -   -   - 174
DISCUSSION, the term explained.   -   - 219
DISTRACTION, the term explained.   -   245
DUARENUS, quoted, *passim.*
EFFECTS saved, see Liens.
EVIDENCE, parol, of the contract, whether admis-
    sible.   -   -   -   -   -   -   45
    It is incumbent upon the lender to prove
        the ship's arrival.   -   -   38, 157
    In case of loss of the ship, the borrower
        must prove effects on board to the
        amount of the sum borrowed.   33, 156
    The proof of the application of the money
        lent is not thrown upon the lender.   158
EXCHANGE, how the term is used by French
    writers.   -   -   -   -   -   56
EXECUTION, PAREE, explained,   -   -   45
EXERCITOR, explained (see *master.*)   . 271
FRAUD, to borrow beyond the effects is a,   151
    For which the security is liable.   - 192
    But not for maritime interest.   -   - 152
FREIGHT, may be insured under certain cir-

cumstances. - - - - 39
Cannot be the subject of a Maritime
    Loan. - - - - *ib.* 130
Penalty on such a contract. - - 134
GROSS adventure explained. - - - 25
GREEK vessels, how navigated. - - 42
GUIDON LE, quoted, *passim.*
HAZARD, see *Risk*
HOSTAGE, see *Ransom.*
IMPRISONMENT of the body for debt, when
    allowed in France. - - - 63
IMPLICITA explained. - - - - 42
INSURANCE, how it differs from bottomry. 38
    In what respects the two contracts are
    alike. - - - - - 39
    The owner of a ship, covered by a bot-
    tomry bond to an amount beyond her
    value, has not an insurable interest. 231
INSTITOR, explained. - - - - 65
INSTRUMENT, simple and notarial, in France,
    effects of, - - - - - 218
INTERNAL DEFECT, the lender is not liable
    for - - - - - - 166
INTERDUM, the law commented upon. 216
    Has been adopted in France. - - 217
INTENTION, in a question of usury the inten-
    tion is the material thing. - - - 34
INTEREST, maritime, accrues only during the
    continuance of the risk. - - 146
    Even though the risk be avoided by the
    act of the borrower. - - - 51
    And though he has stipulated to perform
    the voyage. - - - - 60
    And in proportion to the amount at risk. 248
    In case of a rescission of the contract
    the borrower is entitled to legal interest. 150
    If the contract was void *ab initio* no mari-
    time interest is due. - - - 34
    Is implied in the contract. - - 36, 50
    May be stipulated for, to any amount. 52

It is, generally, payable in money, but may
 be paid otherwise. - - - 50

The rate stipulated is not affected by the
 unexpected arrival of war or peace. 53

The whole premium is due, the moment
 the risk ceases, though the voyage be
 interrupted, or the risk cease before the
 expiration of the stipulated term. - 53

Sed quære, in note. - - - - 54

Whether legal interest be due on the maritime interest. - - - - 60

Generally, in France, interest does *not*
 commence to run but from the time of
 action brought. - - - - 61

In the U. S. when verdict is rendered for
 principal and interest and the judgment
 is entered for the aggregate sum, the
 whole bears interest from the date of
 the judgment, *in not.* - - 62

INVENTORY, benefit of, explained. 246

JETTISON, see *appendix.*

JUDGMENTS, money may be ordered to be paid
 over, in most commercial cases, notwithstanding an appeal, upon the party
 receiving it, giving security to refund. 187

But not in cases of bottomry bonds. - *ib*

JURISDICTION, of the admiralty. - 43, 231

The court of Judges and consuls. - *ib*

Tribunal de commerce. - - *ib*

Council of prizes. - - - *ib*

Cour de Cassation. - - - 200

Tribunal de Senechansée. - - 243

LOSS, The lender is not prejudiced by a loss
 which happens at sea through the fault
 of the borrower. - - - 22, 60

Notwithstanding the loss of the ship, the
 contract continues as to effects landed. 59

MASTER, who is so called in the civil law. 65

When he becomes so. - - - 69

Is the representative of the owner during
the voyage. - - - - *ib*
It is a general rule that the owner is bound
by his acts. - - - - 67
May substitute another in his place, even
although it has been prohibited. - 69
The owners are not bound by bottomry
bonds executed by the master in the
place where they reside, unless they
consent. - - - - - 70
But he is personally bound by them, and
if he can prove that the money borrowed
was usefully employed about the vessel, he may sustain an action against
them. - - - - - 71
Is bound to follow the advice of the owners
in taking freight. - - - *ib*
But a third person who contracts with him
bonâ fide for freight is not bound to inquire whether he is acting according to
his instructions. - - - *ib*
The owners are liable though they abandon
ship and freight. - - - *ib*
And they are bound by a judgment rendered against the master as such, in *not.* 72, 93
He may borrow money for account of those
part owners who refuse to contribute
their proportion and pledge their shares. 73
After due notice to them. - - 74
Or he may commence suit against them to
compel them to contribute or abandon
their interest. - - - - 75
The provisions of different codes respecting the power of the master to borrow. 77
Whether he may borrow at bottomry in
order to complete his return cargo? 82
If the owners have correspondents in the
port, their advice should be taken. - 85

Q q

But a third person who was ignorant that they had correspondents is not to suffer from the master's neglecting to consult them. - - - - - *ib*

Punishment of a master who acts unfaithfully. - - - - 86, 88

His infidelity shall not affect third persons who contract *bonâ fidê*. - 87, 8, 90

If money be borrowed by him in a place where he could not make use of it, the lender has no action against the owners. 89

Of a master who sells part of his cargo during the voyage. - - - 92

How far and under what circumstances he may make such sale. - - - *ib*

The action *de exercitoriâ* was given in addition to that against the master and therefore we may sue the master or owner or both. - - - - 96

There is no limitation against the exercitory action. - - - - 97

The power of the master does not cease by the loss of the ship. - - - 108

In case of wreck he must seek another vessel; he may borrow money for salvage and pledge the freight of the things saved, and in case of capture he may ransom the vessel and draw upon his owner. 101

Of abandonment by the owners in order to avoid being bound by his acts *ib*

If he bind his own person and property he is liable. - - - - 117

Whether the master is bound personally for contracts made by him in that capacity? - - - - - 114

But not when he contracts *co nomine* unless in cases of borrowing money without necessity, or in places where the owners reside and without their assent. *ib*

The power of the master being restricted
to the borrowing of money on bond or
by pledging a part of his cargo, or to
the raising of it by partial sales, he
ought not to draw bills of exchange, and
if he does he is personally bound to the
holder. - - - - - 110
But if he has incurred necessary expences
for the ship and cargo, he has a lien
upon it. - - - - - *ib*
And the owners are obliged to honour his
bills if they have received a part of the
freight or other returns, as far as they
are in funds. - - - - *ib*
Of stipulated penalties against a master
who violates his contract. - - 118
He who furnishes necessaries has a right
of action against the master. - 119
MONEY, maritime what shall be so called. 22
NAVICULARIUS, his office. - - - 66
NOTARY PUBLIC, effect of his acts. - 45
NOTICE, if the lender has notice how far the
master's powers are restricted, he con-
tracts with him at his own peril. - 90
NOVATION, explained. - - - 262
OWNERS, observations on the actions against
them for the acts of the master. - 65
See *Maritime Loans. Master.*
Who shall be understood to be, - 168
PART OWNER, see *Owner, Maritime Loans.*
Master.
PARTNERSHIP, difference between Maritime
Loans and, - - - - - 36
The property of the partnership consi-
dered in one point of view is not the
property of the individuals in their par-
ticular capacity. - - - 249
PARERE's *Savarys* quoted. - - 47
PATRON, explained. - - - - 79

PAYMENT, See *Maritime Loans.*

PEACE, the unexpected arrival of, does not diminish the rate of interest. - - 53

PERIL, See *Average. Maritime Loans.*
The lender is not affected by any accidents on land which happen to goods exported. - - - - 169

PREMIUM, explained. - - - - 56

PRIORITY, where there are several loans, there is no priority. - - - - - 41

PROFITS, money cannot be borrowed on expected, - - - - - 39, 130

MARITIME, how understood by French writers. 56

PROOF, See *evidence.*

PROMISSORY NOTE, for value received in money but at gross adventure is not a bottomry bond. - - - - 47
In blank forbidden. - - - 48

PROVISIONS, the master may pledge his vessel or cargo to purchase provisions. - 85

PROVISIONAL JUDGMENTS in France, what. 187

PURCHASER, a bonâ fidê, is not protected in France unless a receipt is endorsed on the bill of sale. - - - 240, 5

RANSOM, money paid for a, is a charge upon the property. - - - - 56
To which lenders must contribute. 161
And owners cannot be discharged by abandonment. - - - - - 114
The master may pawn his own person, which he may redeem by borrowing money, and recover it in admiralty. 234

RECESANTS, See *Owners.*

REGLEMENT, explained. - - - 133

REPAIRS, See *Master. Average.*

RENEWAL, money left by, explained. - 133
Those who have been security for money lent at bottomry are discharged on the completion of the voyage, if the credi-

tor leave the principal in the hands of the debtor for another voyage, without their consent. - - - - 190

Those who are creditors by *renewal* are among the youngest privileged creditors. - - - - - 237

RESIDENCE, what is understood by the *residence of the owners.* - - - 83

REVENDICATION, explained. - - 235

RISK, the money is not at the risk of the lender until the vessel has set sail. - 19

As soon as it commences the whole sum becomes due. - - - - 54

Is an essential part of the contract and must be borne by the lender. *Ib.* 33, 49, 146

If the money has not been at risk it bears only legal interest. *Ib.* - - 22, 51

The maritime interest ceases with the risk. - - - - 22, 34

Simple average is not one of the risks incurred by the lender. - - 158

But gross average is, though there be a stipulation to the contrary. - 161

Such a stipulation is unlawful. - 163

So also of a clause restricting the lender to particular risks. - - - 164

In general the lender only bears the perils of the sea. - - - - 166

He is not liable for losses happening by the internal defect of the thing. - *ib*

Or for any acts of the owners, master, mariners or shippers, or a forfeiture in consequence of contraband. - - 167

Secus as to contraband or smuggling if the design appear on the face of the contract. - - - - - 168

The lender does not bear the perils by land on goods which are exported- - 169

See *Maritime Loans. Voyage.*

Role d'equipage, explained. . . 133
Savary's Pareres, quoted. - . 47
Salvage, property found derelict at sea will
be restored on salvage unless there be
proof of an intention to abandon wholly. 105
In such cases one half usually allowed. *ib*
In cases of salvage monition issues to the
owner to show cause it is not a proceeding *in rem.* - - - *ib*
In England there is no salvage upon a bottomry bond. - - - - 160
Salvage is the first lien upon property
saved. - - - - - 253
Seamen, are not permitted to ensure their future wages. - - - - - 40
Are not affected by any conventional penalties between the master and owners. 123
The advances to seamen are among the
expences of outfit and may be the subject of maritime loan. - - 137
The wages of seamen constitute the first
lien on a vessel which returns from a
voyage. - - - - - 232
Wages may be decreed on the captain's
certificate, though the vessel be in port,
not earning freight. - - - *ib*
If the voyage be interrupted without their
fault they shall receive wages during
the time they work on board the vessel
in port. - - - - - *ib*
The act of congress respecting them must
be strictly followed. - - - *ib*
If they suffer imprisonment under the 7th
clause of that act, they must draw wages
under the fifth. - - - *ib*
If the esculents specified in the act cannot
be procured, others may be substituted. *ib*
And the master is the sole judge of the
expenditure. . - - *ib*

The act applies only to seamen bound *from*
the United States and not to those shipped in foreign ports. - - -   *ib*
They do not forfeit their wages by absence
without any fault of their own, or prize
money. - - - - -   *ib*
Or by capture if they were on board.   *ib*
The right to wages is founded on the *ser-*
vice, not the articles. - " -   *ib*
And the owner is bound if the vessel is
insufficient. - - - - -   *ib*
If the seamen die, before the voyage is
ended, whether his representatives shall
be entitled to his wages? - -   *ib*
When the voyage is commenced in time
of war, the wages are not to be diminished by the arrival of peace. -   *ib*
Secus where the voyage, is commenced
before that event. - " "   *ib*
SECURITY, See *Maritime Loans.*
SENECSHANSEE Tribunal, explained. " 243
SEVERANCE of property, what it is - 247
The owner of a thing of which a deceased
person was simply the possessor may
reclaim it. - - - -   247
So we may reclaim a deposit which is
still in existence. - " -   *ib*
Though it be in the hands of the heir of
him to whom it was pledged. -   *ib*
The vender on credit is not strictly enti-
tled to a severance. " - -   248
But if there be a suit for the distribution
of the general property of his debtor, he
may demand a severance of the chattel
which he sold. - - " "   *ib*
In cases of bankrupts the vendor has an
exclusive lien on the article sold by him. *ib*
SHIP AND SHIPPERS, for *Maritime Loans,*
Master. Owner.

SLAVE, if the agent be a slave, the person who
    contracts with him, has no right of ac-
    tion but against his owner.   -   -   87
A vessel with slaves on board, but no
    white person, considered as derelict in
    South Carolina.   -   -   -   105

SMUGGLING, the lender does not bear a loss
    occasioned by smuggling, unless it was
    evidently intended.   -   -   -   168

SYNDIC explained.   -   -   -   -   115

SYNALLAGMATIQUE explained.   -   -   32

USURY, observations on the chap. *extra de
    usuris.*   -   -   -   -   -   26
The intent of the bargain is the material
    thing.   -   -   -   -   -   34

VALUTAM explained.   -   -   -   -   183

VENDOR, the vendor of a vessel which has not
    performed her first voyage is placed in
    the first rank of liens.   -   -   224

VERDICT, when a verdict is rendered for the
    principal and interest and judgment is
    entered for the aggregate sum, the
    whole bears interest from the date of
    the judgment.   -   -   -   -   62

VOYAGE, what is understood by an entire voy-
    age.   -   -   -   -   -   -   169
See *Maritime Loan.*
Of liens upon a vessel which has not com-
    menced her,   -   -   -   -   223
Of liens upon a vessel after her return
    from a,   -   -   -   -   -   232

WAGES, see *seamen.*

WAR, the unexpected arrival of war, does not
    affect the stipulated rate of interest.   -   53

WISBUY, laws of, quoted, *passim-*

WORDS, phrases, terms &c. explained.
    Trajectitia pecunia.   -   -   -   18
    Decretal.   -   -   -   -   -   28
    Squallagmatique.   -   -   -   -   32

Court of the judges and consuls. 43
Tribunal de commerce. *ib*
Council of prizes. *ib*
Chancelier. 45
Porter hypotheque. *ib*
Execution parée. *ib*
En brevet. *ib.*
Parere. 47
Different modes of expressing the consideration of maritime loans. 56
Captains, masters and patrons. 79
Actio institoria. 103
Syndicks, 115
Commissaire de la Marine. 133
Role d'equipage. *ib*
Reglement. *ib*
Renewal, money left by, 152
Mutuum. 138
Armateur. 142
En assistance de cause. 143
En caravane. 174
Girantem. 183
Valutam. 184
Cour de cassation. 200
Actes sous seing privé &c. 218
Decretal sale, discussion. 219
Declatraion of the king. 227
Privilege. 231
Tribunal de Senechansee. 243
Revendication distraction. 245
Benefit of Inventory. 246
Novation. 262

ERRATA.

Page **18.** *l. 7.* For promogenitus read primogeniture.

19	6	Nor		non
24	9	diri forma		di riforma
	21	but its		but by its
27	24	concilianus		conciliandus
	25	—quendam		—quendum
	30	omit the penultimate comma		
	34	ess ex		esse
	35	audsendus		audiendus
28	12	censetur		censetur

In the margin the reference to de Luca should be to dise. III.

29	3	valcaut		valeant
	4	tamcu		tamen
59	27	principle		principal
60	28	judiciously		judicially
62	5	usura		usuræ
	6	piotus		potius
63	17	after entitled, insert, to		
83	19	where		when
88	13	requiring		required
	14	non		cum
90	7	cansa		causa
97	7	ee		ea
	last line	hœre des		hœredes
124		in the margin, cargo—		ship
136	26	effects		affects
174	10	borrower		lender
185	15	postquaim, redict		*postquam rediit*
253		omit these words in the title of Sect. VII. "concurrence between the lenders at bottomry and the insurers."		
260	2	assignor		assignee
	13	assignor		assignee and

correct the margin.

In the title page of the appendix for contracts read contrats.

267		(title)	digest	digests
270	§ 10	for pretio		pretiis
271	§ 14	si		sic
	§ 15	exercitorum		exercitorem
273	§ 23	quamquam		quanquam
274		law II, 9 edictum		9 ad edictum
		non implures		ne in plures
184	§ 1	arbora		arbore
289		labes		labeo
290		before § 1 insert		pro operis
		in law V periculo		periculi
291		before § 1 insert		in his
294		sucharisito		eucharisto
		next line, for trajectitia		trajectitiæ

www.ingramcontent.com/pod-product-compliance
Lightning Source LLC
Chambersburg PA
CBHW021353090426
42742CB00009B/831